State and
Society in
Seventeenth-
Century
France

Modern Scholarship on European History

HENRY A. TURNER, JR.
General Editor

State and Society in Seventeenth-Century France

Edited with an Introduction by Raymond F. Kierstead

New Viewpoints
A Division of Franklin Watts, Inc.
New York 1975

FOR ANDREW AND EVAN

Library of Congress Cataloging in Publication Data

Kierstead, Raymond F   comp.
    State and society in seventeenth-century France.

    (Modern scholarship on European history)
    Bibliography: p.
    Includes index.
    CONTENTS: Major, J. R. Henry IV and Guyenne.—
Deyon, P.   Relations between the French nobility and the abso-
lute monarchy during the first half of the seventeenth century.—
Hurt, J. J. The Parlement of Brittany and the Crown:
1665–1675. [etc.]
    1. France—Politics and government—17th century.
2. France—Social conditions.   I. Title.
JN2341.K53   320.9′44′033   74-32202
ISBN 0-531-05367-9
ISBN 0-531-05573-6 pbk.

6 5 4 3 2 1

ACKNOWLEDGMENTS

J. Russell Major, "Henry IV and Guyenne: A Study Concerning Origins of Royal Absolutism," first appeared in *French Historical Studies,* IV (1966) and is reprinted with the permission of the author and editors of the journal. The *Presses Universitaires de France* and the editors granted permission to republish Pierre Deyon's "A propos les rapports entre la noblesse française et la monarchie absolue pendant la première moitié du XVIIe siècle," *Revue historique,* CCXXXI (1964). John Hurt, "The Parlement of Brittany and the Crown, 1665–1675," was first published in *French Historical Studies,* IV (1966) and is reprinted with the permission of the author and editors. Nora Temple, "The Control and Exploitation of French Towns During the Ancien Régime," is reprinted from *History: The Journal of the Historical Association,* LI (1966) with the permission of the editor.

René Pillorget's "Les 'Cascaveoux': L'insurrection aixoise de l'automne 1630" was originally published in *Dix-septième siècle,* No. 64 (1964) and is reprinted with the permission of the author and of the Secretary General of the *Société d'Etude du XVIIe Siècle.* J. Gallet, "Recherches sur les mouvements populaires à Amiens en 1635 et 1636," *Revue d'histoire moderne et contemporaine,* XIV (1967) is reprinted with the permission of the editor of the journal. Leon Bernard, "French Society and Popular Uprisings Under Louis XIV," first appeared in *French Historical Studies,* III (1964) and is reprinted with the permission of the author and the editors. *Editions Edouard Privat* granted permission to reprint François Loirette, "Un épisode des résistances locales aux empiètements du pouvoir royal: La défense du franc-alleu agenais au XVIIe siècle," *Annales du Midi*, LXXI (1959).

Guy Lemarchand, "Crises économiques et atmosphère sociale en milieu urbain sous Louis XIV," first appeared in the *Revue d'histoire moderne et contemporaine*, XIV (1967) and is reprinted with the permission of the editor of the review. R. G. Grassby, "Social Status and Commercial Enterprise Under Louis XIV," *Economic History Review*, XIII (1960–1961) is reprinted with the permission of the editor and of the author.

The kindness of the persons listed above is gratefully acknowledged.

Translations from the French by Raymond F. and Marilyn J. Kierstead.

CONTENTS

ix

Contents

3

Absolutism and Elites

INTRODUCTION

As one contemplates the grand lines of modern historiography on seventeenth-century France, two broad and distinct modes of interpretation become evident. One, firmly rooted in the traditional notion of the seventeenth century as France's classical age, emphasizes royalty, *grandeur,* and the country's attainment of a preeminent place in the political, diplomatic, and cultural life of old Europe. Louis XIV's palace at Versailles serves as a convenient institutional symbol of this view of France— focusing our attention on the martial spirit, cultural centralization, and the highly personal nature of French absolutism.[1] However, the dominant school of historiography in contemporary France has treated the traditional diplomatic and political mode of interpretation with a scorn that is, indeed, monumental. Richelieu, Mazarin, the Sun King, and their agents appear scarcely at all in the great tomes of social and economic history that have been the special glory of this school.[2] Rather we find ourselves deep in the complex and particularistic world of French peasants, of grasping landlords, and of stubborn and independent provincial notables. And in this world of the *pays* (or region), the impersonal forces of nature were of far greater moment than the personal power of the crown. To the great masses of men and women in rural France, Versailles was a remote and alien place.

The decline of court-centered history and the emphasis upon society and economy at the expense of the state have been, in many respects, salutary developments. French historians of the so-called Annales group have been enormously inventive in raising new problems for study and in designing new methods of research.[3] And the grim hold upon the French historical imagination of a particularly stultifying form of institutional history has been broken. Yet the study of kingship and of the evolution of the seventeenth-century state now lags in France, and this can only be regarded as a loss. For political and institutional history, on the one side, and social history, on the other, are not mutually exclusive. As Robert Mandrou has recently stressed, one might reasonably expect the new history to reinvigorate the old and even to suggest new perspectives on past politics.[4] It is the purpose of this book to illustrate Mandrou's point by raising what, for lack of a better formulation, I have called the state-society problem.

In the following pages, a diverse group of historians —French, American, and British—fixes our attention upon the relations of the Bourbon state and the surrounding society. By no means do these historians comprise a school or even share a common outlook upon the past. But the totality of their work, I believe, does suggest both a fruitful marriage of political, institutional, and social history and a more subtle understanding of the early modern European state than is generally found in the traditional histories.

The broad questions raised by these essays may be posed as follows: how did the modern state, in the early stages of its formation, affect the established social structures and institutions of France? and how, conversely, did established social patterns and assumptions shape or influence the absolutist state? As members of industrialized and thoroughly modernized Western society, we know that the state looms large in our lives and touches us individually or collectively at every turn. As students of history, we know that preindustrial civilization was alien to our own in almost every respect—not only in its characteristic institutions, but also, as the new social historians insist, even in the outlook and mentality of its people. Most certainly the history of political systems cannot resist the general thrust of recent scholarship—which is to treat traditional society on its own terms and to establish the otherness of that society in relation to our own. The seventeenth-century European state belonged to what Peter Laslett has called "the world we have lost." [5] It had its particular scale and scope, and it was not a close blood relation of the modern industrial state. Now precisely at this juncture, some of the concerns of the social historian become pertinent to the political or the institutional historian. Seventeenth-century France offers an excellent example of the possibilities of a dialogue between the fields.

Over the course of the seventeenth century, the French monarchy came to stand as the model of absolutism for the entire European continent. Other princes would seek to imitate the institutions, architecture, manners, and even the language of the French kings. At the same time, the enemies of the Bourbons—in Holland, England, and elsewhere—saw in the French experience an example of despotism to be avoided at any cost.[6] Both the admirers and the detractors of the French monarchy viewed its history through a distorted lens. In fact, Bourbon absolutism was an ambiguous achievement—neither as sinister and despotic as its enemies claimed; nor as radiant a success as its proponents believed. During the seventeenth century, the monarchy did not simply parade from one great domestic conquest to another. The reassertion of royal authority after the religious wars, and again after the Fronde of midcentury, and the extension of royal influence throughout the country were accomplished slowly and, at best, with limited success. From the beginning to the end of the century, the reality of absolutist government fell far short of the rhetoric propounded by the royal lawyers and other propagandists of the crown.

The tensions that existed between the bolder ambitions of the century's kings and ministers, on the one hand, and the very real limitations upon the crown that were imposed by the established institutions and structures of archaic society, on the other, constitute a central historical problem about French absolutism. It is a subject that has been identified with the work of one of the great modern interpreters of the Old Regime, Professor Roland Mousnier of the Sorbonne.

Almost alone among the leading French historians of the

period, Mousnier has maintained a certain continuity between present historical practice and the older forms of legal and institutional history. But his notable achievement—and the principal source of his influence upon a generation of younger French and foreign scholars—has been to infuse that old and respectable tradition with a keen sense of the relations between institutions and society.[7] From his earliest work on the buying and selling of royal offices, to his more recent studies of peasant uprisings in the seventeenth century, Mousnier has sought to delineate the social character of the French state and to explore the social basis of opposition to the crown. Of course, this is not the place to analyze the entire body of Mousnier's scholarly production, but several of his principal themes dominate the articles that follow, and these themes must be highlighted.

In his thesis of 1945, *La vénalité des offices sous Henri IV et Louis XIII,*[8] Mousnier set forth his essential vision of state and society in the seventeenth century. According to this vision, conflict was at the heart of political and social relations in the Old Regime—conflict between the state and the dominant elites, and conflict among the elites as well. To survive and prosper in this Hobbesian world, the monarchy played off one social group against the other in the old political game of divide and rule. The venerable practice of selling offices in the royal service to wealthy families provided the crown with one means of gaining support from the French bourgeoisie. By sharing public power with an ambitious order of venal officeholders, the Bourbons not only filled the state service and the royal treasury, but also benefited politically from the rivalry of the officeholders and the military aristocracy. The upper bourgeoisie, in short, provided the crown with a convenient counterweight to the nobility. However, there was another side to the question of venality, and that concerned the impact of a powerful and widespread order of officers upon the state and its policies. Venal officeholders formed a self-perpetuating elite that was, to be sure, dependent, but that would also resist the monarchy when its vital or selfish interests were threatened. The Fronde of 1648 offered sufficient proof of this. Thus

Mousnier arrived at the following understanding of absolutism as it was practiced in the first half of the century: "The monarchy, with a king who was absolute in principal, was, in fact, a monarchy tempered by venality of offices." [9] Finally, Mousnier argued that, after 1660, Louis XIV determined to break the independent authority of the officers, and that, by doing so, he became a "revolutionary" monarch.

After the publication of his influential thesis, Mousnier went on to refine his ideas about the relations of state and society in the early modern era. In particular, the publication in German translation, of a massive study of French popular revolts by the Russian historian, Boris Porchnev, stimulated Mousnier's mature reflections on the state-society problem.[10]

Porchnev had argued that the rash of popular uprisings in the decades before the Fronde served as the essential key to our understanding of the nature of absolutism. The Bourbon monarchy, according to the Russian scholar, was a "feudal-absolutist" state—an instrument of the dominant social and economic class, the nobility. Rural and urban revolts, in turn, represented a spontaneous popular reaction against the oppressive ruling class and against the political force of that class—the absolutist state. The threat from below caused the aristocracy and the upper bourgeoisie to form a class front against the popular elements and to repress them.

In an important article published in 1958, Mousnier began his counterattack against this Marxist view and disputed Porchnev on almost every important point.[11] France, he quite rightly held, was not a feudal society. Far from representing the interests and outlook of the dominant feudal nobility, he went on to argue, the Bourbon monarchy sustained and increased its power only by constantly opposing the great landed families. Indeed, it was the provincial aristocracy that fomented many of the popular rebellions against the crown, and noblemen often provided the leadership of these uprisings. These points made against Porchnev led Mousnier to restate and refine the conception of French society that he had originally advanced in his study of venal officeholding. In this revised model, class warfare and class divisions played little or no part. Hierarchically arranged orders based upon function, and not classes based upon wealth, formed the fundamental social units in seventeenth-century France.[12] And in this preindustrial society, the lines of loyalty tended to run vertically from peasant to lord, and not horizontally according to class. Thus provincial noblemen, enjoying the traditional prestige and status of their order, commanded the allegiance of their peasantry and used the lower orders to oppose the centralizing state. Popular revolts did not comprise an early episode in the class war; rather they were sure evidence of the continuing vitality of archaic society in its ongoing struggle against the absolutist monarchy and especially against the royal fisc. Particularism or provincialism—and not class antagonisms—served as the vital spark behind the opposition to the crown.

This brief summary does not do justice to the complex, and sometimes subtle, ideas put forth by both Mousnier and Porchnev. But it should serve to define the boundaries within which historical investigation of the problem of state and society in seventeenth-century Frence has been conducted in recent years. Many of the articles in this anthology reflect to a greater or lesser degree the influence of the controversy upon historians, and they particularly reflect the influence of Mousnier. Essays on royal action in the provinces, for example, clearly illustrate his points about the role of local particularism in stimulating resistance to the crown and about the ambivalent relationships that existed between the royal officers and their sovereign. Others support Mousnier's interpretation of popular revolts, although Porchnev too has his followers among the historians who appear here. Above all, each article confirms in some manner the central tenet of Mousnier's lifework: "The state cannot be separated from the society of which it is the product, but which, in turn, it informs and shapes." [13]

But this book has a larger purpose than to honor a distinguished master in the field of early modern French history and to illustrate his influence. Indeed, there are good reasons to take a certain critical stance in regard to the great debate and to free the discussion of state and society from the rather rigid conceptual frameworks imposed by both Mousnier and his

Russian colleague. For example, Mousnier's suggestion that the French monarchy could manipulate whole orders of men to achieve a sort of political balance flies in the face of what social historians have told us about the infinite complexity of social structures in early modern France. So too, the notion that Louis XIV drastically altered the balance of power between crown and elites, and was thus a revolutionary monarch, is, to put the best face on it, an overstatement. Nor does Mousnier's central conceptual scheme, founded on the idea of a society of orders, adequately reflect social realities in the Old Regime.[14] Finally, despite the blinders that his Marxist philosophy has placed upon his historical vision, did not Porchnev discern at least part of the truth in asserting that, in the end, the seventeenth-century French monarchy was an aristocratic institution, and not, as Mousnier would have it, the embodiment of an ill-defined national interest above the social orders?

We must conclude that neither the dialectic of Marx, nor the dialectics of Mousnier, have fully comprehended the subtle relations of state and society in the early modern era. For this reason, the case studies that follow have a particular value. Although some are cast in the mold of Mousnier or of Porchnev, each shows traditional society in all of its bewildering and contentious complexity. Taken together, these articles suggest that no simple sociological mode of explanation can adequately deal with the particularism, the solidarities, or the mentality of provincial French society under the Old Regime. They also suggest that the history of the absolutist state cannot be subsumed under simple models of conflict—class or otherwise.

Like the family, or any other institution in the traditional world, the state was permeated with the assumptions of its age. Thus it acted within a society that valued hierarchy and privilege, that was nourished on patronage, and that was glued together by family connections and local solidarities. Although examples of conflict and opposition are plentiful in the history of the Bourbon monarchy, the fact remains that the state, as a general rule, accepted the provincial world and sought to work within it. Moreover, the state was relatively small in scale. Its principal cutting edge, the provincial intendants, numbered at most about thirty men—hardly sufficient to tame a turbulent society of some eighteen or twenty million people. To the degree that the monarchy expanded its power over the country, this was accomplished not so much by forcing new ways and institutions upon society, as by manipulating the old ways and arrangements for the ends of the state. Thus the judicious use of royal patronage, the selling of great and petty offices, the offering or withdrawal of privileges, and the raising or breaking of families were typical means of governing in the seventeenth century. Finally, over the course of the century, the French monarchy did not increase its authority and institutions at an exponential rate. Institutional, financial, or political victories by the crown over one or another group were always tentative and subject to reversal.

A fragile state in a highly particularistic society—our conclusion undoubtedly robs the history of the Bourbon monarchy of a touch of its *grandeur*. But it does serve to place the state and its agents in the proper framework of a society influenced more directly by the scourges of nature, or by nature's beneficence, than by the crown's administrative or political action. This conclusion also raises questions, other than the conventional ones, about absolutism. What impact, for example, had the royal quest for greatness upon the institutions of a society that, for the most part, lived at the subsistence level? How were local solidarities organized, what motivated them, and to what degree were they antagonistic to the state? What place had the king in the intricate fabric of loyalties and beliefs that bound provincial society together? Did the degree of centralization that was achieved in the seventeenth century change the monarchy's perception of society and of its functions in society? These are but a few of the problems that our authors raise, and, in so doing, they not only illuminate the issues of the Mousnier-Porchnev debate, but also take us beyond it to a view of absolutism more in harmony with the concerns and conclusions of the contemporary school of social historians who have located the heart of seventeenth-century France in the *pays*.

NOTES

1. The distinction, which is made here, between the older and newer approaches to French history is not meant to be an invidious one. Recent, interesting, and highly respected studies that focus on the great political personalities of the seventeenth century are, John B. Wolf, *Louis XIV* (New York, 1968), and William F. Church, *Richelieu and Reason of State* (Princeton, 1972).

2. The new school of social and economic history in France has as its institutional base, the *Ecole Pratique des Hautes Etudes*. Among the major works of this school that pertain to the seventeenth century are the following: Pierre Goubert, *Beauvais et le Beauvaisis de 1600 à 1730* (Paris, 1966); Emmanuel Le Roy Ladurie, *Les Paysans de Languedoc* (Paris, 1966); Pierre Deyon, *Amiens: Capitale provinciale* (Paris and The Hague, 1967); François Le Brun, *Les hommes et la mort en Anjou aux 17e et 18e siècles* (Paris and The Hague, 1971).

3. The "Annales" school derives its name from the historical journal, *Annales: Economies, Sociétés, Civilisations,* founded in 1929 by Marc Bloch and Lucien Febvre.

4. Robert Mandrou, *La France aux XVIIe et XVIIIe siècles* (Paris, 1967), 293–301.

5. Peter Laslett, *The World We Have Lost: England Before the Industrial Age* (New York, 1965).

6. For example, on the English perception of French absolutism, see the thoughtful article of J. P. Cooper, "Differences Between English and Continental Government in the Early Seventeenth Century," in *Britain and the Netherlands,* eds. J. S. Bromley and E. H. Kossmann (London, 1960).

7. Among Mousnier's principal works are the following: *La vénalité des offices sous Henri IV et Louis XIII* (2nd. ed.; Paris, 1971); *L'assassinat d'Henri IV* (Paris, 1964); *Fureurs paysannes: les paysans dans les révoltes du XVIIe siècle* (Paris, 1967); *Les hiérarchies sociales de 1450 à nos jours* (Paris, 1969); and his collected articles, *La plume, la faucille, et le marteau* (Paris, 1970).

8. Quotations and references from Mousnier's *La vénalité* are taken from the second edition noted above.

9. Mousnier, *La vénalité*, 666.

10. Boris Porchnev, *Die Volkaufstande in Frankreich vor der Fronde,* trans. M. Brandt (Leipzig, 1954). A French translation, with a special introduction by Porchnev, was published in 1963: *Les soulèvements populaires en France de 1623 à 1648* (Paris, 1963).

11. Roland Mousnier, "Recherches sur les soulèvements populaires en France avant la Fronde," *Revue d'histoire moderne et contemporaine,* V (1958), 81–113.

12. Mousnier elaborates on this point in his *Problèmes de stratification sociale: deux cahiers de la noblesse pour les Etats généraux de 1649–1651* (Paris, 1965).

13. Mousnier, *La plume*, 11.

14. For a different conception of French social structures under the Bourbon monarchy, see Pierre Goubert, *L'ancien régime*, I (Paris, 1969).

1

ABSOLUTISM AND PROVINCIAL INSTITUTIONS

During the seventeenth century, the royal lawyers described monarchical authority in increasingly extravagant terms. However, the following four case studies of absolutism in action provide a perspective on the monarchy different from that suggested by the inflated rhetoric of the royalists and the dry formulas of the legal texts. Here we see the crown chipping away at the rights, privileges, exemptions, and nepotic power that constituted the liberties of Frenchmen, and seeking to reduce the worst excesses of the days of civil war. Yet, from these studies of the governments of Henry IV, Louis XIII, and Louis XIV, it becomes clear that absolutism did not mean the centralization and rationalization of power in the hands of the crown and its agents. War, and its compelling necessities, tended to undermine the systematic application of royal power to the reform of society and institutions, and to encourage a system of compromise and bargaining between the monarchy and elites. Nor was Bourbon government bureaucratic precisely. Although the intendants were professional administrators, absolutism more commonly appeared in the provinces in the guise of a whole host of freebooting tax farmers and revenue contractors who treated the country, as was said at the time, like some vast cow to be milked dry. Finally, as the provocative conclusions of Major and Deyon suggest, the development of absolutism over the century cannot be treated simply as a lineal evolution in which each king or minister built upon the policies of his predecessors in subduing the social orders beneath the crown. Louis XIV, for example, may have been more supportive of the old social order, in some respects, than Richelieu had been. Thus case studies selected to illustrate certain of the notable confrontations between the crown and elites point up not only the strengths of absolute monarchy, but also its ambiguities and nuances.

Henry IV and Guyenne: A Study Concerning Origins of Royal Absolutism [1]

BY J. RUSSELL MAJOR

The efforts of Henry IV and his principal minister, the Duke of Sully, to restore order and prosperity to France after the long and destructive Wars of Religion have generally been admired. Most historians have agreed, however, that they did not attempt to change the character of the monarchy, but rather were content to try to make the old system of government work.[2] It is my hope to throw doubt on this interpretation and to suggest that Henry and Sully consciously planned and began to implement changes that would have altered the nature of French government and society by undermining the provincial estates and through them the political position of the seigneural nobility and urban aristocracy. They were unable to make much progress in this direction in most parts of France because of the weakness of the crown, but in their dealings with the *généralité* of Guyenne they proceeded far enough to indicate that they desired to transform the Renaissance monarchy into a more absolute state.

The French Renaissance monarchy had been a decentralized state in which town councils and provincial estates had exercised numerous functions of government including, in many instances, the levying and collection of taxes. Even provincial governors and other royal officials had often been more the servants of their own interests or those of a powerful patron than of the king's. Upon occasion provincial estates and towns had claimed that they were unable to vote the taxes the king demanded, but then had given handsome presents to their governor, the secretary of state in charge of their province, and

2

other royal officials to encourage them to persuade the king to accept their pleas of poverty. Clearly the French kings could never become absolute monarchs so long as this situation existed, but to alter it they had to find means to win the loyalty of the bureaucracy and to control the tax collecting machinery. By doing so they could not only deal a deadly blow at the landed and urban aristocracies that controlled the provincial estates and the towns, but also increase their own revenue without adding to the burden on the people. With more money a larger, more trustworthy army could be developed and royal patronage extended to insure wider support. At the same time, by preventing the provincial estates and towns from taxing as they pleased, an important source of revenue that had been finding its way into the hands of the great nobles would be removed. With less wealth the great nobles could afford fewer clients to do their bidding; with fewer clients they would be less dangerous to the king.[3]

It was one thing, however, to talk of winning the loyalty of the bureaucracy and breaking the power of the provincial estates and municipal governments and another thing to put such ideas into practice. Many public officials owed their posts to the kindly offices of a patron to whom they remained more loyal than to the king. Others felt themselves independent because they had purchased their positions and could not easily be removed. To attack the privileges of towns and provinces was dangerous and even dishonest, for Henry IV, like his predecessors, had promised to respect their privileges.

As a result, although all of Henry's close advisors wanted to see royal authority restored, there was a faction led by Chancellor Bellièvre who thought that this could best be done by winning the loyalty of the vocal elements of the population by respecting the traditional privileges of towns, provinces, and social classes. The people as a whole could be won by providing an honest, frugal government administered by a small number of dedicated officials who owed their positions to their ability and served at the king's pleasure.

The Marquis of Rosny, afterwards Duke of Sully, was the leader of the absolutist faction. He had entered the *Conseil des*

3

finances in 1596 and had become its principal member in 1599. From this key position he attempted to spread his influence into other branches of the government. Exactly when the debate between the two factions began is not known, but by the close of 1605 Sully was clearly victorious and Bellièvre had been asked to surrender the seals of his office.[4]

Among the issues that led to the struggle between the two factions were whether the Paulette should be adopted making offices hereditary, and whether *élections* should be established throughout France in which royal officials, rather than those of the provincial estates and towns, would divide and collect taxes. Sully advocated both these measures. By making offices hereditary appointments could be freed from the influence of great noble patrons like the Duke of Guise, who had placed so many of his clients in the bureaucracy during the Wars of Religion that he had become more powerful in administrative circles than the king himself. By using royal tax collectors the crown could be freed from its financial dependence on provincial estates and towns.

Professor Mousnier, who has written such an admirable history of the sale of offices, has shown how the Paulette strengthened royal control over the bureaucracy and weakened the patron-client system. He has also proven by use of pamphlets that as early as 1614 contemporaries recognized that this had happened. Nevertheless, he believes that between 1602 and 1604 when the critical debate over the Paulette took place, Henry IV and Sully were motivated primarily by their desire to increase revenue. As evidence he argues that Bellièvre failed to mention the political motive for the Paulette when he attacked the proposal and that the crown had need of additional revenue.

Questions of motive, however, are always difficult to determine, especially when, as in this case, the two men who sponsored the measure left no contemporary evidence to explain why they acted as they did. Some years after 1605, Sully did tell Cardinal Richelieu that political considerations were of primary importance, but Mousnier attributes this statement to hindsight. He may, of course, be correct, but it is significant that

4

Richelieu seems to have accepted it as true and the usually well-informed Jacques-Auguste de Thou attributed the Paulette to a desire to strike a blow at the patron-client system as well as to increase revenue. Furthermore, it is at least possible that Bellièvre's insistence that the Paulette would weaken royal authority was in answer to a claim made by Sully that it would make officials more loyal. Even if the effect of the Paulette on the patronage system was not discussed in the council, it may have been considered by Henry IV and Sully. An open attack in the council on the patronage system might have made the great nobles aware of how much the Paulette would endanger their position and have caused them to try to block the proposal. Mousnier is on firm ground when he states that Sully wanted to increase royal revenue, but the need was less compelling between 1602 and 1604 when the Paulette was a major issue than it had been before because the treasury was enjoying a surplus. That Sully was more anxious to increase royal power than to increase royal revenue is also suggested by his refusal to abandon the *élections* in Guyenne in return for reimbursement as will be shown below. Therefore, it seems probable that when Henry IV and Sully proposed to establish the Paulette and the *élections* between 1602 and 1604 they were motivated primarily by the desire to win control over the bureaucracy and the tax collecting machinery in the kingdom.[5]

Since the establishment of hereditary officeholding has been studied by Mousnier, the remainder of this paper will be devoted to the issues surrounding the creation of eight new *élections* in the *généralité* of Guyenne in January 1603, an act which was regarded by its sponsors as preliminary to the establishment of *élections* in the remainder of France.

The *généralité* of Guyenne, one of the largest in France, was created in January 1523.[6] During the reign of Henry IV, it included Rouergue, Quercy, Rivière-Verdun, Comminges, Agenais, Armagnac, Condomois, and Landes, where *élections* were established by the 1603 decree. In this region there were periodic assemblies of the three estates in Rouergue, Quercy, and Comminges, that had voted, divided, and collected taxes prior to the edict. In Rivière-Verdun, Agenais, Armagnac,

Condomois, and Landes this task was done in assemblies attended by the deputies of the towns and communities, but rarely by the nobility and clergy. Périgord and the area around Bordeaux known as the *sénéchaussée* of Guyenne were also in the *généralité*, but *élections* had been established here prior to Henry IV's reign. The estates were rarely summoned in the *sénéchaussée* of Guyenne, but the three estates of Périgord met regularly until 1595 when, less than two years after their submission to the king, they ceased to be convoked, strong evidence of Henry's intentions in regard to the estates once he had established his own tax collecting machinery.[7]

In addition to the assemblies of the estates in the individual provinces, there was an Estates General of the *généralité* and government of Guyenne which had met regularly since the closing years of Henry II's reign to deal with matters of interest to all the provinces.[8] Bordeaux did not participate regularly in this huge regional assembly, perhaps because as a *pays d'élection* it was less interested in its financial activities. As a result, leadership fell to the municipal officials of Agen, the next most important town in the region. It is through their activities and those of their deputies to court that the negotiations between the *généralité* and the crown can be best studied during the critical years of the reign of Henry IV.

The earliest clashes between the crown and the inhabitants of Guyenne grew out of the financial disorders that had arisen during the Wars of Religion. In 1597 the *Parlement* of Paris deplored the fact that financial officials were levying a third or half again as much as the king intended on some people while others, more favored, contributed nothing. Minor royal officials and other persons were illegally claiming exemption from the *taille*. To correct these evils the crown dispatched commissioners to a number of provinces.[9] Among them was Michel de Marillac, the future keeper of the seals and rival of Cardinal Richelieu, who was sent to Guyenne.[10]

No report of Marillac's mission to Guyenne has been found, but we know that he established contact with the three estates of Comminges in the spring of 1599. That October their

deputy at Paris wrote that Marillac's initial report to the council
had been unfavorable. To put Marillac in a friendly mood before the council consulted him concerning the provincial *cahier*,
the deputy reported that he had promised that the estates
would pay him 1000 *écus* to which he had some claim.[11]

The recommendations of the commissioners led to a long
edict on the *taille* which was issued in March 1600, and to a
series of measures directed specifically at Guyenne either because Marillac's report indicated that the situation was worse
there than elsewhere or because the provincial estates were
thought to be less able to defend their privileges than those in
other parts of France.[12]

In 1600 and 1601 Jean de Martin, *trésorier général de France*
at Bordeaux, was sent to the various provinces in his jurisdiction to hold the provincial estates, study tax collection, and verify local debts. He found that the provincial estates were needlessly burdening the people by the costs of their frequent
meetings which they often held on their own initiative and by
the sums they levied to support their own activities. He issued
directives that struck severe blows at the independent position
the estates had enjoyed. The length of their sessions, the
number of representatives, and their daily remuneration were
strictly limited. Meetings were to be called only with the express
permission of the king and a limit was set on the amount that
could be voted to support their legitimate activities. Hardly
enough was allowed to pay the costs of holding the assemblies,
sending deputies to the king, and paying the debts incurred
during the Wars of Religion. If enforced, the opportunity to
make handsome presents to royal officials who supported their
cause would be removed as well as many opportunities for
graft and corruption.[13] On November 15, 1601, the king's
council issued a number of decrees supporting Martin's orders.
To prevent possible disobedience the council also ordered that
henceforth the towns and parishes would turn the taxes they
collected over to royal officials rather than to those of the provincial estates.[14] This act was soon followed by a directive sending two commissioners into the provinces with orders to study

7

the tax records since 1585 in search of fraud and illegal exemptions.[15] The final blow fell in January 1603 when the edict was issued creating eight new *élections* in Guyenne.[16]

In evaluating the significance of this last act, one must examine the intentions of the crown. Since the offices in the *élections* were venal, it might be argued that the edict was a fund raising measure rather than one designed to break the power of the privileged classes and move in the direction of royal absolutism, just as Mousnier has suggested that the Paulette, which made offices hereditary, was initially designed to fill the royal coffers, not to undermine the patronage system. The financial motive had evidently been paramount in the minds of Francis I, Henry II, and Henry III when they each in turn had established *élections* in Guyenne only to abolish them almost immediately when the provincial estates offered to reimburse the *élus* for the offices they had just purchased from the crown.[17] For example, in July 1581 *élections* had been created in Guyenne, but they had been abolished "forever" the following year in return for 70,000 *écus*.[18] At times the government frankly stated that it created offices to secure revenue as in January 1587 when it established additional posts in those parts of France where there were *élections*.[19] When Henry IV desperately needed money after the Spanish captured Amiens in 1597, Sully himself suggested that part of the needed sum be raised by creating and selling new offices. Included among the proposed financial positions were offices in the *élections*.[20] Therefore, only by a careful study of the actions of the crown and the leading citizens of Guyenne can it be determined whether the edict creating *élections* in January 1603 was intended as a move towards royal absolutism or merely as another stopgap measure by the Renaissance monarchy to obtain funds.

The decrees issued by the royal government between 1601 and 1603 caused a strong reaction in Guyenne. In the controversy that followed, Sully's desire to alter the nature of the Renaissance monarchy is revealed.[21] To defend their privileges which they clearly saw were threatened, the town councils, provincial estates, and Estates General of Guyenne swung into action. Efforts were made to block the royal edicts by winning favorable decisions in the sovereign courts in Bordeaux and Toulouse, by securing the support of Marshal Ornano, the king's lieutenant in Guyenne, and other powerful personages, and by sending one deputation after another to king and council.

The *consuls* of Agen secured Ornano's permission to summon the Estates General of Guyenne to meet in their town in November 1602. Once assembled, the deputies prepared a statement charging that the creation of commissioners to examine their tax records was a clear violation of their privileges and named two deputies to take it to court.[22] Aided by Marshal Ornano their suit was partially successful and on December 31 the decree was suspended by order of the council.[23]

The first round had gone to Guyenne. Anxious to show their gratitude and to insure further favors, Bayonne, Condom, Agen, and perhaps other towns each gave Ornano a fine horse.[24] Ornano, in turn, authorized the Estates General to meet in February and in May 1603 to name delegations to go to the king to secure the permanent revocation of the commissioners and the suppression of an unpopular tax.[25] To support their cause Ornano wrote letters to the king and the chancellor on January 25 expressing the satisfaction of the urban aristocracy of the region at the decision to suspend the edict creating the commissioners and on July 19 he pleaded with the chancellor to look favorably upon the *cahier* of the estates.[26]

Once more victory went to Guyenne and on August 2 the edict on the commissioners was permanently revoked.[27] Joyfully the Estates General met in October to express the gratitude of the *généralité* in a tangible way. Taxes were voted to raise 6000 *livres* for Ornano, 1500 for his son, and 600 for his secretary. In addition, each of the successful deputies was voted 4500 *livres,* a handsome sum well in excess of the espenses they had incurred.[28] In November the Estates General met once more, this time to follow up its victory by trying to get the king to revoke the January edict authorizing the new *élections.* The support of the sovereign courts and the *trésoriers généraux de France* at Bordeaux was sought and a new deputation was sent to the king.[29]

This time the government stood firm. The *trésoriers généraux* at Bordeaux refused to permit the tax to be levied to reward Ornano and the others because the king had not given his authorization, the deputations to court met with little success, and in April 1604, the *Parlement* of Bordeaux verified the edict creating the *élections*.[30] Nevertheless, Guyenne continued to resist in the hope of getting rid of the new financial officials and preventing the actual establishment of the *élections*. The *consuls* of Agen arranged for the assistant syndic of Agenais to purchase one office for 3000 *écus* and frightened a less friendly officeholder so much that he abandoned his post.[31] In March 1604 the three estates of Comminges adopted regulations designed to reduce the costs of holding the estates in order to silence criticism in the province itself, but continued to levy illegal taxes with the result that they were rebuked by the king's council. Rivière-Verdun was likewise reprimanded.[32] The *trésoriers généraux* at Bordeaux reported to Sully in August 1603 that Rouergue was resisting new taxes and the following year the president of the *Parlement* of Toulouse wrote the king that the estates were stirring up trouble and preventing the decrees of *Parlement* from being executed.[33] A voluminous correspondence was carried on by the *consuls* of the towns in the hope of devising some means of defending their privileges and in the fall of 1604 it was decided that the individual provinces should send deputations to the king and council to seek the revocation of the edict creating the *élections* and other concessions.[34]

Agen's municipal officials chose their first *consul,* Julien de Camberfore, Sieur de Selves, to represent their town and the province of Agenais.[35] Selves arrived in Paris around the middle of December 1604 and quickly contacted the king who referred him to Sully and his council.[36] There followed a ten month battle between the powerful minister and the outspoken defender of municipal liberties. Their frequent engagements are clearly revealed by Selves' numerous letters to the *consuls* at

Agen and by other sources. Neither Sully nor Selves were intel-
lectuals and one looks in vain in Sully's utterances for learned
explanations of royal prerogative such as James I was then
regaling the elected representatives of the English people, and
in Selves' for comments on the concept of popular sovereignty
that had lately found so many defenders in France. Sully justified his acts in terms of the corruption of the estates and the
welfare of the people; Selves in terms of tradition and privilege.

The contest between the two men was not as uneven as it
may initially seem. Selves alone was nothing, but as the spokesman of traditional privileges and procedures he found many
supporters both in the provinces and in the king's council itself.
Sully, on the other hand, owed his power solely to royal favor.
His proud demeanor and fiery temper had won him many
enemies whose numbers were augmented by his firm opposition to the graft and corruption that had lined the pockets of
courtiers and officials for so long a time. In the early months of
1605 he felt that he was on the verge of disgrace.[37] Even when
he was clearly master of the council, progress was slow. He
never managed to have an edict issued establishing *élus* in the
other *généralités* and they did not begin to function in all of
Guyenne until 1609.[38]

Sully was thoroughly convinced that the officials of the
provincial estates and towns were using their position to exempt themselves and their friends from taxation and to vote
handsome sums for those who attended the estates, served as
deputies to court, or performed other duties that might seem
to justify reward. He was equally certain that large sums were
granted to great nobles and royal officials in return for defending local privileges. Such practices, he thought, overburdened
the people and denied necessary revenue to the crown. His information was derived from the investigations that had been
held in Guyenne by financial officials, from reports from the
Parlement of Bordeaux, and from disgruntled local inhabitants.
In their first meetings in December 1604, therefore, Sully told
Selves that the current financial administration in Agenais
made the establishment of *élections* necessary and that most of

11

the inhabitants of the province favored this step. Later Sully made revealing comments about the small revenue the king received from Agen and the heavy burden borne by the people, comments accompanied by a question of whether money was levied for gifts and local purposes, a question to which he well knew the answer.[39] This is not to suggest, however, that Guyenne alone was set aside for punishment. Sully made no attempt to hide the long range objectives of the crown. The king, he declared to Selves, "wants the *taille* to be levied in all of France in the same fashion." He specifically said that Languedoc, Dauphiné, and Provence were earmarked for *élections*.[40]

Sully evidently did not feel secure. Selves often reported that Gilles de Maupeou, intendant of finances, was the only member of the council who supported Sully on the *élections*. Villeroy, the influential secretary for foreign affairs, Sillery who was soon to become keeper of the seals, Forget de Fresnes, the secretary of state in charge of Guyenne, and other councillors told Selves that they did not believe that the *élus* were necessary.[41] Perhaps it was for this reason that Sully did all he could to discourage and frighten the deputies so that they would depart without submitting their petitions to the council. From the beginning he insisted that there was no chance that the king would revoke the edict creating the new *élections*. When Selves persisted in his mission, Sully threatened to throw him in the Bastille on the grounds that he had a faulty procuration. When this did not suffice, he threatened him with his cane, and when Selves finally managed to appear before the council, Sully stormed out of the room in anger.[42] Little wonder Selves arrived at the conclusion that "those who come here for the welfare of the people are hardly welcome." [43] "There is nothing so odious here," he wrote, "as syndics and deputies." [44]

Since Selves and many other deputies braved his anger, Sully did all he could to discredit them and the cause they represented by obtaining letters and documents charging them with dishonest practices. He was not above tampering with the mail, Selves charged, and as a precaution the intrepid deputy usually entrusted his dispatches to friends going to Guyenne rather than to the post. He often repeated information given in an earlier letter and in several instances wrote twice the same day to insure that one letter would arrive safely.[45] When it became necessary to send very secret information to Guyenne around the first of April, the deputies from the *généralité* decided that one of their number should go in person.[46]

Sully tried to discourage deputies from coming to court with petitions that might be favorably received by refusing to authorize payment for their services. Indeed, he even attempted to prevent assemblies from meeting to elect deputations to court. One of Selves' tasks was to try to get the council to authorize the tax voted by the estates in 1603 to reward those who had participated in the negotiations to secure the revocation of the edict on the commissioners. On January 22, 1605, the council decided to permit Ornano and his son to keep the 7500 *livres* that had been voted them, perhaps because they were fearful of offending a marshal of France at a time when his aid was needed in his restless government. The deputies, however, were not even permitted to receive compensation for their expenses.[47] Little wonder that as his mission extended month after month, Selves raised the question of his own payment.[48] He also found his efforts to get permission to have an assembly of the estates temporarily blocked by Sully.[49]

From the first, Selves clearly realized the threat that the establishment of the *élus* posed for the towns and estates. In moments when he despaired of success he punctuated his letters with such phrases as they want "to abolish the privileges of the towns in order to be able to do as they please, and remove the means of complaining." Or "Adieu liberties! privileges! Consular offices will no longer have their luster or power." Or again "They have created the *élus* in order to reduce the authority of the consulat. . . . If we do not take care, we will be consuls only to have the streets cleaned." [50]

On his arrival in Paris Selves had quickly recognized the advisability of joining forces with the deputies of the other provinces in Guyenne in order to have "a stronger battery against the canons of M. de Rosny." [51] Cooperation, however, proved difficult. Some deputies failed to recognize the serious threat that the *élus* posed to their privileges. Others, like those from Rouergue and Quercy, preferred to try to persuade the sovereign courts in Toulouse and Montpellier to refuse to verify the edicts creating the new *élections,* a type of resistance not as promising for Agen because the courts in Bordeaux in whose jurisdiction it lay were less friendly. As a result, Selves cooperated closely only with the deputy from Condomois who found himself in a similar position.[52]

To accomplish his mission Selves soon saw that he would have to by-pass Sully and reach the king. To aid in this project he turned to the great personages of Guyenne and the court. Few of his letters fail to mention Marshal Ornano, the lieutenant general in Guyenne, whose aid Selves constantly sought and whose assistance he often received. It was Ornano who wrote the king and members of the council to secure a hearing for Selves when Sully wanted to send him away without presenting his petition, it was Ornano who sought permission for the estates to meet so that action could be taken against the *élus* and taxes voted for provincial affairs, and it was Ornano who warned the king that there would be popular disturbances in Guyenne if the *élus* were established.[53] Others Selves turned to included the seneschal of Agen, the secretary of state responsible for Guyenne, members of the council, lesser royal officials, and, of course, the king's mistress. Most of them probably expected a reward for their services although no one was so blunt as Nicolas de Netz, a counselor in the *Cour des Aides.* "Send a well-filled purse," Selves wrote on September 12, ". . . to pay M. de Netz because he has frankly told us that he will do nothing without money," a request that he repeated on October 17.[54]

Apparently Selves' instructions called for him to ask for the revocation of the edict creating the *élus* on the grounds that the *élections* had been abolished "forever" in 1582 in return for a substantial sum. He knew, however, that he would have no success unless the government was compensated for the revenue it anticipated from the sale of the new offices. It was probably to prevent him from making such a proposal that Sully tried to deny him access to the king and other councillors. The minister's efforts to prevent a financial offer from being made is the initial proof that he aimed at royal absolution, not additional revenue, for he knew how tempting a large sum would be to the other councillors and perhaps the king.

To circumvent Sully, Selves met with a group of the other deputies around the middle of March and prepared a plan that had to be kept so secret that it was agreed that one of their number would go to Guyenne to win the support of Ornano and their constituents rather than entrust their proposals to the mail. The plan called for getting Ornano's permission for the provincial estates to meet so that a definite financial offer could be made in return for abolishing the *élections*. Ornano was also to write the king telling him of the growing unrest in Guyenne. In this manner, the king would be confronted with a choice of adhering to his absolutist designs and of keeping the *élus* at the risk of rebellion, or of accepting a substantial sum of money accompanied by a reduction of local discontent. It is true that some revenue would be achieved by the sale of the new offices, but as these officials would have to be paid salaries, this approach would be less profitable than accepting the offer of the estates.[55]

There was no doubt in Selves' mind that Sully would choose the road to absolutism. He therefore by-passed him and the council and made the offer to the king through the Countess of Moret, his current mistress. If she was successful, he warned the *consuls* on June 22, it would be necessary to give her "a fine present." Selves originally hoped for a reply in several weeks, but Sully's absence at a Protestant assembly and, perhaps, the indecision of the king and his other councillors led to a long delay. On August 23 Selves was recalled by the *consuls* of Agen, but he lingered on at court until October grasping at every hope of success. Sully remained determined, however, and his influence on the king increased. Slowly resistance was stifled in the badly divided provinces of Guyenne, the sovereign courts verified the necessary edicts, and the *élus* were appointed. By 1609 they had begun to collect taxes in all of Guyenne.[56]

Selves and his fellow deputies had failed.[57] With the coming of the *élus* the Estates General of Guyenne became inactive,[58] and the provincial estates maintained a precarious existence by virtue of a royal decree permitting each of them to levy 3000 *livres* annually for local expenses, a sum too small to pose a threat to the crown or to justify for long the existence of the estates in the minds of the inhabitants.[59] Had Henry IV lived or Sully remained the leading figure in the council, royal absolutism would have become firmly established in Guyenne at this time, but this was not the case. Henry was removed from the scene by the hand of an assassin in May 1610 and Sully resigned his principal posts in January 1611.

The regency of Marie de Medici has generally been interpreted as a disorderly period in which the crown unsuccessfully attempted to purchase the obedience of the great nobles at home and to establish friendly relations with Spain abroad. To me it was more than this for it marked the abandonment of Henry IV and Sully's attempt to establish royal absolutism and the return to the consultative tradition of the Renaissance monarchy with its respect for the rights and privileges of towns, provinces, estates, and social classes. No longer did Sully dominate the council; in his place stood Villeroy, Jeannin, and Sillery, three men who Selves had believed to be sympathetic to his cause. The new government tried to modify the Paulette [60] and in February 1611 revoked the edict of 1603 creating the *élections* in Guyenne in return for the provincial estates reimbursing the *élus* for the cost of their offices.[61]

There followed a period of increased activity for the Estates General and the provincial estates of Guyenne in spite of efforts of the crown to prevent a renewal of their past abuses, but a few years after Louis XIII personally assumed the reins of government, he reverted to the policies of his father. In September 1621 he ordered that *élections* once more be created in Guyenne. As a result the Estates General soon died and the provincial estates slowly decayed and finally disappeared during the course of the century. In July 1622 Louis issued an edict creating *élections* in Languedoc, but that province was temporarily saved through the intervention of its lieutenant general.[62] Both of these events took place before Richelieu came to power but at a time when Sully's lieutenant, Gilles de Maupeou, was the superintendent of finances in charge of Guyenne and Michel de Marillac, whose investigation of the financial abuses in Guyenne in 1599 had been partly responsible for the temporary establishment of the *élections* there a few years later, was one of the king's councillors with specific responsibility for Languedoc.[63]

The assault on the provincial estates was renewed with unparalleled vigor between 1628 and 1630 when orders were issued creating *élections* in Dauphiné, Burgundy, Languedoc, and Provence. The plan of Henry IV and Sully seemed about to be put into effect, but the Day of Dupes (November 10, 1630) led to a reversal of policy. Michel de Marillac, now keeper of the seals and largely responsible for domestic affairs, was dismissed. His victorious rival, Cardinal Richelieu, abandoned the effort to create an absolute monarchy and permitted Burgundy, Languedoc, and Provence to buy back their privileges just as the government of Marie de Medici had acceded to the wishes of Guyenne in 1611. Because of this act the dream of Henry IV and Sully was never fully realized. Even Louis XIV permitted the provincial estates to function in some parts of France.[64]

NOTES

1. This paper was read at the meeting of the American Historical Association in December 1965. The material upon which it is based was gathered during a leave of absence in 1961–1962 made possible by a Social Science Research Council Fellowship and Emory University. To both I would like to express my appreciation. The following abbreviations have been used: "AC" for Archives Communales; "AD" for Archives Départementales; "BN" for Bibliothèque Nationale; "IAD" for *Inventaire sommaire des archives communales antérieures à 1790.*

2. See for example Jean-H. Mariéjol, *Histoire de France illustrée depuis les origines jusqu'à la Révolution,* ed. E. Lavisse (Paris, 1911), VI, pt. II; Georges Pagès, *La Monarchie d'ancien régime en France* (Paris, 1946), and R. Barbiche, "Étude sur l'œuvre de restauration financière de Sully, 1596–1610," *École Nationale des Chartes, Positions des Thèses* (Paris, 1960), pp. 11–18. In a sense Poirson sees a reorientation of the monarchy, but in the direction of greater popular participation, not royal absolutism. Auguste Poirson, *Histoire du règne de Henri IV* (Paris, 4 vols.; 2nd ed., 1862–67). Exceptions, however, are Roland Mousnier, *La Vénalité des offices sous Henri IV et Louis XIII* (Rouen, 1946); and William F. Church, *Constitutional Thought in Sixteenth-Century France* (Cambridge, Mass., 1941).

3. For essays on the nature of the Renaissance monarchy and aristocracy see J. R. Major, "The French Renaissance Monarchy as Seen through the Estates General," *Studies in the Renaissance,* IX (1962), 113–25; "The Renaissance Monarchy: A Contribution to the Periodization of History," *Emory University Quarterly,* XIII (1957), 112–24, reprinted in *The "New Monarchies" and Representative Assemblies—Medieval Constitutionalism or Modern Absolutism?* (Boston, 1964), 77–84, ed., A. J. Slavin; and "The Crown and the Aristocracy in Renaissance France." *American Historical Review,* LXIX (1964), 631–45.

4. R. Mousnier, "Sully et le conseil d'état et des finances: La luttre entre Bellièvre et Sully," *Revue Historique,* CXCII (1941), 68–86.

5. Mousnier, *Vénalité,* pp. 557–66. Jacques-Auguste de Thou, *Histoire universelle* (Basel, 1742), IX, 716. For Bellièvre's argument see "Contre la Paulette," *Revue Henri IV,* I (1906), 182–88. Jean R. Mallet, *Comptes rendus de l'administration des finances du royaume de France* (London, 1789), esp. pp. 194–95.

6. L. Desgraves, "La Formation territoriale de la généralité de Guyenne," *Annales du Midi,* LXII (1950), 239–48.

7. L. de Cardenal, "Les États de Périgord sous Henri IV," *L'Organisation corporative du moyen âge à la fin de l'ancien régime* (Louvain, 1939), III, 163–81. Other evidence of Henry's dislike of the provincial estates is not lacking. Concerning a request from the town of Bordeaux that the estates of Guyenne be assembled, he wrote to Matignon in 1595: ". . . il me semble que le temps n'est pas propre pour faire telles assemblées, lesquelles ordinairment tendent plus à descharges mes subjects de despenses que à me fortiffier et assister en mes affaires; car chacun ne regarde pas plus loin maintenant que à sa commodité particuliere, de sorte que je veulx que vous vous passiés de la dicte assemblée s'il est possible et qu'elle soit remise en temps plus opportun, . . ." Berger de Xivrey, ed., *Recueil des lettres missives de Henri IV* (Paris, 1848), IV, 343. On December 30, 1608 Henry told the deputies of the estates of Burgundy "Qu'ils lui parloient toujours des privilèges du pays; que ces privilèges n'étoint que pour faire des mutineries; que les plus beaux privilèges que les peuples pouvoient avoir, étoient quand ils étoient aux bonnes grâces de leur roi." Poirson, III, 14.

8. J. R. Major, "French Representative Assemblies: Research Opportunities and Research Published," *Studies in Medieval and Renaissance History,* I (1964), 201–208.

9. B. Barbiche, "Les Commissaires députés pour le 'régalement' des tailles en 1598–1599," *Bibliothèque de l'École des Chartes,* CXVIII (1960), 58–96.

10. Barbiche did not mention Marillac's participation in the investigation and believed that Normandy was the only *pays d'états* to which investigators were sent, *ibid.,* p. 62. Marillac's biographer, Nicolas Le Fevre, sieur de Lezeau, said that Chancellor Chiverney sent Marillac to the *généralités* of Limoges and Guyenne. He was given virtual "carte blanche" to do what was necessary. Included in his orders were commissions to assemble the estates of Agenais, Rouergue, Quercy, Comminges, and Rivière-Verdun. BN, ms. fr. 14,027, ch. 2.

11. AD, Hauté-Garonne, C 3764, nos. 7–10; C 3676, nos. 53–54. The estates of Agenais contacted Marillac during the winter of 1599. AD, Lot-et-Garonne, C 95, fols. 88V, 101.

12. Barbiche, "Les Commissaires . . . ," p. 84. François-A. Isambert and others eds., *Recueil général des anciennes lois françaises depuis l'an 420 jusqu'à la Révolution de 1789* (Paris, 1821–33), XV, 226–38. Noël Valois, ed., *Inventaire des arrêts du conseil d'étate, règne de Henri IV* (Paris, 1886–93), II, nos. 6094, 6114, 6117, 6151, 6159, 6164, 6263, 6294, 6344, 6465, 6479, 6488, 6491, 6511, 6543, 6575, 6577, 6610, 6611.

13. Martin was directed to visit the estates of Comminges, Rivière-Verdun, and Quercy in the spring of 1600. AD, Gironde, C 3873 bis, fols. 26v–27v. AD, Haute-Garonne, C 3680, nos. 1–16. His regulations for the estates of Quercy are at BN, ms. Clairambault 360, fols. 12–14v. Sully praised Martin for his efforts. AD, Haute-Garonne, J 103, no. 97. In January and February 1601 Martin held the estate of Condomois, Armagnac, and Agenais. AC, Mézin, BB 2, fols. 65–73v; AC, Condom, BB 18; AD, Gers, E Suppl. 23,936, fols. 191v–94; AC, Isle-Jourdan, BB 2, fols. 52v–55. His regulations on the receipts and expenses in Agen are in AC, Agen, BB 17. An order of the king's council concerning the estates and taxation in Guyenne that was based on Martin's work was issued on Feb. 12, 1611. *Édit du roy, contenant revocation et suppression des huict bureaux d'élections, establis en la généralité de Guyenne par edict du mois de janvier 1603* . . . (Agen, 1612), pp. 29–52. There are copies in AD, Lot-et-Garonne and BN, *Actes Royaux,* F. 46,923, no. 3.

14. Valois, II, nos. 6630, 6639, 6641, 6643–50. AD, Gironde, C 3873 bis, fols. 10v–11v.

15. G. Tholin, "Des Tailles et des impositions au pays d'Agenais durant le XVIe siècle jusqu-aux réformes de Sully," extract from *Recueil des travaux de la société d'agriculture, sciences et arts d'Agen,* XIII (1875), 28–29. It is unfortunate that this significant work has been neglected by historians.

16. *Edit . . . portant création et establissement de huict sièges d'eslections . . . de la généralité de Guienne* (Paris, 1603). There is a copy at BN, *Actes Royaux,* F. 46,912, no. 1.

17. AD, Haute-Garonne, C 3416; C 3804, esp. nos. 1–5, 8, 15, 41, 50, 51. In the 1550's the inhabitants of the villages of Comminges and a few other persons wanted royal tax collectors to avoid the expenses of holding the estates and perhaps for other reasons. C 3804, esp. nos. 6, 7, 9–14, 40, 50c. In their petition to the king's council in 1611 to obtain once more the abolition of the *élections,* the deputies from Guyenne cited five previous instances when *élections* in all or part of Guyenne had been suppressed. Their list was not complete. See pp. 17 and 75–78 of the printed edict of Feb. 12, 1611 cited in fn. 13. See also Tholin, pp. 26–27.

18. *Edict du roy contenant révocation des édicts de création des sièges d'élections au pais de Guyenne* (Paris, 1582). Copies are at BN, *Actes Royaux,* F. 46,872, no. 8; and in AC, Agen, AA 17.

19. *Edict du roy pour le restablissement des offices des bureaux d'élections cy-devant supprimez* (Paris, 1587). A copy is at BN, *Actes Royaux,* F. 46,884, no. 1.

20. Sully, *Mémoires des sages et royales oeconomies d'estat . . . , Nouvelle collection des mémoires pour servir à l'histoire de France* (Paris, 1837), eds. J. Michaud and J. Poujoulat, 2nd sér., II, 248.

21. Sully failed to mention this controversy in the *Mémoires . . .* probably, as Mousnier has suggested in regard to the Paulette, because he did not want to associate himself and or his master with these generally unpopular measures. Mousnier, "Sully et le conseil . . . ," p. 73, fn. 5; and *La Vénalité . . . ,* p. 209, fn. 664. For this reason and because Sully left no extensive correspondence, his quarrel with Guyenne has been overlooked by nearly all students of the period including Poirson, Mariéjol, Barbiche, and Mousnier himself. There is little on the subject in the Bellièvre correspondence (BN, ms. fr. 15,890–15,911) probably because the chancellor was not directly concerned with financial administration. Furthermore, by the time the struggle reached its height in 1605 he had lost most of his influence. Jean P. Charmeil, *Les Trésoriers de France à l'époque de la Fronde* (Paris, 1964), pp. 360–61, mentions the edict creating the *élections,* but only a few local historians, especially Tholin, *op. cit.,* have recognized its significance.

22. AC, Agen, AA 33; BB 40, fols. 132v–138; CC 116. AD, Dordogne, 5C 29, fol. 23–23v. Tholin, pp. 29–30.

23. Valois, II, no. 7387. AC, Agen, BB, 40, fols. 143–144v.

24. AC, Agen, BB, 40, fol. 148v–149.

25. AC, Agen, BB, 40, fols. 145v–47; CC 116, procès-verbal of May 1603. AC, Mézin, BB 2, fols. 153v–154. For some relevant correspondence see also AC, Agen, AA 33.

26. BN ms. fr. 15,897, fols. 339 and 351. *Archives historiques du département de la Gironde,* XIV (1873), 387–89.

27. AC, Agen, CC 118, extract of the *cahier* of Aug. 2, 1603.

28. AC, Agen, CC 116, procès-verbal of Oct. 11, 1603; BB 40, fols. 166–68, 191–92. BN, ms. fr. 18,168, fols. 17–18v.

29. AC, Agen, BB 40, fols. 168v–169v; CC 116, procès-verbal of Nov. 18, 1603.

30. AD, Gironde, C 3874 bis, fol. 135–35v, AC, Agen, CC 120, Bazas to Agen, July 24, 1604.

31. Tholin, p. 32.

32. AD, Haute-Garonne, C 3686, nos. 16–17. Valois, II, no. 9305.

33. AD, Gironde, C 3874, fols. 39–40v. BN, ms. fr. 23,198, fols. 288–95.

34. AC, Agen, AA 33, Correspondance of 1604. AC, Condom, BB 18, esp. entries in October and November 1604.

35. Selves's valuable correspondence has been utilized by Tholin, pp. 32–50.

36. AC, Agen, CC 111, Selves to Agen, Dec. 21, 1604; CC 120, letters of Selves to the consuls of Agen, Dec. 1604; CC 123, Selves to Agen, Jan. 1, 1605.

37. Sully, III, 20–25, 34–40. Sully reported that his enemies accused him of disbursing royal funds in such a manner as to win the support of certain great nobles.

38. Marc -A. -F. de Gaujal, *Études historiques sur le Rouergue* (Paris, 1858–59), II, 482.

39. Selves's December 1604 letters from Paris are in AC, Agen, CC 111 and CC 120. His 1605 correspondence is in CC 123, including the Jan. 1 letter containing Sully's question concerning the gifts. Selves wrote of Sully's insistence that the *élus* were necessary on Jan. 12 and 30, Feb. 11, March 16 and 20, May 2, 18, and 20, and on other occasions. The most serious attack on the administration of the Agen *Consuls* was launched by the *procureur du roi* in Agenais. He claimed that he had been threatened by the *consuls* when he had tried to examine their financial records as instructed by the *Parlement* of Bordeaux. He sent a report to the king charging the *consuls* with financial disorders and abuses, charges which Selves was called upon to answer. AC, Agen, CC 122; CC 123, Selves to Agen, Feb. 15, March 3, and March 8.

40. AC, Agen, CC 123, Selves to Agen, Feb. 11 (no. 13). See also letter of Jan. 30. This correspondence helps to confirm Richelieu's comment that Henry IV would haved liked to establish *élections* in Languedoc. *Mémoires du Cardinal de Richelieu* (Paris, 1929), eds. G. Lacour-Gayet and R. Lavollée, IX, 302–303. Selves reported on April 6 that the crown wanted to treat Brittany in the same manner as Guyenne.

41. AC, Agen, CC 111 and CC 120, Selves to Agen, Dec. letters, 1604; CC 123, Selves to Agen, March 3, 10, and May 14, 1605.

42. AC, Agen, CC 123, Selves to Agen, Feb. 11 (nos. 12 and 13), March 3, 8 (no. 19), 20, and 27.

43. *Ibid.,* Feb. 11 (no. 12).

44. *Ibid.,* March 10, 1605. For similar statements see letters of March 8 (nos. 18 and 19), April 22 and 29.

45. Selves usually told the *consuls* how he dispatched each letter. He wrote twice on Feb. 11, and March. 8.

46. AC, Agen, CC 123, Selves to Agen, March 27 and April 6.

47. BN, ms. fr. 18,168, fols. 17–18v. Vicose was later permitted to keep 1800 of the 4500 *livres* voted him, fols. 219v–220, but I have found no evidence that the other deputies were compensated for their expenses. AC, Agen, CC 123, Selves to Agen, Jan. 22, Jan. 30, Feb. 11, April 6, and June 22, 1605. For a brief but interesting account of how Vicose combined the roles of a royal official investigating financial matters in Guyenne and of a deputy of the estates defending local privileges, see D. Buisseret, "A Stage in the Development of the French Intendants: The Reign of Henry IV," *The Historical Journal,* IX (1966), 28–30.

48. *Ibid.,* April 6 and Sept. 12, 1605.

49. *Ibid.,* May 14, May 18, and May 20, 1605. Permission was, however, eventually granted.

50. *Ibid.,* CC 123, Selves to Agen, Jan. 22, March 8 (no. 19), and March 10, 1605.

51. *Ibid.,* Jan. 1, 1605.

52. AC, Agen, CC 120, Selves to Agen, Dec. 1604; CC 123, Selves to Agen, Jan. 1, Feb. 11, March 3 and 8 (no. 19), 1605.

53. AC, Agen, CC 123, Selves to Agen, March 8 (nos. 18 and 19), March 10, April 29, May 14, May 20, and July 11, 1605. *Mémoires authentiques de Jacques Nompar de Caumont, duc de la Force* (Paris, 1843), ed., LaGrange, I, 402–404. BN, ms. fr. 23,198, fols. 321–22. Many of Ornano's letters to the king and the chancellor supporting the desires of the inhabitants of Guyenne may be found in BN, ms. fr. 15,897, fols. 325–86; and *Archives historiques du départment de la Gironde,* XIV (1873), 352–438.

54. AC, Agen, CC 123, Selves to Agen, January 5, 6, 22, Feb. 11 (no. 12), March 3, May 14, June 22, Sept. 12, and Oct. 17, 1605; CC 124, Verduc to Agen, July 29, 1605. On Netz mission to Agen see CC 118.

55. AC, Agen, CC 123, Selves to Agen, March 16, 27, April 6, 22, 29, May 14, 18, 20, and June 4, 1605. To persuade the consuls of Agen to accept the proposals of the Paris deputies, Selves pointedly told them in his letter of April 22 of a deputy sent by the *Parlement* of Bordeaux to protest against some tax farmers who Sully wished to send home without being heard, but the king, fearing an uprising, gave reasonable satisfaction. There was already considerable unrest in southwestern France because of the activities of some nobles and Protestants and the suffering of the agricultural classes. Mariéjol, VI, pt. 2, 4–5, 44–45, 66–72.

56. Selves's correspondence between June 22 and Oct. 17 is in AC, Agen, CC 120 and CC 123 except for some letters which appear to have been lost. Letters of Verduc, who joined Selves in Paris during the latter part of his mission and remained as Agen's representative after his departure, are at CC 124, along with letters from some deputies from other provinces in Guyenne. After Selves's departure from court, most of the resistance to the *élus* was carried on by other provinces. The syndic of the nobility of Armagnac visited the estates of Comminges in Dec. 1605 and suggested that the provinces of Guyenne unite in an effort to block the establishment of the *élus.* Comminges sent a deputation to Ornano to seek his advice and assistance. AD, Haute-Garonne, C 3690, nos. 15–16. On Jan. 7, 1606, Ornano wrote the king telling him that the establishment of the *élections* was causing strong resentment in Guyenne because there was a tradition passed on from father to son that the *élus* would subvert their privileges, franchises, and liberties which had been preserved for so many years under the crown. The bourgeoisie and the inhabitants of the *plat pays* were especially fearful that they would be over-taxed because the *taille* was *réele.* He expressed fear that the edict would lead to unrest and, in conjunction with the seneschal and governor of Quercy, urged that the edict creating the *élections* be revoked. BN, ms. fr. 23,198, fols. 321–22. In 1606 the deputy of Comminges to court borrowed 10,250 *livres* as a down payment and purchased the offices in the *élection* in the name of the *pays* de Comminges for 25,250 *livres.* AD, Haute-Garonne C 3691, nos. 3–4; C 3692, nos. 53–54; C 3693, nos. 3–5; C 3694, nos. 1–6. Comminges still owned the offices when they were abolished in 1611. See pp. 25–26 of the printed copy of the edict of Feb. 1611 cited in fn. 13. Rouergue, Quercy, and other provinces continued to protest and in Dec. 1608 the *élus* were still not established in the first named province. *IAD, Aveyron,* ser. G, 89, AD, Aveyron, C 1903. In May 1609 the Estates General of Guyenne was permitted to meet once more to elect deputies to go to court to protest against the *élus.* AD, Gironde, C 3977. Valois, II, no. 14,891. AD, Agen, BB 40, fols. 368v–69v.

57. Selves attributed his difficulties to the failure of the provinces in Guyenne to cooperate more closely. AC, Agen, CC 123, Selves to Agen, March 8 (no. 19) and March 12. He may have been partially correct because the Estates General of Guyenne had never been able to relegate the smaller estates to secondary status as the estates of Languedoc had its diocesan and seneschalsy assemblies. However, other rivalries lessened Guyenne's capacity to resist. The failure of the nobility and clergy to participate in many of the provincial estates must have weakened them. It is noteworthy that the most effective resistance was offered by the estates of Comminges and Rouergue where the three estates acted as a unit. To make matters worse the third estate of Agenais was then quarreling with the nobility over whether the *taille* was *réele* or *personnelle.* Part of Selves' mission was to support the suit at court. See AC, Agen, CC 123, Selves to Agen, Feb. 15; March 3, 6, 10, and 27. See also CC 108, CC 118, and CC 121. A similar dispute was a major factor in the establishment of *élections* in Dauphiné during the reign of Louis XIII. The towns in Agenais also quarreled among themselves and Selves devoted much of his time trying to thwart Villeneuve-sur-Lot's special deputy to court who was seeking a general levy on the region to repair a bridge. *Ibid.,* May 25, June 4, July 3, 11, Aug. 27, and Sept. 12; CC 120, Selves to Agen, Aug. 6, 1605. On this long dispute see also Valois, II, nos. 6212, 8721, 12,011, and 14,686.

58. I have found no evidence of a meeting of the Estates General of Guyenne in 1605, 1606, 1607, or 1608.

59. This decree of July 14, 1607 reaffirmed the rule regulating the estates established by Martin in 1601. AC, Agen, CC 128; and Valois, II, no. 11,190.

60. Mousnier, *La Vénalité . . . ,* p. 568.

61. The printed copy of this edict cited in fn. 13 also contains a copy of the *cahier* the deputies of the Estates General of Guyenne presented the council on Nov. 20, 1610 asking that the *élections* be suppressed.

62. Major, "French Representative Assemblies . . . ," 201–208. *IAD, Haute-Garonne,* Sér. B, no. 420. Claude de Vic and Jean Vaissete, *Histoire générale de Languedoc* (Toulouse, 1874–1905), XI, 981.

63. R. Mousnier, "Les Règlements du conseil du roi sous Louis XIII," *Annuaire-bulletin de la société de l'histoire de France,* (1946–1947), p. 157.

64. My suggestion that Marillac, not Richelieu, was responsible for the attempt to create the new *élections* has been anticipated by Mariéjol, pp. 405–406 and Pagès, pp. 104–105. In the hope of resolving some unanswered questions, I have begun a detailed study of the relations between the crown and the provincial estates during the first half of the seventeenth century. For bibliographical material, see Charmeil, pp. 359–74.

Relations Between the French Nobility and the Absolute Monarchy During the First Half of the Seventeenth Century

BY PIERRE DEYON

More than ten years ago, B. P. Porchnev sought to substitute for the traditional accounts, which complacently described the battle between Richelieu and the great nobility and the opposition of the nobility to the development of royal absolutism, the idea of a common front that united the monarchy, the seigneurial lords, and the urban bourgeoisie against the lower classes of the cities and the countryside. This thesis, doubtlessly too bold, had the great merit of focusing attention once again on the importance and the frequency of popular uprisings before the Fronde. The debate that it stimulated has not ended, and an investigation intended to clarify all facets of the problem and to collect information is underway.[1]

Certain of the objections raised against the theories of the Soviet historian evoked the responsible role of members of the privileged orders in the origins of several provincial uprisings. This is the perennial and unresolved problem concerning the relations between the nobility and the absolute monarchy: if we know a great deal about the endless plots directed against the cardinal ministers, we understand poorly the collective psychology and the material situation of the noble order as a whole.[2] While waiting for the results of the investigation in progress and for the precise knowledge it will bring concerning the effective participation of diverse social groups in the riots and rebellions that troubled the kingdom from 1624 to 1653, we would like to draw attention to certain particular aspects of noble discontents and noble demands.

25

1

It would be completely wrong to imagine that the nobility was perfectly protected from the fiscal pressure that the government of Louis XIII and the regency imposed upon the country. Engaged in a vast European competition, at a time when the reversal of economic conditions shook the prosperity of the kingdom, the monarchy was forced to increase existing taxes, to multiply duties and expedients, and it also sought to reduce the extent of fiscal privileges. In order to study this financial policy, it is advisable to distinguish the regions where the *taille personnelle* prevailed, and those where the *taille réelle* was levied. In the one, the treasury took into account only the quality of the persons involved; in the others, the noble or plebeian character of the lands decided whether a tax would be imposed or an exemption granted.

In the regions of the *taille personnelle,* where noble status was probably the most advantageous, the regulations concerning the *taille* that were promulgated during the first half of the seventeenth century sought progressively to limit fiscal privilege. The edict of March 1600 ordered to be inscribed on the tax rolls all of the tenants of ecclesiastics, gentlemen, and other privileged persons "as much for their property as for the profits they could make from the said farms." The regulations of 1634 and 1643 prescribed that intendants and *trésoriers de France* tax on their own authority "privileged persons whose exemptions have been revoked by the edict of 1640 . . . powerful inhabitants of the parishes who, by their own power or by intimidating others, have previously been exempted or have been assessed at low rates . . . and the tenants of gentlemen . . . who have, up to the present, carried little or no tax burden, through the authority of their masters who have exempted them." [3]

These insistent repetitions eloquently suggest the difficulties and the obstacles that were encountered. The solidarity of the seigneurial lords, nobles and officers, significantly paralyzed the will of the government and of its representative, the intendant. But these initiatives and decisions led to a whole series of investigations—most often confided to private tax contractors—that immediately stimulated anxiety, as is seen, for example, in the "Journal of the Noble Assembly of 1651."

The regulations of 1634, 1640, and 1643 contained other innovations that were contrary to the interests of the order. Thus article 33 of the edict of 1634 authorized nobles, ecclesiastics, and other privileged persons to work "by their hands only one of their lands and estates" and ordered that the receivers and servants overseeing other fields be taxed "just as the property of tenants would be." [4] These restrictions sought to eliminate fraud by certain privileged persons who declared as their servants farmers who were, however, bound to them by secret contracts. They provoked the complaints of the entire nobility, and the Estates of Normandy protested in 1643 against the relentlessness shown by the tax commissioners in the application of this measure.[5] The privileged thought up other methods to circumvent royal legislation and to protect their domains from the tax. They regrouped several small farms under the direction of one steward—"combining three or four farms together and buying the houses of the peasants in order to pull them down." [6] A study of noble inheritances confirms this evidence. Thus we have found in the inventory taken after the death of Lemaître de Bellejamme, who was a councillor of state when he died in 1666, traces of more than one hundred contracts of exchange and purchase that were concluded between this personnage and neighboring peasants, and all of which were designed to consolidate his seigneurial domain.[7] It would be easy to offer other examples taken from family archives or notarial minutes, but only a systematic comparison of a great number of land plans would give us an appreciation of the importance of the phenomenon, which was, in any case, real enough to arouse the concern of the government and led it to reduce in 1667 the effects of its benevolence: "Abusing the right granted them by the regulations of 1643 and 1664 of working one farm themselves without paying the *taille*, certain people joined several farms into one and tilled an area covered by eight or ten ploughs." [8] The extent of the area under exemption was restored to the land tilled by four ploughs for the ecclesiastics and gentlemen, and by two ploughs for the bourgeois of Paris.

In the interval, other edicts proceeded against usurpers of nobility and against the recently ennobled. The latter submitted to new investigations and were obliged to pay for the confirmation of their nobility.[9] Two edicts of 1610 and 1614 sought to combat the abuses from which members of the royal and princely households (*commensaux*) benefited. These titles were widespread, and a great number of *commensaux* served only honorifically.[10] Henceforth, only officers who rendered effective service, at wages of more than sixty livres, and whose names were listed in the annual registers, were admitted to the exemption.[11] These decisions responded to a desire often expressed by the old nobility, but their application, confided to revenue farmers, led to investigations that were harmful to the entire body of the nobility. Thus in December 1634 and 1635, the Estates of Normandy complained about the proceedings of the revenue farmers and of the *trésoriers de France* who were engaged in verifying letters of nobility.[12] The same grievance was again invoked in 1658 by the organizers of the rebellious assemblies in Normandy.[13]

In the regions where the *taille réelle* applied, sharp conflicts had for centuries divided the different orders of the provinces on the subject of the *tailles*—should nobles pay, or not pay, taxes on their non-noble lands? Almost everywhere, during the first part of the seventeenth century, the monarchy intervened to restrict their privileges. In Provence, a judgment of the *Parlement* in 1552 had already established the principle: all non-noble land payed the *taille,* whoever the proprietor. But certain provisions of this warrant having caused serious disputes, there had to be a decision of the royal council, of January 21, 1625, to reaffirm the obligation weighing on all non-noble properties. Only those lands of which the proprietors could prove that the acquisition was in compensation for the alienation of fiefs effected after 1556 were spared.[14] In Languedoc as well, at the end of the reign of Louis XIII, the "real" character of the land tax was asserted, and "no privilege could any longer exempt someone from inheritance and estate duties." The treatise on the *tailles* by Antoine Despeisses, a lawyer at the Cour des Aides of Montpellier, specified in the edition of 1643 that "it had thus been judged" by the decrees of April 28, 1633, and of March 15, 1634.[15]

The development in Dauphiné was even clearer. Until 1639, the nobility of the sword and robe and the clergy remained exempt from all taxes. The regulation promulgated by Louis XIII on October 24 of that same year compelled all non-noble estates to pay the *tailles,* the *taillons,* and garrison duties.[16] Finally, in the *élections* of Condom and Agen, the new land survey, established between 1604 and 1622, included for the first time all of the non-noble lands in the parishes, without considering the status of the proprietors.[17]

It is far from our intention to affirm that fiscal privilege no longer existed in the regions of the *taille réelle.* Because they possessed a certain number of fiefs, nobles did not contribute to the royal tax exactly according to their landed wealth. Moreover, the lords often excluded from the land surveys taxable lands that they kept in their own domain, or those they were able to compensate for through former alienations of the family's noble patrimony. However, it is too often forgotten, in our opinion, that they were taxpayers and probably resented, along with other taxpayers, the increase in the total volume of the *taille* and direct duties.[18] One can guess the possible consequences of such a development. D'Epernon, governor of Guyenne, certainly knew how things stood, when he wrote Seguier, on March 25, 1649, "The nobility, principally in the regions of the *taille rélle,* show an interest in the welfare of the people." [19]

The fiscal grievances of the nobility did not, moreover, concern only direct taxes; it complained also about the increase in the *octrois,* the *aides,* and customs duties, of which it bore its share. "Subject to all sorts of taxes and duties, it [the nobility] also pays what is imposed on merchandise," the assembly of the nobility recalled in 1651.[20] Finally, the taxes of the *ban* and *arrière-ban* were equally a source of discontent. Already in the six-

29

teenth century, the monarchy had, on several occasions, substituted a compensatory contribution for the active military service of the *ban* and the *arrière-ban*. After the failure of the summons of 1635, the government of Louis XIII revived the procedure, and the service of the *ban,* as a system of recruitment, seemed to be transformed, little by little, into a veritable fiscal system applicable to nobles and the holders of fiefs.

From the *Testament* of Richelieu, we know what was the exact intention of the king and his minister on this subject—to recruit, using the contributions of the *ban* paid by those who did not serve in person, regular companies of light-horse cavalry and militiamen, whose valor and military effectiveness would have been infinitely superior to the feudal mob produced by the traditional levies.[21] But there was not enough time for the realization of this project, of which they retained mainly the financial aspect. The blow thus aimed at fiscal privilege was so serious that, in order to hide its importance, they pretended each time to prepare for an actual mustering of the noble troops, which, before the opening of the campaign, was turned into a collecting of funds. The summons of February 1639 contained severe strictures against "those who remain at home in shameful idleness." [22] Its fourth article recalled the obligation upon nobles to march, armed, mounted, and equipped, in the companies of the *ban* and *arrière-ban.* However, some weeks later, at the beginning of the campaign, and without fearing accusations of inconsistency, service was converted into a financial loan, and the offers of the provincial country gentlemen, determined to serve in person, were rejected. In 1642, gentlemen were excused from personal service, but compelled to provide for the maintenance and armament of a foot soldier, and the same comedy of the muster, annulled at the last moment and "generously" transformed into a compensatory tax, was revived during the Dutch war of 1675.[23] Here was a formidable precedent: not only did the tax reach 15 to 20 percent of the presumed income of the fief,[24] and thus constituted a significant expense, but again it aimed a serious blow at the very principle of fiscal exemption.

All these measures were strongly resented by a nobility whose material situation was hardly prosperous, and whose revenues were diminished by the interconnected effects of the war and of the economic reversals that occurred between 1630 and 1650. Like other social groups, the nobility had been tempted to attribute to the monarchy responsibility for the family difficulties which the reduction of its seigneurial rights and its land revenues brought about. The initiatives of a hard-pressed government, coming under such circumstances, assumed for many a vaguely provocative aspect, and the pursuit of the war appeared almost nonsensical. Still incapable of the lucidity that has sometimes been attributed to them, all social groups feverishly sought out a scapegoat—the revenue farmer, or the Mazarin who had deprived them of the paternal protection of the king.

The registers and the accounts of the lay landlords are, unfortunately, too rare, but there does exist a bundle of grievances and sorrowful representations, all of which point out the mediocre material situation of a part of the nobility during the reign of Louis XIII and the Regency.

The memoir submitted to the king after the assembly of notables of 1626–27 invoked the financial distress of the entire order: "It is in the most pitiable state that it ever was . . . poverty overwhelms it . . . idleness renders it vicious . . . oppression has nearly reduced it to despair." [25] Perhaps a stylistic exercise, but Richelieu confirmed the essential of it in his *Testament politique* and made allusions on several occasions to the misery of the country nobility.

During the Fronde, a certain number of pamphlets and *mazarinades* expressed this theme. The "Plaintes de la noblesse contre les partisans et mange-peuple," after the customary protests against the venality of offices and the insolence of magistrates, described those gentlemen "grown old in the service, dying in their lodgings without rewards, being compelled to trample on the common man and to pillage the peasant in order to live according to their rank and quality." [26] In the same way, the noble "confused on the question of money" is presented to us as a picaresque hero, with an empty belly, beating the pavement of Paris, in search of an invitation to dinner or of a loan from his friends, who were, however, also drained of cash: "O heavens, what pitiable reign is this? must the nobility be treated so . . . poor nobility which passes away like time." The protagonist of this little comedy had the merit to tell us about the origins of his financial difficulties: his tenant had not been able to pay him what he owed.[27] Such failures made recourse to credit, which the nobility had abused for a long time, ever more necessary. Borrowing assumed the form of mortgage loans, very dangerous for the future of noble patrimonies. The author of a memoir of 1655–57 treated this problem clearly and passionately. "There has appeared another kind of people among us . . . the rentiers, ignorant and illiterate people who amass large estates painlessly, without work and without risk, great good-for-nothings who do business only with notaries . . . it is they who have driven the two pillars of the state—the gentlemen and the tillers—from their former patrimonies, and who have, by decree, caused to disappear the greater part of the noble and non-noble lands held for 150 years. Three things have ruined the nobility—the ease of finding money, luxury, and war." [28] A very moving picture, but which, just like the preceding evidence, calls for statistical verification. We shall have only a conjectural knowledge of these problems, as long as we lack sufficient studies on the evolution of noble property and on the influence of economic circumstances on the movement of landed and seigneurial revenues.[29]

While awaiting the result of these long and difficult investigations, it is possible to make use of the dossiers and lists drawn up on the occasion of the convocations of the *ban* and *arrière-ban,* a source that is only approximate, but one that is easily used and that quickly provides interesting information.[30] The declarations, either made verbally or in writing, by the gentlemen at the time of the preliminary review offer us numerous personal appraisals. One recalled that he had served His Majesty for forty years, that his son was in the service of the regiment of Rambures, but that in order to equip him, he had to contract several large loans.[31] Another, aged sixty-five and handicapped in both arms, invoked the mediocrity of his estate: "A little thatch-covered house and garden at Boves, with 100 livres in rents, and he added with bitterness, that he had passed his youth in the service of the king where he had ruined his body and his estate." [32] One, "who had squandered his estate in the service of the Piedmont regiment," declared himself ready to respond to the convocation "provided that they give him equipment," while another begged His Majesty to let him serve in person, because his land had been burned by the Spaniards, and he could receive nothing from his tenants.[33] But beside these moving witnesses, what is one to make of this country gentleman, who invoked his sciatic gout and the pleas of a neighbor, [and who claimed that he] was obliged, as the former commendatory prior of a nearby community, to say the mass each morning? [34] Without underestimating the revealing and typical character of these declarations, it would be difficult and, indeed, hazardous to establish on this basis the degree of loyalty to the monarchy and the level of wealth of the provincial nobility.

Happily, other archival documents permit us, on occasion, to moderate the pathos, true or false, of the witnesses by the reassuring simplicity of numbers. When we possess both the muster roll, with the declarations of the gentlemen of the jurisdiction, and the final definitive list, after eventual changes in the substitution taxes have been made, it becomes possible to establish some representative statistical data on the conditions of the nobility. Here, by way of example, are the results that can be gleaned from the archives preserved from the *ban* and *arrière-ban* in the *bailliage* of Amiens from 1639 to 1675. Before the Fronde, the rolls were very succinct. Generally they only mentioned the names of men ready to serve and those who were already fighting in the king's armies, without any precision concerning their financial condition. In 1639, the particular roll of the *prévôté* of Amiens contained only 58 names, but 14 heads of family presented a valid excuse, because their eldest son already bore arms, and, finally, two of the nobles summoned had already rejoined the troops. In 1642, in the *prévôté* of Saint-Riquier, the officer charged with establishing the roll came up with the names of 6 horsemen ready to serve, of 4 old and infirm men, and of 3 gentlemen already in the service. The one who did the same work in the *prévôté* of Vimeu provided us with 101 names, of which 9 were of persons serving in the king's armies. The roll of the *prévôté* of Fouilloy is the exception. It specifies the material and financial situation of the country gentlemen of the region. Four were in the army; 8 were able to serve under the usual conditions; a ninth could do it only with very inferior equipment; 2 were "very poor; 1, poor only; 3 were barely comfortable; 3 others did not possess a fief and could not serve." [35]

The dossiers for 1675, unfortunately rather late for our concerns, contain more numerous details. There we find the declarations of gentlemen and the roll of the contributions in lieu of service decided by the *lieutenant général.* Three hundred and eighty-six nobles were compelled to appear: thirty already served in the king's army; sixty-two, more aged, had served or had an unmarried son in the service of the king; forty declared that they could not provide for their equipment and maintenance expenses; eighteen asserted that their principal residence was not in the *bailliage;* and the majority of the others declared their readiness to respond to the summons of the king.[36] Thus a little less than a quarter of the gentlemen of the *bailliage* had served, were serving, or had a son in the army. This was little for an order sworn to the military career, but venality of offices and poverty prohibited a great number of family sons from entering upon an honorable service.

The roll of the contribution in lieu of service set by the *lieutenant général* confirmed the majority of excuses that were offered and concerned no more than 230 persons. But it furnishes us with precious information on their presumed financial conditions.[37] At the bottom, there were not only 40, who were exempted because of poverty, but also 89 who were taxed at 40 livres, which corresponded to an annual total revenue of less than 300 livres—if not indigence, most certainly a great mediocrity [of fortune]. At the other end of the hierarchy of fortunes, 51 gentlemen, to whom they attributed more than

2000 livres in revenue, had each to pay 300 livres. Certainly, we would like to possess such precise rolls for the convocations of 1639 and 1642, and for the same jurisdictions. Their comparison would allow us to lay down the first guidepost for a social history of the nobility in the seventeenth century. In other places and in other archival collections, a happy chance will perhaps assist the historian. In any case, let us state that there existed in the middle of the seventeenth century a sort of noble proletariat, an inexhaustible reserve of men for all the trouble-makers. And let us state too, that the reforming efforts of the monarchy appeared under unfavorable circumstances, capable of exacerbating the resistance of the privileged.

3

A great part of the French nobility thus felt that the absolute monarchy, in menacing its privileges, violated the fundamental laws, which sanctified the status of persons. In this regard, nothing is more significant than the comparison between the noble claims that were expressed in the *cahier* of grievances of 1614, and the ones of which we find evidence in the unions of nobility of 1649, 1651, 1658, and in certain *mazarinades*. In 1614, the effort of the order appeared to be entirely directed against venality of office and against the officers of justice and finance, usurpers of noble status. The *cahier* of 1614 claimed for the old nobility a monopoly of offices and places in the king's household, one over the orders of knighthood and over the most honorable positions in the *Parlements,* the reestablishment of seigneurial justice, and the severe repression of usurpations of nobility.

Of course, we again find the same hostility in regard to venality of office and the same complaints against royal justice in the texts contemporary with the Fronde. The assembly of nobility of 1651 repeated that it was scandalous to make representatives of the authentic nobility appear before commoners: "A *prévôt* and the least *présidial* daily hold criminal trials of the nobility . . . a simple priest can be judged only by ecclesiastical judges, a commoner is judged by commoners like him, a gentleman is judged by persons who are not of his rank." [38] Venality of office was all the more unpopular, because it furnished a great number of financiers and revenue farmers with opportunity for scandalous speculations. With the rest of the country, the nobility felt that "hatred for these harpies of finance who, because of shameful and excessive venality, remove the nobles from government and make them despair of ever occupying the places held by their ancestors." [39]

But to these traditional claims, some new grievances were added. A first collective manifestation occurred in 1649 in opposition to privileges accorded by the court "to a few gentlemen and particular houses and to the prejudice of the entire nobility of this kingdom." [40] A union of the nobility was formed against the pretensions of foreign princes and of some dukes and peers, while the king was beseeched not to give, in the future, any commission or letter on this subject.[41] It was the monarchy's pretention to upset, through its favors, the traditional hierarchy of the order that prompted this initiative. In arousing these grievances, the jealous opposition of some great nobles revived in the entire noble order a muted bitterness against the favorites and intimates of the king. The nobility felt vaguely frustrated and incapable of appreciating the necessities of a more regular administration of the court and the government. It believed itself abandoned and neglected to the exclusive profit of a few schemers. Despite its limited objective and its minor political consequences, the union of 1649 thus revealed a new aspect of the noble opposition.

More significant still was the assembly of the nobility of 1651. Its ambitions were broader, its representativeness more assured. If we judge by the circular letters addressed to the provincial gentlemen, and by the journal that was left by the Marquis de Sourdis, first among its preoccupations was the battle against the excesses of royal fiscal policy.[42] First off, it evoked the difficulties of collecting seigneurial dues: "The financiers overburden the subjects of the nobility with enormous taxes, so that, by reducing them to total poverty, they have no means to provide their lords with a significant amount of money." [43] Thus the rivalry between the royal collector and the seigneurial collector, both taking as much as possible of the peasant income, was bluntly exposed. Then the journal of the Marquis de Sourdis alluded to the investigations by the agents of the *gabelles*, who came armed to search the residences of the nobility.[44] He reported the complaints of the gentlemen of the *élection* of Dourdan, who were prosecuted "because they farmed too many of their estates by their own hands, and who were threatened with having themselves or their servants put on the *taille*." He did not hesitate to declare: "For the general welfare, nobles are subject to all sorts of *tailles* and duties, the value of their lands diminishes in proportion to the amount their tenants pay in *tailles* . . . they are still subject to personal service, at their own expense, in the *ban* and *arrière-ban*." [45] The circular letters addressed to the provincial gentlemen added to these grievances an additional complaint—the damages caused by lodging soldiers: "The honor of our wives, of our daughters, our houses, our goods, and our lives remain exposed to the insolence and pillage of the soldiers." On this last point, to which, it seems, they attached much importance, the deputies of the assembly obtained a promise from Gaston d'Orléans, *lieutenant général* of the kingdom.[46] The regulation of November 4, 1651, gave the privilege of exemption to ecclesiastics, gentlemen bearing arms, to the heads of the law courts, and to the king's men sitting in the said courts,[47] but it remained a dead letter under the conditions of anarchy into which the kingdom was plunged in 1652.

The assemblies that took place in June and July at Nogent-le-Roi, La Roche-Guyon, and Dreux begged the king again both for a meeting of the Estates General, promised a year earlier, and for "remedies against the soldiers . . . because it is a feeble recourse to invoke ordinances that today have no effect, except insofar as the sword sanctions them." To assure order in the provinces and to put an end to the exactions of mercenaries, they proposed the formation of noble companies, a suggestion that the regent and the council, rightly suspicious, hurried to set aside.[48] The same reproaches were invoked by the organizers of the assemblies and secret meetings of 1658 and 1659, among whom we find again certain instigators of the gatherings at the time of the Fronde.[49] The royal declaration of

1658 described the motives and pretexts for their agitation in these terms: "For this end, they have taken the occasion of the investigation that we have ordered of those who have usurped the titles and quality of nobility," and they have taken advantage of "a few abuses that were committed against our intention, both in this investigation, and in the establishment of winter quarters and other lodgings by our soldiers." [50] More explicit, the decree of the council of June 1, 1665, allows us to imagine the nature of these abuses: "Often the tax farmers and their agents alarmed some true gentlemen . . . ," then, with regard to usurpers, "they came to terms with some of them." [51]

Thus it seems no exaggeration to say that the fiscal policy of the absolute monarchy in France, during the first half of the seventeenth century, seriously disturbed the order of nobility, and that it contributed, in certain cases to the temporary conjuncture of popular, bourgeois, and noble oppositions—all set against the development of royal finances.

Even though this agitation ended in a major political setback, it had probably obtained, at a more modest level, certain compensations and results. The pleas and the troubles, which had lasted nearly a half century, worked to check the reformist will of the monarchy and to maintain abuses. The archives of the *élections* and *bureau des finances* could furnish precious information in this regard. Henceforth, the fiscal regulations and the administrative correspondence of the first part of the reign of Louis XIV suggest that in the regions of the *taille personnelle,* at least, fiscal privileges had, in 1685, retained their full scope, and, finally, that they had succeeded in surviving through the previous sixty years of monarchical and absolutist history without too much damage. The regulation of March 30, 1673, concerning the *taille,* denounced again, "the ordinary manuevers of the rich who use their authority and tricks to help themselves and their tenants at the expense of the poor." [52] And Colbert had to admit in his instruction of May 28, 1681, "that nearly all, or at least a considerable number of, gentlemen, officers and powerful persons have the *taille* rolls drawn up in their *chateaux,* their homes, or by their order." [53] The effective solidarity of the officers of justice and finance, and of the nobles, all equally landed and seigneurial proprietors, paralyzed the will of the councils and the commissioners in this domain. The royal declaration, of February 12, 1685, noted the frequent ineffectiveness of administrative taxation,[54] and a decree of the Cour des Aides, on September 24, 1688, pointed out one final irregularity of the *élus* who, "in order to favor their tenants, relatives, and friends, send their commissions to the parishes with notes attached, by which they enjoin the *greffier* in the *élection,* and his clerk, from writing down the roll, by means of which they make themselves the masters of the assessments." [55]

Thus behind the facade of the absolute authority of Louis XIV, it is possible to imagine these privileges safeguarded and society temporarily stabilized. Such a guarantee perhaps contributed as much as fear to the new docility of the nobility. Docility toward an authority that had rigorously pursued the authors of the schemes of 1658–59,[56] but docility also toward a conservative authority that was again embodied in the person of the king.[57] The government of this young sovereign, "resolved not to have a first minister," and who associated the nobility in the ceremonial and liturgy that he organized little by little around his person, probably appeared less formidable than the improvisations of the cardinal ministers and the tax farmers during the worst days of the Thirty Years War.

NOTES

1. Roland Mousnier, who initiated this investigation, has discussed the ideas of the Soviet historian in the *Revue d'Histoire moderne et contemporaine,* V (1958), 81–113.

2. Marc Bloch, in 1936, had invited researchers to fill this gap [*Annales d'histoire économique et sociale,* VIII (1936), 238].

3. *Nouveau code des tailles ou recueil par ordre chronologique des ordonnances, édits, et déclarations,* ed. Poullin de Viéville (n.d.), I, 183, art. 19; 277, art. 34; 370, art.8.

4. *Ibid.,* 277, art. 33.

5. Edmond Esmonin, *La taille en Normandie au temps de Colbert* (Paris, 1913), 225; Charles de Beaurepaire, *Cahiers des Etats de Normandie sous les règnes de Louis XIII et de Louis XIV* (Rouen, 1876–1878), III, 106.

6. *Bibliothèque Nationale,* Ms. Clairambault 792, fol. 353.

7. *Minutier central des notaires parisiens,* Etude XC, 162, August 5, 1666.

8. *Nouveau code des tailles,* II, 20, March 1667. Letters patent of August, 1664, had expressly authorized this practice. (*Ibid.,* I, 556).

9. The edict of January 1634, on the regulation of the *taille* ordered those who had pretended to be exempt in the past to be put on the *taille* rolls. See *Nouveau code des tailles,* I, 280, art. 1, and 362.

10. Jean Combes, *Traité des tailles et autres charges et subsides* (Paris, 1598), 82.

11. *Nouveau code des tailles,* I, 215: "Household officers and others exempt from the *taille* will be taxed, if they do not actually serve" (declaration of September 8, 1610).

12. Charles de Beaurepaire, *Cahiers des Etats de Normandie sous les règnes de Louis XIII et de Louis XIV* (Rouen, 1876–1878), III, 7.

13. According to the royal declaration giving pardon to the gentlemen who took part in the assembly of the nobility (September 1658): *Bibliothèque Nationale, Imprimés,* F 5001.

14. *Mémoire concernant les impositions et les droits en Europe,* M. de Beaumont ed., (Paris, 1768), II, 227.

15. Antoine Despeisses, *Traité des tailles et autres impositions* (Toulouse, 1643), 86.

16. *Mémoire concernant les impositions,* 129–132.

17. *Ibid.,* 160.

18. Which probably did not exclude the prosecution of disputes between the privileged and commoners regarding the classification of lands.

19. *Archives historiques du Département de la Gironde,* II (1860), 39.

20. Marquis de Sourdis, *Journal de l'assemblée de la noblesse* (Paris, 1651): *Archives Nationales,* K 118, no. 24, 43–44, and *Bibliothèque Nationale,* Lb 37 1858.

21. Richelieu, *Testament politique,* Louis André ed. (Paris, 1947), 218–223.

22. *Archives Départementales de la Somme,* Bailliage d'Amiens, B 334.

23. *Ibid.,* B 333 (royal declaration of May 14, 1639), and B 336 (royal letter of June 5, 1642). The crown acted in the same fashion in 1675. After having announced a convocation for effective service, the king, in a letter of January 14 to the intendant, justified the establishment of a compensatory tax in these terms: "Considering the great expense that the *ban* and *arrière-ban* entails for my nobility . . . I have judged for this reason and for the little service I get out of it . . . I doubt not that my nobility will be happy, for such a modest sum, to dispense with their personal service. . . ." Those who persisted in serving were finally deterred (*Ibid.,* B 337).

24. In the Bailliage of Amiens in 1675, for a fief with 300 livres of revenue, or less, one paid 40 livres tax; from 300 to 600 livres, 80 livres in tax; from 900 to 1500 livres, 150 livres; from 1500 livres to 2000 livres, 200 livres; and for a fief with a revenue superior to 2000 livres, 300 livres in tax.

25. *Requêtes et articles pour le rétablissement de la noblesse,* A. de Montluc ed., cited by Ernest Lavisse, *Histoire de France* (Paris, 1914), VI, Part 2, 390. This memoir also demanded the suppression of venality of offices in the royal household, the monopoly of a part of ecclesiastical benefices for younger sons, the creation of military schools, and the authorization to engage in commerce without losing noble status.

26. *Bibliothèque Nationale, Imprimés,* Lb 37 1886, Paris, 1651.

27. *Ibid.,* Lb 37 930.

28. *Bibliothèque Nationale,* 500 Colbert, fol. 257.

29. On the former subject, see the remarkable note of Jacques Jacquard, "Propriété et exploitation rurale au sud de Paris dans la deuxième moitié du xvie siècle," *Bulletin de la Société d'Histoire Moderne,* Nos. 15–16 (1960).

30. As Pierre Goubert has already done in his *Beauvais et le Beauvaisis* (Paris, 1960).

31. *Archives départmentales de la Somme,* B 333.

32. *Ibid.,* B 338 (Prévoté de Beauvaisis).

33. *Ibid.*

34. *Ibid.,* B 338 (convocation of 1675).

35. *Ibid.,* B 336.

36. Declaration without any detail—70
   Illness and age—18
   Son in the service, long personal service, or wounded—62
   Presently in service—30
   Ready to serve—134
   Other residence —18
   Doubtful excuse—6
   Inhabitants of Amiens invoking the city's privileges or their status as
      officers of justice—11
   Too poor to equip themselves—40
   Will pay the compensatory tax—6

37. Tax	Presumed Revenues	Number of Gentlemen
40 livres	Less than 300 livres	89
80	300 to 600	26
100	600 to 900	17
150	900 to 1500	33
200	1500 to 2000	14
300	More than 2000	51

38. Sourdis, *Journal*, 43.

39. *Bibliothèque Nationale,* Lb37 1856, 11: *Déclaration des prétentions de la noblesse assemblée aux Cordeliers de Paris* (1651).

40. *Archives Nationales,* K 118, 24: *Union de la noblesse de France touchant leurs prééminences* (Paris, 1649).

41. All of these problems, which occupy such an important place in the memoirs of Saint-Simon, were debated again at the end of the reign of Louis XIV and during the Regency.

42. Already in 1616, the nobility of Normandy complained, "that by means of several taxes levied indifferently on all people, they have robbed the nobility of its prerogatives . . . making it contribute to charges that are unworthy of its status," (Beaurepaire, *Cahiers des Etats,* I, 124).

43. *Déclaration des prétentions de la noblesse,* 11.

44. Sourdis, *Journal,* 2.

45. *Ibid.,* 44.

46. *Bibliothèque Nationale,* Lb37 1849 and 1859: *Lettre circulaire envoyée dans les provinces à tous les gentilshommes par ordre de l'assemblée de noblesse,* and *Lettre envoyée sur le sujet de l'assemblée de noblesse.*

47. *Nouveau code des tailles,* II, 422.

48. See in particular, *Lettre circulaire à tous les gentilshommes pour leur adresser l'arrêt fait à l'assemblée de La Roche-Guyon (Bibliothèque Nationale,* Lb37 2700); the results of the assembly held at Dreux (*Ibid.,* Lb37 2833); letter of the nobility for the convocation of the Estates General on November 1, 1652 (*Ibid.,* Lb37 2832); and, finally, a letter of a gentlemen on the present movements—"The troops do not distinguish any longer between gentleman and peasant"—(*Ibid.,* Lb37 3128).

49. On this subject, see the numerous letters published by Pierre Clément, *Lettres, instructions, et mémoires de Colbert* (Paris, 1861), I.

50. *Bibliothèque Nationale,* F 5001: *Déclaration du roi portant pardon aux gentilshommes.*

51. An order of the royal council on June 1, 1665, suspending the investigations of the nobility of Normandy (cited by Esmonin, *La taille,* 208).

52. *Nouveau code des tailles,* II, 103.

53. "His Majesty has received diverse reports that . . . in almost all the parishes, the principal inhabitants and the rich easily find the means to avoid the *tailles* and to overcharge the average and poor inhabitants, and that these latter even accept the avoidance by these rich people, because they give them work and give them help in time of need" (Clément, *Lettres de Colbert,* II (part 1), 154).

54. "Direct administrative taxation has been introduced to maintain equality in the imposition of taxes and to oblige the rich and the powerful to carry their share in proportion to their faculties . . . whatever care we have taken to order those who have the job of drawing up the *taille* to continue the said administrative taxation, those who were subject to it have done all they could to evade the effect of our ordnances and regulations, by using an appeal to our *cours des aides,* where they easily obtain relief from the said taxes by decrees of default . . . the *syndics* in the parishes not being able to undertake the expense of a trial" (*Nouveau code des tailles,* II, 189).

55. *Ibid.,* II, decree of September 24, 1688. It was probably after noticing this reversal, that a certain number of persons in the entourage of the controller general came to forsee the suppression of the *taille personnelle* and the generalizing of the *taille réelle.*

56. Once again, on the occasion of these events, a part of the nobility had been able to see that the princes and great nobles scarcely cared for its collective interests and easily accommodated themselves with the monarchy by abandoning the demands of the gentlemen. The development of a more centralized royal administration and the increased role of the intendants and commissioners was, in any case, to break noble solidarities, thus depriving the whole order of part of its cohesion and dynamism.

57. The royal government would show great severity toward the popular revolts of 1675, and it allowed, in several provinces, a seigneurial reorganization that was seriously harmful to peasant interests. On this subject, see, in particular, Georges Livet, *L'intendance d'Alsace sous Louis XIV* (Paris, 1956), and Pierre de Saint-Jacob, *Les paysans de la Bourgogne du Nord au dernier siècle de l'Ancien Régime* (Paris, 1960).

The Parlement of Brittany and the Crown: 1665–1675

BY JOHN J. HURT

In the years 1665–1675 the Parlement of Brittany repeatedly quarreled with Louis XIV and Colbert. The members of this hostile Parlement hoped to thwart Colbert's projected reform of the French judiciary in order to preserve their investments in court offices, which they had purchased or inherited. But the government triumphed in the quarrel. The crown admonished and humiliated the Parlement and finally expelled it from its seat at Rennes for alleged complicity in the local rebellion of 1675, which erupted throughout Brittany. In addition to repeated humiliation and the exile of 1675, the Breton *parlementaires* suffered financial losses after 1665 owing to a sharp decline in the price of their offices.

We propose to describe the origin, development, and culmination of this struggle between the Rennes Parlement and the crown. Insofar as it is possible to do so, we will examine the effect of the struggle upon the financial interests which the members of the Parlement held in their offices. Before proceeding to these issues, however, it is necessary to begin with a brief summary of the judicial reform which, to the distress of the Rennes Parlement, Colbert sought to impose throughout France.

1

The institution of the venality of office was a fundamental part of the French economy and social structure in the Old Regime. Its preponderance was evident in the sheer numbers of officials who owned their offices as property. An estimate prepared for Colbert placed the total number of venal offices at 45,780, their official value at something over 187 million livres, and the capital invested in them at almost 420 million. This estimate was known to be incomplete when it was prepared. Another indication of the extent of the venal system was provided when the Old Regime was liquidated in 1789–1790, for at that time the offices of the legal profession alone were valued at 426 to 456 millions.[1]

Among the many factors which gave rise to the extent of the venal system, none was more important than the Paulette, the name given to the royal decree of 1604 which permitted an officer to bequeath his office to a surviving member of his family, even to his wife, provided that he paid annually to the crown a sum equal to one-sixtieth of the designated value of his office. The Paulette virtually guaranteed the heredity of office, for it did away with certain conditions under which the office of the deceased magistrate would revert to the King without reimbursement to his heirs. Thus a venal office, virtually hereditary after 1604, became a highly desirable investment, almost as sound as real estate, which the occupant could mortgage if necessary, sell at an auction, or include in a marriage settlement. Offices were in demand especially by the bourgeoisie, for whom they represented positions of influence and sometimes titles of nobility. In addition to increasing the demand for offices, the Paulette stimulated a general and continuing increase in the price of offices, whether purchased from the occupant or the King.[2]

However much the third estate thirsted for office through the venal system, Colbert harbored bitter feelings toward venality. He wished to put an end to property in office and to reduce the number of officers, especially legal officers. Colbert outlined his views in 1664 and 1665 in several memoirs for the King.[3] The offices available in the administration of finance and law, he wrote, were occupied by about 100,000 persons, needlessly diverting their productive labor and their capital from the four occupations he considered most useful to the state: agriculture, commerce, the army, and the navy. Colbert believed that 70,000 magistrates were fastening a "heavy and tyrannical yoke" upon the people: the magistracy ". . . occupies, by chicanery, more than a million of them [i.e., the people], and eats away at more than a million others and reduces them to such misery that they can no longer think of any other profession during their entire life." Colbert proposed a drastic reduction in the offices of the judiciary and the eventual termination of the Paulette, not only for the judiciary but for all officers whom the Paulette protected. Colbert freely admitted that a substantial retrenchment in legal offices would ruin an "infinite number" of families, especially those of the members of the *parlements* and other sovereign courts. He suggested, therefore, that reform take place gradually and in secret, its goal being the abolition of the Paulette within four years and the substantial reduction of the number of legal officers within eight years. He recommended that for the time being measures to reduce the number of magistrates be restricted to the simple redemption of the office upon the death of the occupant. In order that redemption of these offices should not become more expensive in the future, Colbert asked that the King place ceilings upon the prices of judicial offices, which, as we have seen, were continually rising. Ceilings, once established, could be lowered when the King desired.

Colbert also wanted a sweeping reform of jurisprudence. He longed for a codification as comprehensive as the Justinian Code of the conflicting laws, a weeding out of the unenforced laws, and the imposition of uniform procedures throughout the kingdom.[4]

One of the objectives of this legal reform would be to make justice "free," for Colbert could not tolerate the universal practice by magistrates of extracting payments known as *épices* from litigants in civil cases. Originally a present, such as sugared almonds, which the litigant presented as a courtesy to the judge who heard his case, the *épices* had been converted into money payments and made obligatory, though no payments were exacted in criminal cases. The magistrates derived most of their financial receipts in office from their *épices* and their valuable tax exemptions, salaries being of comparatively less value.[5]

Magistrates could therefore be expected to oppose any attempt to regulate, decrease, or abolish these payments.

Within the next few years portions of Colbert's projected legal reform began to be enacted into law. A specially constituted Council of Justice, guided by Colbert's uncle, Pussort, prepared new legal codes and in 1667 published the first, which was a code of civil procedure. Additional codes appeared at intervals through 1681 and covered the full range of French law: forestry (1669), criminal procedure (1670), land commerce (1673), and maritime law (1681).[6]

Since they altered local custom in the courts, the new legal codes, especially civil and criminal procedure, aroused the hostility of the *parlements,* including those of Paris, Toulouse, Rouen, Bordeaux, Grenoble, and Rennes.[7] But such opposition worried neither Colbert nor the King. Colbert had spoken acidly of the *parlements* as "so-called sovereign companies," and Louis XIV had expressed his strong views upon the proper role of the *parlements.* The remonstrances of the *parlements,* he said, could not trouble him less. He would consider any valid objections to new laws which the *parlements* raised but ignore other objections at his pleasure.[8] Reforms specifically affecting the *parlements* followed. In December, 1665, the King issued an edict which embodied Colbert's ideas on the reform of venality in judicial office. It fixed maximum figures for the prices of offices and minimum ages at which magistrates might take office. The Paulette was renewed for only three years instead of the customary nine.[9] There will be more to say of this edict later. In 1667 and again in 1673 the crown struck at the power of the *parlements* to present remonstrances, or objections, to royal ordinances, a practice which sometimes resulted in the substantial revision of the ordinance or even an outright rejection of it and a refusal to enforce it within the *parlement's* jurisdiction. The *parlements* held that their power to remonstrate against an ordinance derived from their function of registering or verifying that ordinance before it could be enforced. But in 1667 the ordinance of civil procedure required that all ordinances be registered without modification and at once. Remonstrances might be submitted within a time schedule based upon the distance of the *parlement* from Paris. The effect of these provisions was to require that registration of an ordinance precede any remonstrance against it. In 1673 the crown reinforced and made this requirement explicit by decreeing that all ordinances be registered unaltered within seven days of receipt. The schedule of 1667 for remonstrances was retained, but any remonstrance would be a formal gesture only, which the King would accept or reject as he pleased.[10] The crown also regulated *épices* in 1673, tolerating the payments if exacted by a presiding officer in a court, but holding out the prospect that *épices* might some day be abolished altogether.[11]

In the end most of these reforms of court practices came to nothing. By 1676 the King's need for finances had led him to suspend the age limits for entrance into judicial office. The price limitations of 1665 were not rigidly enforced. Pressed to finance the war against Holland, Colbert, who had wanted to reduce offices, resorted to selling them, though only on a small scale. The Paulette remained. And the last thirty years of Louis's reign witnessed a tremendous expansion in the sale of office. In one respect, however, the King remained firm. The *parlements* were so neutralized politically that in 1679 Colbert spoke of their weakness with utter contempt. They did not recover the full power of remonstrance until after Louis's death in 1715.[12] In another respect the work of Colbert was lasting, for the legal codification which he invoked formed the framework for the codes of Napoleon.[13]

The response of the *parlements* and other sovereign courts to these reform measures is eminently worthy of study. For the time being their established position was seriously threatened. It was not immediately clear that the reforms would fail, nor does their failure prove that they had no immediate or permanent effects. There was certainly a response in Brittany and pronounced effects upon the Parlement at Rennes. To these matters at Rennes we may now turn.

2

The old province of Brittany included what are today the departments of Côtes-du-Nord, Ille-et-Vilaine, Morbihan, Finistère, and Loire-Inférieure. The province was formed by the long Breton peninsula, which, with its excellent harbors, tended to orient the maritime Bretons toward Spain, England, and Ireland and even to Central Africa, the Orient, and the West Indies. This outward orientation also resulted from Brittany's physical isolation from the interior of the kingdom, for Brittany was sealed off by swamp land and rough forest, so that its principal route of communication with the rest of France ran through the Loire Valley. The temper of Brittany was distinctly particularistic, and until late in the reign of Louis XIV the crown treated Brittany with prudence and reserve.[14]

In the sixteenth century the kings of France hesitated to create so powerful an institution as a *parlement* in this province of intense local feeling, which had merged definitively with the kingdom as late as 1532. However, the Estates of Brittany petitioned for a local *parlement,* whose existence they sought in order to end the jurisdiction in Brittany of the Council of the King. The governors of Brittany supported the Estates and argued that litigation was excessive in the existing royal court, the Grand Jours, owing to the fact that a litigant could appeal from it to the Parlement of Paris. At last Henry II yielded and in 1553 created the Parlement of Brittany, the supreme court for the province. In forming the Parlement, however, he weakened it from the start by requiring that its members divide into two sessions, one session meeting in Nantes from February through April, the other in Rennes from August through October. The King also stipulated that only half of the *parlementaires* could be of Breton origin; the other half would be introduced from outside the province. (In practice these *non-originaire* members were selected from the neighboring provinces of Touraine, Anjou, and Poitou.) With these reservations, therefore, the King endowed the Parlement with a first president, four presidents, and thirty-two councillors, as well as the "king's men," who were the solicitor general and the two advocates general. The Parlement took up permanent residence in Rennes in 1560 and began to expand the length of its sessions and to increase the number of its officers. Beneath its jurisdiction came four *présidiaux,* and beneath these again were a number of *sièges royaux,* of which, on the eve of the Revolution, there were twenty-five.[15]

In the early seventeenth century Brittany was in effect governed by the Estates, the Parlement, and the governor.[16] It is true that there was a parade of intendants in the years 1636–1640 and 1646–1648, but each intendant, holding powers of justice and police, inevitably collided with the Parlement, a condition which ended only with the general suppression of the intendancy in 1648, during the Fronde. Not until 1689 did an intendant take up permanent residence in Brittany, and that event opened a new chapter in the history of the province.[17]

What manner of institution was the Parlement, which one king hesitated to create and which quarreled with the intendant of another? It is important, first of all, to realize that the Rennes Parlement was not merely a law court, considering only abstruse legal questions. In addition to administering the law, the Parlement acted as an administrative arm of the executive through its function of registering royal ordinances. It was, for example, through the Parlement that the crown in 1625 forbade Brittany to export foodstuffs, not only to neighboring provinces but to Spain as well.[18] The Parlement held other important powers. Henri Carré, having studied seventeenth-century Rennes, disclosed the remarkable political influence in municipal affairs which was wielded by the Parlement, the source, he wrote, of decrees forbidding gambling in the town, regulating its nighttime traffic, and outlawing hoarding.[19] All the Breton municipalities and provincial corporations, including the University and the clergy, lay within the jurisdiction of the Parlement, which registered the "letters of provision" of all officers of the province, watched over their execution of office, and even imposed its regulations at the level of the parish.[20] Throughout Brittany, from Rennes to the farthest seigneurial court, the Parlement exercised powers of general police, keeping an eye on foreigners and the press, attending to the transport of arms and safety on the highways.[21] The monument to so much enterprise and importance was the Parlement's own *palais de justice,* constructed between 1618 and 1655 at a cost in excess of two million livres, a figure said to have astounded even Louis XIV.[22]

Certain information has come to hand about the officers who held seats in this Parlement. For this information we are indebted to Louis XIV and Colbert, who in 1663 dispatched agents throughout the realm with instructions to examine, among other things, the quality, personality, and loyalty of the officers of justice.[23] The King's official commissioned to Brittany reported of the Rennes *parlementaires* that some of them were gregarious and personable, schooled in affability and the arts of committees, while others were secluded and withdrawn, preferring solitude to the company of their colleagues. Some were industrious and learned, assiduous in the daily work of the law court; others were given to wine and debauchery, scarcely bothering to attend court sessions. Of about sixty *parlementaires* whom the official listed only six did he consider to be wealthy, the highest annual income recorded being forty thousand livres. One of the officers was a brother of the Descartes "who wrote." [24]

Whatever their personal traits and habits, all the *parlementaires* derived important privileges from their office, such as immunity from any legal jurisdiction except that of the Parlement, which meant that each officer had the right to bring his civil and criminal suits immediately before his own court, thus avoiding the expense of proceeding through the lower courts. The members also enjoyed the privileges of nobility, which in Brittany included exemption from the *taille, aides,* the *ban* and *arrière ban,* and other impositions.[25] In addition, most of these officers were landed proprietors, exercising seigneurial justice, an additional means of income on their domains.[26]

Family ties were important within the Parlement, where frequently father and son, uncle and nephew, or two or three brothers came together in the same courtroom.[27] What the influence of the *parlementaires* could mean to relatives outside the court was indicated by Colbert's brother, Charles, who visited Brittany in 1665. He accused Breton noblemen of employing the authority of relatives in the Parlement to exploit litigants in the seigneurial and other courts and to absorb church property and tithes.[28]

The social rank of these magistrates was an exalted one. By the eighteenth century it was taken for granted that all members of the Rennes Parlement were nobly born.[29] Our knowledge of their social standing in the sixteenth and seventeenth centuries is less certain, but Saulnier has found that all the Bretons who entered the first Parlement in 1554 were nobles by birth.[30] A few Breton bourgeois were admitted in subsequent years, he tells us, and many of the magistrates entering the court from outside the province were of bourgeois origin. Bourgeois magistrates were accepted as nobles by virtue of their membership in the Parlement. They enjoyed all the exemptions and immunities associated with nobility, and if no royal ordinance proclaimed their new status, it was guaranteed by custom and repeatedly confirmed by the edicts of the Parlement. But nobility became a rigorous condition of admission after the reformation of the nobility in 1668–1671, when the Breton nobles had to prove their rank before a royal commission. It happened that this commission was composed entirely of members of the Rennes Parlement, and almost all *parlementaires* who appeared before it emerged as nobility of ancient extraction, though the rank of some went back no more than one hundred years.[31]

It may be seen from the foregoing that membership in the Parlement of Brittany endowed the magistrate with profound advantages. The Parlement with its salaries and *épices* was a fine source of private income, and there were also tax exemptions and other perquisites of office. It was convenient, especially if the officer were a seigneur, to be responsible only to the legal jurisdiction of the Parlement, even if we leave aside the accusation of Charles Colbert that magistrates permitted their relatives to exploit litigants in the seigneurial courts. A seat in the Parlement sustained the officer's claim to nobility and gave him a voice in provincial affairs, in which the Parlement played a considerable role. Then there was an aura of prestige, cultivated for generations, which always enveloped the magistrate, especially when he paraded in formal ceremonies in his splendid red robes. The *parlementaires* of Brittany could not be expected to accept any threat to their position with complacency. Nor did they.

3

On January 15, 1666, the Parlement listened to the reading of the King's letters patent of December, 1665, in which Louis announced his intention to "reform perfectly all the orders of Our kingdom." This reform would include a reduction in the "great number of our officers and particularly those of Judicature through the vacancies which may occur." The King expressed concern about the rising prices of the legal offices and the age at which members entered his courts. He therefore set the following limits upon the price of offices: president—150,000 livres; Breton councillor—100,000 livres; *non-originaire* councillor—50,000 livres; solicitor general—150,000 livres; advocate general—90,000 livres. In the case of the death or resignation of an officer, the King warned, he might redeem the office of the deceased at these fixed prices.[32]

The members of the Parlement did not register the King's edict; they ignored it until June 5, 1666, when they voted to submit a remonstrance to the crown. On June 30 the remonstrance was read, approved, and dispatched to the King. In this interesting document the writers made haste to express their submission and obedience to the wishes of the King, whose attention, however, they directed to the financial ruin which his ordinance implied for the *parlementaires* and their families. The King's failure to extend the Paulette for more than three years would, they felt, result in a decline in his own financial receipts. Worse than that, the King was surrendering control over his officers, which, secured under Henry IV, was the one sure way to make the King absolute.

Turning to the new restrictions on the prices of offices, the Parlement stated:

> *It is, Sire, of natural right to sell what one has purchased; liberty is the soul of contracts, and if it is taken away all trade is disrupted. No price will be necessary for what one cannot sell, and*

*one will not be able to negotiate with offices, since there will be no
one to buy them. . . . Your Majesty can regulate the price of offices, but he cannot oblige those who wish to have them to give
[these prices], Your power can restrain the immoderation and
prodigality of your subjects, but it cannot cause them to do more than
in this instance they wish; the preference which Your Majesty reserves
to himself is beneath his dignity, he can make use of his seal at his
pleasure . . . as the finest characteristic of . . . royal power,
However Sire the officers will be deprived of . . . help, their families
ruined by this loss and instead of receiving some reward for the
services which they have rendered your state during the course of
their lives, they will see their fortunes and their persons enclosed in
the same tomb.*

The Parlement went on to call for:

*. . . the offices filled by persons of quality and of great wealth
than by people who are poor and of undistinguished birth; wealth
is not incompatible with knowledge. It is the best means to attain to
it, but nobility and honor are inseparable; the advantage of the offices is to know the profession thoroughly and to be removed from
all avarice. To fight under the laws is to fight for your state and
the nobility who compose your Parlement believe that they display
signs of generosity when they render justice.*

The King was therefore asked to rescind the new price and age
regulations and to continue the Paulette for nine years instead
of for three.

To sum up, the *parlementaires* correctly interpreted Colbert's reforms as a threat to their financial future and class
standing, as an attack upon privilege. They pressed their own
claims to noble rank, and they used stern and unflattering language with their King. One may add that it is ironic that the
personal ruin which they so bleakly forecast as an argument
against the reform was about what Colbert had in mind.

Louis replied in letters patent of November, 1666, which
the Parlement registered on December 22, 1666. There were
no real concessions to the Parlement, and very few changes in
the letters patent of 1665. Revocation of offices, foreshadowed

in 1665, actually took place in 1666, as the King suppressed the offices of two deceased councillors and announced his intention to redeem their offices from the heirs. What passed through the minds of the *parlementaires* we can only conjecture; perhaps they contemplated some further action, for the letters patent were not actually inscribed in the Parlement's register until the August session, 1667.[33]

In addition to a fear for the permanence of the Paulette, the Parlement's opposition to the new regulations of offices resulted from the conditions under which offices were normally exchanged in the local market. While the market for offices in Brittany has never been studied thoroughly, a few suggestions about its workings may be ventured with respect to the years preceding 1665. In the first place, it was a live and active market, in which offices were highly negotiable and practices resembling speculation appeared. Two examples illustrate this point. There was the Marquis de Troche, who, resigning from the Parlement, exchanged his office of councillor for the less prestigious office of councillor and commissioner, but immediately sold this latter office, presumably at a profit, to a third party.[34] Another officer, Gilles Martin, sold his councillorship in November, 1662, but in May, 1663, purchased another office and continued to sit in the Parlement.[35] In a market in which offices might be so easily exchanged no one could look with favor upon restrictive government measures.

Secondly, the Breton market was one in which youth prevailed. Not one of the magistrates who voted to remonstrate in 1666 was over twenty-seven when admitted to the Parlement, and twenty-seven was the minimum age which the new rules laid down. Raising the age limit tended for the immediate future to reduce the number of young men able to buy offices. It also threatened the future of such practices as *concurrence,* whereby a councillor's son was permitted, upon a payment to the crown, to occupy an office jointly with his father. While the son did not receive a salary, he acquired valuable seniority in the Parlement and held a guarantee of succession in the office. One office of solicitor general was subjected to *concurrence* for three successive generations.[36]

Finally, this was a market in which prices had climbed steadily after the enactment of the Paulette in 1604 and had become especially steep in the period 1638–1665. For example, an office purchased for 12,000 livres in 1598 sold for 60,000 in 1645. The following represent the prices paid for the office of councillor by men who sat in the Parlement in 1666: 115,000 (1660); 120,000 (1661); and 135,000 (1663). Colbert's restrictions in this inflated market would destroy investments above 100,000 livres in Breton offices and above 50,000 in *non-originaire* offices, and such investments appear to have been substantial. Although not every councillor would have paid more than Colbert's maximum rates, each councillor could hope to sell his office for more than Colbert permitted. Hence the intense tone of the Parlement's remonstrance.

As it turned out, the prices of offices fell far below the ceilings Colbert fixed in 1665. An office obtained for 120,000 livres in 1661 sold for only 58,000 in 1667. Other prices received after 1665 were: 57,000 (1673), 40,000 (1676), 57,000 (1676), 64,000 (1678), 45,000 (1682), 40,000 (1689). This decline in prices was touched off by the reforms of Colbert. Clearly it was both sudden and steep. The fact that prices fell so far below the ceilings Colbert imposed may reflect both the general economic depression which had begun to trouble France after 1660 and the *parlementaires'* loss of confidence in a market which had become subject to unprecedented government regulation.[37]

The anxiety over coming financial losses no doubt contributed to a certain ill temper in the Parlement, which soon became apparent. In December, 1666, Colbert was informed that the Rennes Parlement, in delaying to establish a royal postal service, had shown disrespect for the King.[38] Colbert found it necessary in 1670 to admonish the first president to insure that the Parlement adhered strictly to the new schedule of registering ordinances unaltered. The Parlement had recently modified a royal ordinance, Colbert observed, but the first president should take care to observe the will of the King, for his own sake as well as that of the court.[39]

A new threat to the Parlement and to the Breton nobility

arose in 1672. The crown gave notice that it intended to appre-
hend those who exercised seigneurial justice without official authority. In order to prove his right to administer the law, a seigneur would have to produce the letters patent awarding him
that authority. Anyone who administered the law without the
authority of the crown would pay a fine of 1,000 livres, and it is
estimated that almost all the noblemen of Brittany would have
had to pay. There was also talk of a tax to be placed upon
judicial offices. After much commotion the Breton Estates in
1673 obtained the temporary withdrawal of this project by
making over a large grant to the crown. But the idea of reforming seigneurial justice created much bitterness among the
Breton nobles, especially in the Parlement.[40]

Matters were further complicated on December 23, 1672,
when the Parlement received letters patent creating several
minor offices at the court, including four substitutes for the solicitor general.[41] By custom Parlement alone selected the substitutes of the solicitor general, without recourse to the King, but
the new regulations brought these offices under the exclusive
control of the crown.[42] This was objectionable in itself. It is possible that the *parlementaires* also resented the sale of new offices
out of fear of competition in the sale of their offices.

Parlement determined to remonstrate, and on January 6,
1673, a delegation left Rennes, carrying a remonstrance against
the creation of these new offices.[43] Contrary to the 1667 enactment governing ordinances, the Parlement did not register the
letters patent which it was protesting. Two weeks later, perhaps
after this remonstrance had been read at court, Colbert wrote
that he was waiting impatiently for news of important events at
the Rennes Parlement. Colbert did not believe that the Parlement would resort to "formal disobedience," notwithstanding
". . . the noise of that city and the stubbornness which appears
up to now in the business of this Parlement." Colbert continued: "As this is the only company of the kingdom which
resists the wishes of the king, His Majesty cannot suffer that to
last any longer. . . ." He predicted ominously that if the Parlement did not conform it would have "much to suffer."[44]

The events which Colbert anticipated had already unfolded in Rennes. On January 17, 1673, two visitors entered the Parlement, the Marquis de Coëtlogon, governor of Rennes, and M. de Chamillart, a master of requests and intendant at Caen. Chamillart produced a decree from the Council of State and announced that the King ordered the registration of the letters patent against which Parlement had remonstrated. Chamillart seized the secret register from the Parlement's clerk and directed a soldier to locate the entry providing for the remonstrance. When the soldier found the entry, he cut it out with scissors and inserted the Council's decree in its place. Chamillart declared all royal decrees officially registered, and asked for comments from the magistrates. One of the presidents declared, "Monsieur, we owe on this occasion only our presence." Chamillart retorted. "I do not believe, Messieurs, that there are any in the Company who wish to defy the orders of the King." The visitors then stalked out. Chamillart took the secret register with him and did not return it until the next day.[45]

On January 21, 1673, the Parlement dispatched a second delegation to the King, this one instructed to protest not only the objectionable letters patent but "what has happened in consequence." But this delegation returned empty-handed in April. On April 29 the first substitute to the solicitor general, appointed by the crown, won admission to the Parlement.[46]

Thus was the Parlement humiliated, but the abandonment of Colbert's earlier plan for reducing judiciary offices was evident in this attempt to sell new offices in Brittany. Of similar futility was the idea of suppressing offices as their occupants died, for the two offices so suppressed in 1666 were reoccupied in 1673.[47]

The strained relations between the Parlement and the crown worsened in 1675, when, following a riot in Bordeaux, Brittany rose in open rebellion, with mob uprisings occurring first in Rennes and then throughout the countryside. The mob uprisings at Rennes were touched off by new taxes introduced in 1673 and 1675 in the forms of a government tobacco monopoly, a seal to be stamped upon pewter utensils, and the imposition of specially marked legal paper, *papier timbré,* to be used henceforth by everyone in all contracts, agreements, wills, and generally in all authentic legal documents. These were taxes upon commodities in general use and exempted no one from payment. They produced a widespread hostility in Rennes and throughout Brittany, of which the first important manifestation was a serious uprising in Rennes in April, 1675. This was primarily a lower class uprising, featuring the destruction by an angry mob of the royal tax offices. The second riot in Rennes occurred in June. It was related only indirectly to the new taxes, for its prime cause was resentment among both bourgeois and the lower classes at the introduction by the Duc de Chaulnes, the governor of Brittany, of three companies of royal troops into a town historically free of quartering troops. In this instance Chaulnes acquiesced, sent his troops away, and temporarily suspended the taxes upon tobacco and pewter utensils. But the governor restored the crown's legal paper to use, so that the offices of *papier timbré* became a target for a third uprising in Rennes, which took place in July. Once again the *papier timbré* office was ransacked and destroyed in what apparently was another lower-class manifestation, for members of the bourgeois militia finally dispersed the mob. Meanwhile, peasant uprisings erupted throughout lower Brittany, characterized by the destruction of manorial records and involving many complex issues which need not be recorded here. The governor, having quitted Rennes in July, passed the summer in suppressing the peasants with six thousand troops and the severest measures. On October 12 he returned to Rennes at the head of his infantry and began to inflict a severe punishment upon the town. As a part of this punishment, the King exiled the Parlement to Vannes, a small town about sixty miles from Rennes where there was no sumptuous *palais de justice*. The intention was to deprive Rennes of its income from the spending of the *parlementaires* and visitors who had business at the court. Income from rent, for example, fell rapidly.[48]

The question is what part the Parlement took in the repeated manifestations at Rennes. At one extreme there are the numerous accusations against the Parlement which the Duc de Chaulnes expressed in his letters to the crown. Chaulnes said of the June uprising in Rennes that ". . . the parlement is directing this whole revolt . . . from the solicitors to the *présidents à mortier* the greatest number is going to contest the authority of the king. . . ." [49] Modern scholars have rejected his accusations. An eminent historian of Brittany, having studied the Breton revolt of 1675, exonerated the Parlement of complicity in it and accused Chaulnes of casting blame upon the Parlement in order to conceal his own mistakes. [50] Another student concluded that neither the Parlement as a body nor any of its members instigated the uprising of 1675 but instead exerted all their energies in repressing it. [51] An American scholar, who examined the available French studies, recently concluded that the Parlement actually tried to restrain the Rennes mob and never resisted an official of the crown. [52]

But we suggest that in the revolt of 1675 the Parlement arrayed itself against the crown in an important if undramatic way. This does not mean that the Parlement whipped up the Rennes mob, as Chaulnes said that it did. On the contrary, there is ample evidence that the Parlement tried to preserve order in Rennes. As for the King's taxes, that was a different matter, for the Parlement disliked the taxes and resisted them when it could. To this extent the Parlement encouraged and made use of a rebellion which it did not in fact provoke. The best way to illustrate this point is to employ a narrative.

Almost two weeks before the April rioting in Rennes, the first president of the Parlement, d'Argouges, having learned of the rebellion in Bordeaux, took pains to warn the authorities in the Breton towns and municipalities of the need to maintain order as news of the Bordeaux uprising spread. [53] At the first riot in Rennes, which occurred on April 18, the Parlement on its own initiative prohibited the gathering of crowds and the illegal bearing of arms and expelled vagrants from the town. [54] When Chaulnes brought troops into Rennes in June, he did so with the advice of d'Argouges and others that without military force order could not be maintained. [55] It is clear that the instinctive reaction of the Parlement was to maintain discipline in the town.

But the Parlement's preference for good behavior did not imply a willingness to restore the wrecked tax offices to operation. It was not until early May that the Parlement took steps to restore these offices and then it was only after prodding from Chaulnes, who had just arrived in Rennes. When the office of *papier timbré* was again ransacked, this time on July 17, the Parlement did not reestablish it until September 26, again after a pointed request from Chaulnes.[56] Furthermore, d'Argouges himself, pleading financial hardship in the province, formally asked Colbert to suspend the taxes pending a meeting of the Breton Estates, precisely the request which Chaulnes, fearing royal displeasure, wished to avoid.[57] It was with the greatest difficulty that Chaulnes dissuaded the Parlement and the Rennes municipality from dispatching a delegation to the King to seek revocation of the taxes. He could never persuade the Parlement to agree to send deputies throughout Rennes and the Breton countryside to exhort the people to abandon their revolutionary manifestations.[58]

Failure of the Parlement to enforce the tax decrees with promptness and decision could only rekindle the latent wrath of Colbert. As early as 1673 he instructed d'Argouges to insure that the new tax of *papier timbré* was in effect in Rennes and that the magistrates, by their firmness and their conduct, maintained order over public unrest. Colbert even suggested that d'Argouges show these instructions to the *parlementaires* in order to make their duty clear.[59]

If in 1675 Colbert was exasperated with the Rennes Parlement and advised the King to exile it to Vannes, there can be no mystery as to why he was so provoked. The Parlement, having resisted royal edicts, had required disciplinary action in 1666 and in 1673. Now the Breton governor blamed the Parlement for a serious insurrection, which at any rate it had failed to prevent, and, as if to confirm his reports, d'Argouges himself had protested the unwisdom of the crown's taxes and made himself the mob's spokesman. To the government the Parlement of Brittany must have appeared an incorrigible nuisance.

As for the Parlement, in 1675 it was outwitted and distraught, humbled before the royal will, all of its demands rejected. Each of the points on which it had resisted the crown was lost. A remonstrance had not diminished the threat posed in 1665 by the reform of venality of office, and a general decline in the price of offices took place in a market subject to increased government regulation. If it was clear by 1675 that the reform of venality had been abandoned, there was no guarantee that it would not be resumed in the future. In 1673 the *parlementaires* lost control over the appointment of their officers, the substitutes of the solicitor general, and the King had proved able to impose his decrees upon them, if necessary by force. An appeal for relief from the taxes of 1673–1675 had proved fruitless and efforts to resist them in a passive way unavailing. There was also the lingering threat of a reform of seigneurial justice. All of these measures implied some financial disadvantage, if not an outright loss of income, and it is interesting to note that in resisting the will of the crown in 1665–1675 the *parlementaires* sought only to preserve their own economic interests. They evolved no radical constitutional ideas and proclaimed no new political conceptions. They wished merely to retain the old social and economic order to which they were accustomed. There was much else. Together with the other *parlements,* the Parlement of Brittany faced the implications of the new law codes, the regulation of *épices,* and an economy upon which royal exactions were increasingly brought to bear. We have concluded that the members of the Parlement suffered financially as the prices of their offices declined. If one projected this conclusion into the other sectors of their private financial affairs, including their income from *épices,* the impression would be one of general economic reversal. What is needed is a rather precise estimate of the sources and amount of individual income in the Parlement. But this estimate remains to be made.

NOTES

1. Koenraad Wolter Swart, *Sale of Offices in the Seventeenth Century* (The Hague, 1949), p. 16; Marcel Marion, *Dictionnaire des institutions de la France aux XVIIe et XVIIIe siècles* (Paris, 1923), pp. 405–406.

2. Swart, *Sale of Offices*, pp. 9–12; Marion, *Dictionnaire*, pp. 433–434.

3. Jean Baptiste Colbert, *Lettres, instructions et mémoires de Colbert*. Edited by Pierre Clément (7 vols.; Paris, 1861–1873), VI, 3–4, 10–12.

4. *Ibid.,* pp. 5–11.

5. *Ibid.,* p. 12; Roland Mousnier, *La vénalite des offices sous Henri IV et Louis XIII* (Rouen, 1946), pp. 55–56; Marion, *Dictionnaire*, p. 212.

6. James Edward King, *Science and Rationalism in the Government of Louis XIV* (Baltimore, 1949), pp. 264–273.

7. Pierre Clément, *Histoire de Colbert et de son administration*. Third Edition (2 vols.; Paris, 1892), II, 314–316; Pierre Adolphe Chéruel, *Histoire de l'administration monarchique en France depuis l'avénement de Philippe-Auguste jusqu'à la mort de Louis XIV* (2 vols.; Paris 1855), II, 268–269; Ernest Désiré Glasson, *Histoire du droit et des institutions de la France* (8 vols.; Paris, 1887–1903), VIII, 190.

8. Colbert, *Lettres, instructions et mémoires,* VI, 5, 11; Glasson, *Histoire du droit,* VIII, 189.

9. Ernest Lavisse, *Louis XIV. La Fronde. Le Roi. Colbert. (1643–1685)*, Vol. VIII, part i of *Histoire de France depuis les origines jusqu'à la Révolution* (9 vols.; Paris, 1903–1911), p. 362; Francois A. Isambert, and others, eds., *Recueil général des anciennes lois françaises* (29 vols.; Paris, 1821–1833), XVIII, 66–69.

10. Gaston Zeller, *Les institutions de la France au XVIe siècle* (Paris, 1948), pp. 155–160; Roger Doucet, *Les institutions de la France au XVIe siècle* (2 vols.; Paris, 1948), I, 210–222; Isambert, *Recueil général,* XVIII, 105–106; XIX, 70–73.

11. Marion, *Dictionnaire*, p. 212; Isambert, *Recueil général,* XIX, 86–88. This edict did promise that the wages of the magistrates would be increased if *épices* were abolished. It appears doubtful, however, that any such wage increases would fully compensate for the loss of *épices*. In any event, the magistrates would lose all control over whatever payments might be forthcoming.

12. Franklin L. Ford, *Robe and Sword: The Regrouping of the French Aristocracy after Louis XIV*. Second Edition (Cambridge, Mass., 1962), pp. 82–84, 110–111; Lavisse, *Louis XIV,* pp. 276–277.

13. King, *Science and Rationalism,* pp. 264–265.

14. Henri Fréville, *L'intendance de Bretagne (1689–1790): essai sur l'histoire d'une intendance en Pays d'États au XVIIIe siècle* (3 vols.; Rennes, 1953), I, 17, 25–30.

15. Bernard de la Roche-Flavin, *Treize livres des Parlemens de France. Esquels est amplement traicté de leur origine et institution, et des présidens, conseilliers, gens du roy, et de leur charge, devoir, et jurisdiction: ensemble de leurs rangs, seances, gages,* *privileges, reglements, et mercurialles* (Bordeaux, 1617), Book I, chapter xii, pp. 19–20; Henri Carré, *Le Parlement de Bretagne après la Ligue (1598–1610)* (Paris, 1888), pp. 1–6; J. de la Martinière, "Le Parlement sous les rois de France; 1491–1554," *Annales de Bretagne,* XXXVII (1926), 110–113, 114–115, 118, 122–123; J. Trévédy, "Organization judiciare de la Bretagne avant 1790," *Revue historique de droit,* XVII (May, 1893), 217–220, 234–235, 249; *Édits, déclarations et lettres patentes du roy, et réglemens concernant le Parlement de Bretagne, depuis son érection en 1554 jusqu'en 1754* (2 vols.; Rennes, 1754), I, 9–10. The chief of the Parlement was the first president, who was appointed by the King. The presidents, or *présidents à mortier,* to use their full title, followed the first president in rank and precedence. They, like the councillors, purchased their offices.

16. Fréville, *L'intendance de Bretagne,* p. 35.

17. *Ibid.,* pp. 30, 35–43.

18. Archives Départmentales, Ille-et-Vilaine, IBb, 144 (13 May 1625); 145 (17 December 1625). (Hereinafter cited as AD.)

19. Henri Carré, *Recherches sur l'administration municipale de Rennes au temps de Henri IX* (Paris, 1909), pp. 12–13.

20. Arthur Le Moy, *Le Parlement de Bretagne et le pouvoir royal du XVIIIᵉ siècle* (Paris, 1909), pp. 12–13.

21. Carré, *Le Parlement de Bretagne,* pp. 488–500; André Giffard, *Les justices seigneuriales en Bretagne aux XVIIᵉ et XVIIIᵉ siècles (1661–1791)* (Paris, 1903), pp. 230–231.

22. Hippolyte Bourdonnay, *Le Palais de Justice de Rennes: Histoire et description du Palais—ses salles, ses richesses artistiques* (Rennes, 1902), pp. 2–16.

23. King, *Science and Rationalism,* pp. 130–132.

24. See Georg B. Depping, ed., *Correspondance administrative sous le règne de Louis XIV* (4 vols.; Paris, 1850–1855), II, 70–77.

25. Carré, *Le Parlement de Bretagne,* pp. 281–285.

26. Giffard, *Les justices seigneuriales,* pp. 230–231.

27. Le Moy, *Le Parlement de Bretagne,* p. 57. I have identified forty councillors from the February session of 1666. Of these forty, seventeen succeeded their fathers, and thirteen were succeeded by their sons. The forty names were found in AD, IBb, 226, their precedessors and successors in Frédéric Saulnier, *Le Parlement de Bretagne, 1554–1790. Répertoire alphabétique et biographique de tous les membres de la cour, accompagné de listes chronologiques et précédé d'une introduction historique* (2 vols.; Rennes, 1909).

28. Jean Lemoine, "La Révolte dite du Papier Timbré ou des Bonnets Rouges en Bretagne en 1675," *Annales de Bretagne,* XII (1897), 320–322.

29. Le Moy, *Le Parlement de Bretagne,* p. 21; Saulnier, *Le Parlement de Bretagne,* I, lxi–lxii of "Introduction"; Gustave Saulnier de la Pinelais, *Les gens du roi au Parlement de Bretagne* (Rennes and Paris, 1902), p. 103.

30. Saulnier, *Le Parlement de Bretagne,* I, lx of "Introduction." However, the social rank of one of the Bretons is unknown.

31. *Ibid.,* pp. lix–lxii. Of the forty councillors I have identified, there were four barons, two viscounts, and four counts. All the rest were seigneurs. The royal agent who visited Brittany in 1663 reported that one of the councillors was from a Rennes bourgeois family (Depping, *Correspondance administrative*, II, 75). That this item was considered worthy of mention suggests that the remainder of the *parlementaires* were of noble birth or belonged to families whose claim to nobility was generally accepted.

32. AD, IBb, 225 (15 January 1666).

33. *Ibid.*, IBb, 227 (22 December 1666); IBa, 22 (395–398). The only substantial change was that the price limitation for *non-originaire* councillors was raised from 50,000 to 70,000 livres.

34. Saulnier, *Le Parlement de Bretagne*, II, 802–803 (No. 1122).

35. *Ibid.*, p. 629 (No. 872).

36. *Ibid.*, pp. 513–515 (Nos. 696–698); Saulnier de la Pinelais, *Les gens du roi*, pp. 71–75.

37. Saulnier, *Le Parlement de Bretagne*, I, xxxvi of "Introduction." All the prices listed here refer to Breton offices. However, the *non-originaire* offices may have been as badly inflated; one of these offices sold for 103,000 livres in 1663 (*Ibid.*, II, 629, No. 872). Since the maximum price permitted for *non-originaire* offices was considerably lower than that for the Breton offices, the *non-originaires* would stand to lose more than their Breton colleagues if their offices were selling at the same prices. However, evidence is not available to establish the prices for *non-originaire* offices with confidence. The prices quoted here may be found in: Saulnier, *Le Parlement de Bretagne*, I, 237 (No. 290), 291 (No. 375), 297 (No. 384), 310 (No. 401), 399 (No. 515 *bis*); II, 629 (No. 872), 769 (No. 1070), 858 (No. 1200). On the question of economic depression in France see Philippe Sagnac, *La formation de la société française moderne* (2 vols.; Paris, 1945–1946), I, 204–205.

38. Guibert to Colbert, 19 December 1666, in Depping, *Correspondance administrative*, II, 175–176.

39. Colbert to d'Argouges, 28 November 1670, in Colbert, *Lettres*, IV, 49–50.

40. Giffard, *Les justices seigneuriales*, pp. 167–175.

41. AD, IBb, 239 (23 December 1672).

42. Saulnier de la Pinelais, *Les gens du roi*, pp. 64–65.

43. AD, IBb, 239 (24 December 1672, 6 January 1673).

44. Colbert to Chamillart, Caen intendant, 20 January 1673, in Colbert, *Lettres*, II, pt. i, 264.

45. AD, IBb, 239 (17 January 1673). The mutilated register may be found in IBb, 569, the missing pages falling between 24 December and 29 December 1672. The latter register was the one which the clerk actually used to record the daily sessions of the Parlement. A second register, prepared on parchment, was compiled as the permanent record.

46. *Ibid.*, 239 (21 January 1673); 240 (24 April and 29 April 1673).

47. Saulnier, *Le Parlement de Bretagne*, I, 226 (No. 275); II, 263 (No. 865).

48. Marion, *Dictionnaire*, p. 536; Arthur de la Borderie, *La révolte du papier* *timbré advenue en Bretagne en 1675* (Saint-Brieuc, 1884), pp. 11–14, 27, 43–48, 60, 77, 105–109, 165; Lemoine, "La révolte du papier timbré," *Annales de Bretagne,* XIII (1898), 191–193; Barthélemy Pocquet, *Histoire de Bretagne* (Rennes, 1913), V, 526–527. For a recent synthesis of the whole Breton revolt of 1675 see Leon Bernard, "French Society and Popular Uprisings Under Louis XIV," *French Historical Studies,* III, no. 4 (Fall, 1964), 468–472.

49. Duc de Chaulnes to Colbert, 15 June 1675, in Lemoine, "La révolte du papier timbré," pp. 241–242.

50. La Borderie, *La révolte du papier timbré,* pp. 54–55, 83. In these pages La Borderie is referring only to the Rennes uprising of June, 1675, but nowhere else does he suggest that Parlement instigated or expected any of the other manifestations.

51. Sigismond Ropartz, "Exil du Parlement du Bretagne à Vannes, 1675–1690," *Bulletin archéologique de l'Association Bretonne. Mémoires,* IX (1874), 105.

52. Bernard, "Popular Uprisings Under Louis XIV," p. 470.

53. D'Argouges to *syndics* and *échevins* of the principal towns and municipalities of Brittany, 5 April 1675, in Lemoine, "La révolte du papier timbré," p. 198.

54. Pocquet, *Histoire de Bretagne,* V, 484.

55. La Borderie, *La révolte du papier-timbré,* p. 42.

56. *Ibid.,* pp. 30–31, 105–109, 153–154.

57. *Ibid.,* p. 54; d'Argouges to Colbert, 21 June 1675, in Depping, *Correspondance administrative,* III, 261, n. Theoretically the Breton Estates retained the right to consent to royal taxes, but the crown had imposed the taxes of 1673–1675 without submitting them to the Estates in advance. Apparently it was hoped that the Estates, if convoked, could obtain some tax relief.

58. La Borderie, *La révolte du papier-timbré,* pp. 67, 69–71.

59. Colbert to d'Argouges, 22 September 1673, in Colbert, *Lettres,* II, pt. i, 292.

The Control and Exploitation of French Towns During the Ancien Régime

BY NORA TEMPLE

A paradoxical feature of modern France is that while civic pride and loyalty are strong and persistent, local government in towns is weak, stunted by generations of close control by the central government. This tutelage dates back to the seventeenth century. It was introduced by Colbert as part of his plans for reforming the whole administrative and financial structure of the country. He placed municipal finance under the strict supervision of the *contrôle général* and the *intendants,* in order to put an end to the exploitation of towns by unscrupulous municipal officials and local notables. This apparently minor, limited reform had considerable repercussions. It encouraged the development of a network of permanent officials in the provinces; it introduced new standards of honesty and public service into the administration of towns. At the same time it deprived them of their independence and inhibited the growth of healthy local government, which depends above all else on local control of revenue and expenditure. Consequently, it enabled the royal government to exploit the towns even more ruthlessly and systematically than their old oppressors.

Certainly when Colbert came to power some reform of municipal finance was necessary, for the towns were afflicted by the kind of financial disorder that also crippled the state: expenditure exceeded revenue, taxation was arbitrary, municipal funds were squandered and misappropriated, deficits were met by borrowing, and debts were allowed to snowball unchecked.[1] The *intendants* tended to attribute this sorry state of affairs to

67

the dishonesty and rapacity of the municipal officials. The *intendant* of Dauphiné summed up their attitude when he wrote: "Les communautés n'ont pas de plus grands ennemis que leurs consuls et leurs officiers; ils les pillent par toutes les voies qu'ils peuvent imaginer. Je travaille autant que je puis pour arrêter l'avidité de ces mangeurs de communautés." [2] Such strictures were all too often amply justified. Many municipal officials, if not guilty of outright embezzlement, had frittered away revenue entrusted to them in a frivolous and self-indulgent fashion—on banquets and entertainments, on extravagant gifts for influential persons and for retiring municipal officials, on specially minted *jetons* which were distributed to those who attended council meetings, on litigation, on deputations to Paris, ostensibly on the town's business, but often, it was alleged, to attend to their private affairs or simply for a holiday.

In theory, such dissipation ought not to have been possible. Municipal officials were supposed to be answerable for their administration to the general assembly of all inhabitants, which elected the officials, authorized their expenditure, and ratified their accounts. These had also to be submitted to the local *bailliage* (or *sénéchaussée*), which audited accounts of *deniers patrimoniaux,* and to the appropriate *chambre des comptes,* which audited accounts of *deniers d'octroi.* [3] In practice these checks proved illusory. The general assembly usually acted as a timid, subservient rubber-stamp on the activities of the municipal officials, since it lacked the protection of the secret ballot—it voted by a show of hands or by word of mouth—and was easily intimidated by the municipal officials, who were normally the most powerful men in the town. Nor did the *bailliages* and *chambres des comptes* provide an effective scrutiny of the towns' financial administration. They audited municipal accounts in the narrowest, most technical sense—they checked that the figures were accurate and balanced—but it was no part of their responsibility to decide whether municipal funds had been usefully spent for the public benefit. The value of even this audit was questionable: the impartiality of the *bailliages* was often suspect, since their officers were frequently members of the *corps de ville,* while the fat fees demanded by the *chambres des comptes* induced towns to avoid submitting their accounts for as long as they could remain undetected. In 1683 the *intendant* of Poitiers, complaining to the *contrôleur général* about the damage which the exactions of the *chambres des comptes* inflicted on the towns' finances, revealed that in his *généralité* the towns of Chastellerault and Fontenay had not presented accounts to the *chambre des comptes* for forty-two and twenty-five years respectively.[4]

The inadequacy of the restraints to which they were subject partly explains the municipal officials' financial management and the towns' indebtedness, but only in part. The royal government itself was also to blame for the disorders deplored and attacked by Colbert. In December 1647, casting round frantically for means of staving off bankruptcy, Mazarin had ordered the revenue from all municipal *octrois* to be diverted into the Crown's empty coffers. This completely undermined municipal finances, since *octrois* were no longer simply a means of paying for occasional, exceptional expenses, but were by this time increasingly drawn on for ordinary, regular expenditure too. Although Mazarin authorized the towns to double their *octrois* to make good this loss, many of them, perhaps reluctant to increase taxes so drastically, preferred to raise loans.[5] As the *Mémoires pour l'Instruction du Dauphin* admitted, the Crown's clumsy and short-sighted efforts to surmount its own financial difficulties were a major cause of the towns' distress;[6] the royal deficit, or at least part of it, was simply transferred to the towns. Colbert placed municipal finance under the control of the central government to cure a condition for which the central government was itself largely responsible.[7]

That the towns should be crippled with debt, their assets squandered, their finances maladministered, was intolerable to Colbert, since it jeopardized royal taxation and his plans for commercial and industrial growth. For twenty years he strove to restore the towns to solvency, and constantly urged the *intendants* to see that their debts were liquidated and their finances put on a sound footing. It was not easy. Colbert originally expected the operation to take six to eight years.[8] It dragged on much longer—in fact it was not completed when he died—

largely because the creditors of the towns were reluctant to co-operate since the terms on which the debts were to be liquidated were extremely unfavourable. Not all debts were to be honoured: only those which the *intendants* considered to have been incurred for legitimate reasons were to be repaid, within ten years, during which time interest on them would be reduced to a uniform $4^1/_6$ per cent.[9] In effect a partial bankruptcy was to be imposed on the towns, and their creditors were to pay for the mismanagement of the municipal officials and the Crown. Colbert was well aware of what he was doing, and justified this ruthlessness in a remarkable series of letters to Morant, *intendant* of Aix, who had the unenviable task of seeing that the king's will was obeyed in one of the most recalcitrant provinces in France, and was encountering especial resistance from the town of Marseilles. Colbert, who plainly thought that Morant was weak and easily swayed by local pressures, insisted that he must adopt a tough line, and not be deterred by arguments that the liquidation of debts was unjust to creditors: if the towns were forced to repudiate a large percentage of their debts, he said, they would not find borrowing money so easy in future.[10] It is hardly surprising that creditors jibbed at facilitating a liquidation of debts conducted in this spirit. They could delay the operation for years, simply by refusing to lodge their claims and produce their bonds. Moulins provides a typical example. The royal council issued a decree on 10 September 1660 ordering the liquidation of the town's debts by the local *intendant*. This order was reiterated in a second decree of 17 November 1661. A third decree of 11 January 1663 revealed that proceedings were being held up by the refusal of the town's creditors to deliver the necessary documents to the *intendant*. A further decree of 4 July 1663 gave them a final six months to produce these papers. When this ultimatum expired in December 1663, they were given another year's grace. And so it went on. The process of verifying the town's debts, which began in 1660, was not completed until 1682,[11] and repaying them took a further seven years.[12]

So Colbert died without the satisfaction of knowing that one of his dearest projects had been successfully completed. At least in some provinces the towns had been freed of their debts. Burgundy was one of these. The *intendant* of Dijon, Bouchu, was as robust and resourceful an official as Colbert could wish, and he was armed with exceptionally wide powers in the form of the *commission pour la vérification des dettes des villes et communautés de la province de Bourgogne,* and enjoyed the confidence and support of the governor of the province, Condé.[13] It would appear from Colbert's correspondence that elsewhere the success of the operation was limited. Arrangements were made in most *généralités* for settling municipal debts, but disorder persisted because some municipal officials were capable of misappropriating even taxation authorized to pay off the debts.[14] Their obstinate abuse of public trust suggested that the once-and-for-all reform originally envisaged would be wasted unless followed by a constant supervision of their activities, and after consulting the *intendants,*[15] Colbert issued the edict of April 1683 [16] which transferred the control of municipal finance from the towns to the royal government and its agents, the *intendants.* Except for a brief interval, from 1764 to 1771,[17] this edict provided the framework of the government's relations with the towns until the Revolution.

The edict laid down that a scheme of expenditure was to be drawn up for every town in France by the local *intendant* [18] upon the basis of the previous ten years' accounts. 'Ordinary' expenses, i.e. predictable items which did not vary much from year to year, were fixed precisely, while a round sum was allowed for 'extraordinary' expenses, such as public works, which could not be budgeted in advance. The municipal officials were required to adhere unswervingly to the budget of ordinary expenditure, and to obtain the *intendant's* prior permission for every item of extraordinary expenditure. They were thus converted into simple executives, responsible to the royal government. If this budget could not be met from existing revenue, the general assembly of inhabitants could ask the royal council to authorize additional taxation. As municipal expenditure increased in the eighteenth century, the towns came to rely more and more on supplementary *octrois* granted by the government, which accentuated their dependence. The government disliked increasing municipal taxes, because this could be detrimental to royal taxation, but it was none the less preferable to the towns' former disastrous policy of financing deficits by borrowing, or selling communal property. To prevent a recurrence of the dissipation of the past, towns were absolutely forbidden to alienate communal property, and were to be allowed to raise loans for three purposes only—to combat plague, to provide lodging and supplies for royal troops, and to rebuild parish church naves which collapsed as a result of fire or decay—subject to the approval of the general assembly of inhabitants and the local *intendant,* and providing satisfactory arrangements could be devised for repayment. Other wasteful habits the municipal officials had been wont to indulge in were severely discouraged. Expenditure on meals and entertainments was prohibited; lawsuits and deputations had to be authorized by the general assembly and the *intendant,* and municipal officials and officers of the royal law-courts were debarred from serving on deputations, except at their own expense.[19]

As a deterrent, Colbert's edict proved successful: the wholesale mismanagement and misappropriation of funds which was such a marked feature of the seventeenth century did not recur, because, by and large, the *intendants* managed to keep a close watch on the towns' finances. It was their scrutiny of municipal accounts which made the *tutelle* effective, and yet this was not prescribed by the edict of 1683, and Colbert did not favour it.[20] He intended that municipal accounts should continue to be audited as in the past by the *bailliage* (or *sénéchaussée*) for *deniers patrimoniaux,* and by the *chambre des comptes* for *deniers d'octroi.* But this procedure was inadequate and impractical, and by the eighteenth century the *intendants* had spontaneously assumed the right of verifying municipal accounts. This was in fact the inevitable corollary of the *tutelle* formulated by Colbert, because checking the municipal accounts was the only sure way of detecting and discouraging unauthorized expenditure. Surviving accounts show that the *intendants* subjected them to a rigorous examination, and would question, reduce, or disallow items of expenditure they thought unjustified. Checking the accounts of every town in a *généralité* was indeed, as Colbert wrote, 'un travail immense', which the *intendant* could not have undertaken without the help of a network of permanent assistants in the localities, the *subdélégués*. This may well explain why Colbert did not wish the *intendants* to be responsible for municipal accounts, because he was notoriously hostile to the appointment of *subdélégués*, and allowed the *intendants* to use them only with great reluctance and emphatic and repeated warnings against delegating authority or letting them use their initiative.[21] He mistrusted *subdélégués* because they were local men, and therefore, in his eyes, bound to be committed to some local faction or interest, their judgement warped by local loyalties or jealousies, and so incapable of impartially promoting the interests of the Crown.[22] Yet it was his own long and arduous campaign to clear the towns of debt which not only helped to convert the roving *commissaire départi* into the *intendant,* the king's settled representative in the provinces, but also forced the *intendant* to organize a team of local subordinates. The new responsibilities created by the *tutelle* of municipal finance confirmed and strengthened this development.[23]

On the other hand, as a means of positively guiding municipal expenditure rather than simply preventing the embezzlement of revenue, the *tutelle* was clumsy and at times oppressive. Much depended on the personalities of those who exercised it and the circumstances in which they worked. A town could count on more lenient treatment from an indolent or trusting *intendant* than from a zealous, suspicious one, and arbitrary changes in policy as *intendants* came and went could be a major headache for municipal officials. Such fluctuations caused the *corps de ville* of Auxerre serious anxiety in the second half of the eighteenth century. Joly de Fleury, who as *intendant* of Dijon supervised Auxerre's finances from 1749 to 1761, seems to have been fairly easy-going and indulgent, allowing the municipal officials to embark on no less than nine lawsuits, and drawing up a revised budget which included several increases in ordinary expenditure.[24] This was harshly criticized by his successor, Dufour de Villeneuve (1761–4), whose immediate reaction to the municipal accounts of 1756–61, sent to him in January 1763, was to strike out much of the expenditure, protesting to the *corps de ville* 'il me semble que vous ayez affecté une dissipation extraordinaire'.[25] He eventually had to relent and pass the account because nearly every item he objected to had been authorized by Joly de Fleury, and the municipal officials, ably supported by the local *subdélégué*, could produce convincing arguments in favour of the disputed increases.[26] Auxerre endured similar sharp fluctuations in the *intendants'* attitudes towards its financial problems later in the century, this time in response to changes in national policy. During the reforming ministries of Terray and Turgot, the municipal officials were encouraged and supported by the *intendants* of Dijon in their efforts to overcome the bitter hostility of local privileged groups to an increase in the municipal *taille* levied by the town; when the more conciliatory Necker became finance minister, they were obliged to abandon this struggle and accept ruthless cuts in expenditure instead [27]—cuts which were restored again during the expansionist era of Calonne.[28]

Such fluctuations were not the only or even the worst drawback of the *tutelle* from the towns' point of view. An even bigger grievance was the long and wearisome procedure which had to be observed when a town embarked on public works and amenities, however minor. Every stage, from drawing up plans and estimates to paying the contractor when the work was finished, required the prior sanction of the *intendant,* who, before giving it, invariably referred to the *subdélégué* for his opinion and advice. The municipal officials were often tempted to cut through this red-tape if public utilities, such as the water-supply, required urgent repairs, or if winter unemployment made labour cheap and available. On several occasions during the second half of the eighteenth century the municipal officials of Auxerre spent revenue on public works without first obtaining the *intendant's* permission. Usually the sums involved were so petty and the work done was so necessary that the *intendants* assumed that retrospective sanction could safely be granted and gave it, but although they always added 'sans tirer à conséquence' these instances of transgression condoned accumulated, and inevitably encouraged insubordination. The

74

municipal officials of Auxerre became increasingly careless of the proper formalities, until by 1787–8 they paid no heed to *intendant* Amèlot de Chaillou, but on the contrary flouted his authority—with impunity, because the *intendant* had no convenient means of disciplining a *corps de ville* determined to assert its independence.[29] However, it was in this field of public works and amenities that the *intendant's tutelle* was of most positive value to the towns. The eighteenth century was a great age of urban development and there was a general movement to embellish towns and make them pleasanter, more salubrious places to live. The initiative often came from the municipal officials—local pride demanded a new, enlarged town-hall, better roads that were regularly cleaned and, at the end of the eighteenth century, lighted too, at public expense, tree-lined walks, a more reliable and plentiful supply of water—but a lot of the credit for the improvements achieved belongs to the *intendants,* whose control over expenditure on public works enabled them to guide the enthusiasm of the municipal officials and co-ordinate their plans. The squares, faubourgs, and tree-lined promenades which towns often named after the local *intendant,* are a permanent testimony to their good taste.

In other matters besides urban development the *intendants* often evinced a genuine if paternalist concern for their *administrés,* but however benevolent and enlightened their inclinations, they were first and foremost agents of the royal treasury whose chief interest in the towns was to wring as much revenue as possible from them. Tapping the wealth of the towns was far from easy, and it is widely assumed that the *contrôle général* failed to devise an efficient system of taxing them, and that in proportion to their resources they contributed less to the royal exchequer than rural society. There can be little doubt that direct taxation was unfairly distributed, simply because it was more difficult to levy in the towns than in the countryside—much more sophisticated techniques were required to assess movable wealth than landed wealth.[30] A few towns enjoyed outright exemption from the main direct tax, the *taille,*[31] while some were allowed to purchase the right of paying an annual subscription or *abonnement* to the royal treasury in its place. In negotiating these *abonnements* the royal government was in characteristic fashion sacrificing long-term fiscal interests to meet short-term needs, because, like any fixed payment, the *abonnement* depreciated with inflation, and prevented the royal government from benefiting fully from increases in wealth and prosperity. However, this defect was partly mitigated by the premium demanded by the treasury when it renewed the *abonnement,* which was granted for a limited period of years only. Some towns raised the *abonnement* by direct taxation, many more by indirect taxation on consumer goods. The royal government was not averse to substituting indirect for direct taxation in towns. In favour of indirect taxes it was asserted that they were paid by members of privileged groups who enjoyed exemption from *taille,* and that they were less obnoxious to merchants than direct taxation, which was believed to have a depressing effect on trade and manufactures in towns where it was levied.[32] The disparity that existed between town and country under the *taille* was slightly modified by the new taxes introduced during the reigns of Louis XIV and Louis XV, but the government never made any real attempt to grapple with the problem of assessing urban wealth. The *capitation,* introduced in 1695, soon became a mere addition to the *taille* in towns where the latter was levied. In the larger *villes non tailliables,* taking a census of inhabitants, assessing their wealth and keeping the assessment up to date was beyond the resources of the municipal administration.[33] The result was that, for want of any better system, the *capitation* became an *impôt de répartition* levied through trade gilds and professional corps.[34] The *vingtième d'industrie* also failed effectively to tap urban, industrial wealth, because the government refused from the start to incur the hostility likely to be provoked by any serious investigation into income and profits.[35]

To consider regular taxation alone, however, is to give a very incomplete and misleading account of the towns' contribution to royal finances. Thanks to the control which the *intendant's tutelle* gave it over the towns, the government extracted substantial payments from them by other, indirect means, its two favourite expedients being the *rachat des offices* and the *don*

76

gratuit. Whenever the government verged on bankruptcy—which it did at disturbingly frequent intervals—one of the ways in which it tried to increase its revenue at short notice was by the sale of offices, including municipal offices. Between 1690 and 1713 hardly a year passed without some category of municipal office being declared venal. Under Louis XV all but the most insignificant posts connected with the administration of towns were offered for sale on three occasions: in 1722 to alleviate the financial crisis caused by the collapse of Law's system, in 1733 to raise funds for the War of the Polish Succession, and in 1771 to tide over a near bankrupt treasury until Terray's fiscal reforms could be put into operation. The political consequences of this policy have been exaggerated—contrary to the generally accepted belief, few towns lost the right of managing their own affairs, because most of them bought up these venal municipal offices themselves. At first they did so voluntarily, anxious to prevent the town's affairs falling into the hands of private individuals, who would be irresponsible and irremovable, and whose salaries would be an unproductive drain on municipal revenue.[36] Private individuals, however, soon lost interest in purchasing venal offices, because Louis XIV's ministers glutted the market for them by creating far too many, far too often, and discredited them as an investment by alternately suppressing and recreating them in rapid succession. The *traitant* handling the sale of these offices gave the government no peace until all had been disposed of and he had recovered his outlay. Therefore the towns had to be bullied into acquiring them by threats to suspend elections to municipal offices until they had complied. During the reign of Louis XV little effort was made to sell them to private individuals: they were simply a means of extorting extraordinary subsidies from the towns, which had to buy them or lose such measure of independence as they had. How much the government obtained altogether from *rachats des offices* cannot be calculated, but the cost to particular towns can sometimes be established. The account that follows is drawn largely from the archives of two towns: Auxerre, in the *pays d'états* of Burgundy, a community of just over 2000 households in the early eighteenth century,[37] dependent on the production of wine for its living and not very prosperous; Moulins, capital of Bourbonnais, *pays d'élections,* a market town and administrative centre, economically stagnant, with a population of 11,339 (2879 households) at the end of the seventeenth century.[38]

Auxerre's long series of *rachats des offices* began in 1694 when it offered to buy the office of *greffier alternatif des rolles des tailles,* created in November of that year, for 6930 *livres.*[39] This was one of the many offices invented by the royal government which were a threat to the towns because they allowed their holders some control over financial affairs, or the right to a percentage on the municipal revenue. This particular office carried with it the right to a fee of 4d. for every *livre* of *taille* collected, and in private hands would have been an expensive liability to Auxerre, where a municipal *taille négociale* was levied as well as the royal *taille.* It was recreated in October 1703 and cost Auxerre 4440 *livres* to buy again.[40] Another office, the chief attribute of which was the collection of a percentage on the municipal revenue, was that of *conseiller de ville auditeur examinateur et raporteur des comptes des communautés,* created in November 1704; this cost Auxerre 16,500 *livres.*[41] Even more menacing to a healthy financial administration was a venal treasurer. Little pressure was needed to persuade towns to buy this office, and no doubt aware of this, the royal government recreated it at frequent intervals. Four times during the reign of Louis XIV the provincial estates of Burgundy, which usually negotiated *rachats des offices* on behalf of the towns in the province, bought the suppression of venal municipal treasurerships. The cost to the province was 546,446 *livres,* and to Auxerre, 74,117 *livres.*[42] *Augmentations des gages* attributed to these offices cost Auxerre a further 3823 *livres.*[43]

The most important municipal offices in any town were those of the *maire* and *échevins* (or *consuls* as they were known in the South), who formed the *corps de ville,* or executive committee, which directed urban administration. In Burgundy the *maire* was also ex-officio deputy to the provincial estates, and usually one of the *échevins* was nominated to accompany him, so that if these offices became venal, not only municipal, but also provincial administration would be affected. Consequently the provincial estates of Burgundy had a special incentive for buying these offices, which they did promptly whenever they were declared venal. For the suppression of the venal offices of *maire* and *échevins,* and for the acquisition of the new office of *lieutenant général de police,*[44] the towns of Burgundy paid altogether 4,205,062 *livres* 13s. 6d. between 1696 and 1709.[45] Unfortunately, information on Auxerre's contribution to these purchases has not survived.

Raising the frequent and heavy sums demanded for venal offices was a serious problem for municipal officials and often caused severe distress to the townspeople. The normal method was to obtain the government's permission to levy additional taxes on consumer goods, which were farmed out for a period of years—the shortest possible—to a private individual who in return advanced to the town the price of the *rachat des offices.* In 1696 when Auxerre had to raise 26,609 *livres* demanded for the offices of *receveur* and *contrôleur des deniers patrimoniaux et d'octroi* created in 1694, it was authorized to levy special *octrois* on wine, bread, and butcher's meat, which were farmed out to one Collinet, bourgeois of Dijon, for six years, in return for the price of these offices, plus 1200 *livres* to cover certain petty expenses connected with the negotiation of this purchase.[46] In 1697 to finance the purchase of the office of *juré mouleur de bois* and pay off several other debts, the town was allowed to levy the dues on firewood attributed to this office, and a further tax on wine.[47] These *octrois* caused considerable hardship in Auxerre, since, with the exception of a small tax on the transit wine trade, all fell on prime necessities consumed by the townspeople, and the tax-farmers' efforts to prevent and detect the evasion of these taxes were vexatious. It is hardly surprising that there were grumbles and protests. On 14 September 1698 the general assembly of inhabitants demanded the suppression of the extra *octrois* authorized to pay for the venal offices, alleging that the tax-farmers—always bloated extortioners in the public mind—were making immense profits.[48] This charge may have been exaggerated: according to accounts submitted to the *chambre des comptes* in Dijon, Collinet made a profit of only 361 *livres* os. 6d., and the farmer of the *octrois* on wood and wine introduced in 1697, a loss of 1003 *livres* 13s. 4d.[49] So notoriously unprofitable were these *octrois* that when they were renewed in March 1705 to raise 63,013 *livres* 10s for a batch of assorted venal offices, no one submitted any bid for them; not until a year later could anyone be persuaded to accept the farm.[50] The temper of Auxerre continued to be truculent and unco-operative for some time. A general assembly of inhabitants was summoned for 11 October 1699 to discuss how to raise the cost of the offices of *voyer expert priseur et arpenteur* and *greffier de l'Ecritoire* for which Auxerre was required to pay 14,300 *livres.* The townspeople went on strike: no one attended the meeting, so no decision could be taken.[51] A general assembly held on 25 April 1700 protested against the price of the office of *conseiller garde scel,* for which Auxerre was ordered to pay 5500 *livres.*[52] Again, attendance at a general assembly held on 18 January 1705 to discuss the purchase of 65,488 *livres* 10s. worth of venal offices was so poor that nothing could be decided, except that all absentees should be fined 3 *livres.*[53]

Compared with Auxerre, Moulins escaped lightly during Louis XIV's reign. It appears to have incurred only two *rachats des offices:* in 1696 it paid 24,522 *livres* 17s. 6d. for the office of *juré mouleur de bois,*[54] and in 1705 it paid 92,849 *livres* 19s. for an assorted batch of municipal offices.[55] This inequality of treatment can probably be explained by Auxerre's membership of a *pays d'états,* which was not an unmixed blessing. The well-known advantage of provinces with representative estates which controlled the levy of taxation was that they could bargain with the royal treasury to secure favourable terms or even outright exemption from regular taxes. The disadvantage, which is less often appreciated, was that the very existence of this corporate organization facilitated the negotiation of irregular subsidies. The provincial estates' ardour for preserving local independence and privileges made them vulnerable to government pressure and extortion, while their willingness to act as broker for *rachats des offices,* offer the treasury a lump sum on behalf of the whole province and then recover it from the towns, dividing it among them according to their size and resources, made the disposal of venal offices much easier to organize in *pays d'états* than in *pays d'élections,* where the government had to deal with each town individually. As a result, towns in *pays d'états* may have succumbed to *rachats des offices* more promptly and more frequently than towns in *pays d'élections.* This tentative conclusion is suggested by the experience of Moulins and Auxerre.

In the euphoria that followed the end of the War of the Spanish Succession and the death of Louis XIV, the government resolved to abolish venality from municipal life. In 1714 it ordered the suppression of all unsold venal municipal offices, and empowered towns to buy out private individuals who had acquired them.[56] Few towns could afford to take advantage of this authorization, and in order to achieve a return to normality, the government itself undertook to reimburse private holders of municipal offices.[57] It expected the financial ingenuity of John Law to liquidate these and the other debts that comprised Louis XIV's bankrupt estate. When 'the system' collapsed, the government sought to extricate itself from an embarrassing situation by once again putting all municipal offices up for sale and demanding *titres de rentes, billets de liquidation d'offices supprimés,* and other government stock in payment, coolly proclaiming that its object was the cancellation of government debts.[58] Towns were pressed to acquire these offices *en bloc* and to buy up *titres de rentes* and *billets de liquidations* if they did not own sufficient: the government was simply transferring part of its debts to the towns. Some towns, among them Moulins, did not respond to this appeal; the towns of Burgundy paid 600,000 *livres,* of which Auxerre paid 16,000 *livres,* to be quit of the whole business;[59] but enough cooperated to persuade the government that it could safely bring this demeaning transaction to an end in July 1724, when it once more abolished venal municipal offices, and ordered the capital invested in them to be converted into government *rentes.*[60] This move was premature and regretted; the financial outlook had been optimistically misjudged; a further sacrifice was required from the towns. The venal offices of *receveur* and *contrôleur des deniers patrimoniaux et d'octroi,* which had not been

81

included in the mutations of 1714–24, were simultaneously suppressed and recreated, and the *assignations* issued to compensate the holders of the suppressed offices were demanded as half the price of those newly created.[61] It was a not very subtle way of extorting a forced loan.[62]

The royal government had been too unscrupulous and had pushed the towns too far. In 1733, when municipal offices were again declared venal,[63] this time to help to finance the War of the Polish Succession, the province of Burgundy as usual promptly offered to buy its exemption,[64] but most towns resisted pressure to purchase these offices, which took the usual form of the suspension of elections and nomination of municipal officials by the government.[65] As soon as the Polish crisis was settled, the sale of municipal offices was abandoned and towns were allowed to hold elections again.[66] The respite was only temporary. During the War of the Austrian Succession the government resumed its efforts to dispose of municipal offices not sold between 1733 and 1737 and elections were once more forbidden.[67] Still the towns refused to buy and could not even be induced to do so by a drastic cut in price offered in 1744.[68] The bulk of the offices remained on the hands of the *traitant* until 1746, when the government made a last attempt to salvage what it could from the wreckage of this transaction.[69] It attributed all unsold municipal offices to the towns and imposed on them special *octrois,* known as *octrois municipaux,* which it levied for its own profit, not merely until the cost of these offices had been raised, but until the Revolution. Moulins paid a tax on wine which on average produced over 13,000 *livres* a year.[70]

It is not surprising that when municipal offices were put up for sale for what proved to be the last time in 1771,[71] the government experienced great difficulty in selling them, and by and large, the prices fetched were much lower than on previous occasions. The town of Laon, which had given 66,740 *livres* for the venal municipal offices of 1733, paid only 12,000 *livres* for those created in 1771.[72] The towns of Burgundy were not affected directly. In negotiations for the purchase of these offices, the provincial estates offered 600,000 *livres,* the *contrôle général* demanded exactly twice that amount, and 1,000,000 *livres* was eventually agreed on as a compromise. This was not divided among the towns of Burgundy as in the past: the provincial estates were authorized to prolong certain *octrois* on goods travelling on the Saône for six years to raise this sum.[73] Moulins adamantly refused to purchase these offices, and whenever pressed to do so, indignantly reminded the local *intendant* that the *octroi* on wine authorized to pay for the last batch of offices was still being levied to the profit of the Crown, and that it had raised more than four and a half times the price originally demanded for those offices.[74] No threats were of any avail and eventually the government had to give up.

In the second half of the eighteenth century, when venal offices were proving less and less successful as a device for extorting money from the towns, the government turned to the so-called *don gratuit*. This had occasionally been used by Louis XIV's ministers, who at first even tried to maintain the polite fiction that it was a voluntary donation to an impoverished king by his loyal and enthusiastic subjects. In 1689 the *intendants* were urged to use the utmost tact in prodding towns into volunteering subsidies and to conceal from them the fact that the king had asked for help.[75] Whether taken in or not, the towns responded handsomely.[76] By 1710, the time for face-saving pretence had long passed and the government simply ordered all *octrois* levied by the towns to be doubled, the Crown to enjoy this *doublement* for six years as a *don gratuit*.[77] If enforced this would have been an intolerable burden as the towns were already crippled with extra *octrois* to pay for *rachats des offices* inflicted on them earlier in the War of the Spanish Succession. Consequently many of them offered the government a ready cash payment to be exempt from this measure—which was perhaps what they were intended to do.[78] The *don gratuit* remained a relatively minor, spasmodic source of revenue until the middle of the eighteenth century when it was transformed into what was virtually a regular urban tax. An edict issued in August 1758 required every town in France to pay a *don gratuit extraordinaire* annually for a period of six years.[79] The amount the government expected from each was stipulated,[80] and new *octrois* were authorized to raise the money. The municipal officials could decide on which goods these taxes would be levied, providing their recommendations reached the *contrôle général* within a month of the edict's publication, a proviso that was intended to counteract the towns' probably lukewarm, dilatory response to the demand for a *don gratuit*. Those towns which did not meet this deadline were to have their tariff of *octrois* drawn up by the government. Before the first period of six years had ended, the government, unable to dispense with the additional revenue the *don gratuit* yielded, prolonged it for a further six years, though with the end of the Seven Years' War the amount demanded was gradually scaled down.[81] This was far from being the prelude to its complete extinction. In April 1768 the government ordered a further extension of the *don gratuit* [82] and completely transformed it by ordering that the *octrois* authorized for its payment were to be levied by the *ferme générale des aides* from 1770.[83] From the beginning the government had wanted the *ferme générale* to collect these *octrois,* but the *parlements* had thwarted it by stipulating that 'le recouvrement du droit ... ne pourra être fait que par ceux qui sont ou seront préposés par les Officiers Municipaux, ou ceux qui les représentent'.[84] Many towns had taken advantage of this clause to organize the collection of the *octrois* themselves, instead of farming them out. Unfortunately, municipal officials were rarely efficient tax collectors, and such towns were usually late with the payment of their *dons gratuits.*[85] The government used this as an excuse for insisting that the *ferme générale* collect these *octrois.* The *don gratuit,* as such, was forgotten,[86] and the *octrois* it had occasioned were unobtrusively converted into a kind of *aide,* paid by the urban population, and known as the *droits réservés.*

This change seriously injured the material interests of some towns, as well as their pride and independence. Moulins was one of these. It was among those towns which had not submitted proposals for *octrois* within the stipulated month: the general assembly which met on 3 November 1758 to discuss the *don gratuit* protested that the 20,000 *livres* a year demanded by the government was grossly inflated, and insisted that the *corps de ville* must first petition the *contrôleur général* for a reduction.[87]

This was granted, Moulins' *don gratuit* was cut to 12,000 *livres* p.a.,[88] but meanwhile the *contrôle général* had drawn up for it a tariff of *octrois* on wine, butcher's meat, wood and hay.[89] The town complained that the taxes on wood and hay would cause great hardship, and the government allowed it to forgo these.[90] However, all such adjustments and special agreements were abrogated in 1768, when the *ferme générale* was empowered to levy the *octrois* originally devised by the government. The *corps de ville* protested vehemently against this, denouncing the over-zealous, prying methods of the *ferme générale,* and alleging that the townspeople would be unable to afford fires in winter if wood was taxed, and that unemployment would be created if hay was taxed: 'un tiers au moins des habitants de cette ville étants obligés de gagner leur vie avec leurs chevaux se trouveroient hors d'état de le faire par l'augmentation que ce droit sur le foin apporteroit à la nourriture de leurs chevauz'.[91] The government was deaf to all pleas and protests and enforced the *ferme générale's* right to collect these odious taxes.

Auxerre was also very badly and even more unfairly hit by this change. With the approval of the *contrôle général,* it had been raising the *don gratuit* by means of a direct personal tax similar to the *capitation,* instead of *octrois,* and was under-standably shocked to discover that it was included among those towns in which the *ferme générale* was to collect *droits réservés.* This had come about as the result of a complicated misunder-standing which illustrates the injustice that could be caused by the administrative confusion of the *ancien régime.* As a result of its union with the province of Burgundy in 1668, Auxerre came within the jurisdiction of the *parlement* of Dijon for all fis-cal matters, or so *intendant* Joly de Fleury concluded, although it was otherwise still subject to the *parlement* of Paris. The edict of August 1758 was registered by the *parlement, cour des aides* and *chambre des comptes* of Paris on 6–7 September 1758, but the municipal officials of Auxerre did not discuss how to raise the *don gratuit* until April 1759, having been advised by Joly de Fleury that since this edict was a fiscal measure, it was not valid in Auxerre until it had been registered by the *parlement* of Dijon. Meanwhile, some bureau in the *contrôle général,* assuming that Auxerre came within the jurisdiction of the *parlement* of Paris (even locating it in the *généralité* of Paris), included it among those reprehensible towns which were too disaffected to submit their own suggestions for *octrois,* and drew up a tariff for it.[92] This tariff was quite unsatisfactory from Auxerre's point of view, and would have been vigorously contested by the municipal officials had there been any question of enforcing it, because it included heavy taxes on wine, which would be calamitous in a *pays vignoble* such as Auxerre. When the *ferme générale* claimed the right of levying these *octrois,* angry objections were sent to the *contrôle général* by the municipal officials, who argued that since the decree authorizing the *ferme générale* to collect these *octrois* had not been registered by the *parlement* of Dijon, it could not be enforced in Auxerre.[93] Their arguments were rejected with characteristic harshness by *contrôleur général* Terray—the last minister to be deterred by the legal niceties that were at the crux of this dispute—who dismissed the notion that before a fiscal measure could be applied in Auxerre it had to be passed by the *parlement* and *chambre des comptes* of Dijon— thus in a stroke depriving Auxerre of the advantage of union with Burgundy—and roughly asserted that registration by the *parlement* and *cour des aides* of Paris was adequate.[94] Complaints that the *droits réservés* were ruining Auxerre's wine trade were treated with equal asperity. Although Terray did eventually agree to a slight reduction in the taxes on wine, he maintained the principle that the *droits réservés* should be levied in Auxerre by the *ferme générale.*[95]

These extraordinary payments, *dons gratuits* and *rachats des offices,* extorted so frequently that they became almost normal, helped to rectify the inadequacy of the regular methods of taxing the towns. They were a clumsy, inefficient, and arbitrary way of tapping urban wealth, and probably sapped the moral authority of the Crown, but ruthless exploitation of these time-honoured expedients was politically and administratively easier than enforcing a fair and effective system of regular, direct taxation, since this meant devising new fiscal techniques, and overcoming the relentless hostility of privileged interests. Of course the towns were damaged by this short-sighted policy. Essential public works were often pruned, postponed or abandoned altogether, in order to meet the government's fiscal demands; municipal budgets carried chronic deficits, and towns were seriously in debt when the Revolution broke out. The wheel had come full circle: thanks to the royal government's financial exactions, municipal finances on the eve of the Revolution were in as parlous a condition as when Colbert took office. Most deplorable were the social consequences of relying so heavily on indirect taxation of prime necessities in towns to finance *abonnements, rachats des offices, dons gratuits,* as well as municipal expenditure. Well-intentioned royal officials mistakenly approved such taxes because they were paid by those who were privileged in respect of direct taxation, whereas in fact the *octrois* were one of the most unjust forms of taxation, since they heavily penalized the poor, and one of the most foolish, since they inflated the price of staple foodstuffs. For the mass of the urban population, the government's control of the towns brought little real benefit: abuse and exploitation by local notables had been stamped out only to be replaced by the more systematic exploitation of the State—an unkind critic might describe the *ancien régime* as the substitution of State extortion for private extortion—and it is hardly surprising that there was a sharp, if temporary, reaction in 1789 against centralization.

NOTES

1. This disorder was vividly described by Bouchu, *intendant* of Burgundy, in letters to Colbert. *Vide* M. Marion, *Histoire financière de la France depuis 1715*, vol. I (1914), pp. 61–2, and C. Normand, *Saint Quentin et la royauté* (1881), pp. 103–4.

2. Cited by P. Clement, *Histoire de Colbert et de son administration* (1874), vol. II, p. 34, footnote.

3. Ordinance of Orleans, January 1560, art. 95. Isambert etc., *Recueil général des anciennes lois françaises*, vol. 14, p. 87. *Deniers patrimoniaux* signified revenue from assets which belonged absolutely to the town, *deniers d'octroi* revenue from taxes conceded by the king for a limited number of years to meet specified 'extraordinary' expenses. The distinction between the two was proving impossible to maintain by the late seventeenth century, when increasingly *octrois* had to be authorized by the government to meet 'ordinary' expenditure, and it was becoming difficult to observe the traditional practice of assigning categories of expenditure to specific sources of revenue.

4. Bâville, *intendant* of Poitiers to the *contrôleur général*, 10 December 1683. A. M. de Boislisle, *Correspondance des contrôleurs généraux des finances avec les intendants des provinces*, vol. 1 (1874), no. 34, pp. 8–9.

5. E. Lavisse, *Histoire de France*, vol. VII (i) (1906), pp. 28, 207.

6. *Mémoires de Louis XIV pour l'Instruction du Dauphin*, ed. C. Dreyss (1860), vol. II, pp. 550–1.

7. P. Bacr, *Les Institutions Municipales de Moulins sous l'Ancien Régime* (1906), p. 329.

8. *Instruction pour les maîtres des requêtes, commissaires départis dans les provinces*, September 1663. Colbert, *Lettres, Instructions, et Mémoires*, publiés par P. Clement (1861), vol. IV, p. 38.

9. Edict of April 1667. Isambert etc., *Recueil général des anciennes lois françaises*, vol. 18, p. 188.

10. Colbert, *Lettres, Instructions, et Mémoires*, vol. IV, pp. 167, 168, 179, 180. G. B. Depping, *Correspondance administrative sous le règne de Louis XIV* (1852), vol. III, pp. 301–2.

11. Arch. mun. Moulins, 234, 365.

12. Arch. mun. Moulins, 161.

13. C. Arbassier, *Intendant Bouchu et son action financière, d'après sa correspondance inédite* (1667–71), (1919), pp. 120–4, 142, 144–50, 151–2, 154–5, 157. Claude Bouchu, comte de Pont de Veyle, marquis des Essarts, is an interesting figure, whose background and career belie many of the common assumptions made about the *intendants*. He was a native of Burgundy, his father had been *premier président* in the *parlement* of Dijon, and a leading spirit in the Fronde in that province, and the family owed much to the protection of the Condé. Bouchu was appointed *intendant* of Dijon in 1655, at the age of twenty-eight, and held that office until his death in 1683. *Op. cit.,* pp. 7, 25, 29–31.

14. Colbert, *Lettres, Instructions, et Mémoires,* vol. IV, pp. 138, 155, 172.

15. Colbert to all *intendants,* 29 February 1680. Colbert, *Lettres, Instructions, et Mémoires,* vol. IV, pp. 138–9.

16. Isambert etc., *Recueil général des anciennes lois françaises,* vol. 19, pp. 420–5.

17. The only attempt to revise Colbert's edict was made by the *contrôleur général* Delaverdy in his municipal reform edict of August 1764. Isambert etc., *Recueil général des anciennes lois françaises,* vol. 22, pp. 405–17. He retained the principle of government control of municipal finance, but transferred the exercise of that control from the *intendant,* whose discretionary power he curtailed, to the *contrôleur général,* whose authorization became necessary for all financial transactions of any importance. This exaggerated centralization of the *tutelle* was impracticable. In addition, Delaverdy revived obsolescent rights of interference in municipal finances enjoyed by tribunals like the *bailliage* and *bureau des finances,* also at the expense of the *intendant's* authority. The regard he showed for these corporations of venal officials probably reflects Delaverdy's *parlementaire* background and sympathies; it went against the traditional policy of the Crown and produced a confusion of checks and controls which diluted responsibility and did nothing to promote sound and efficient management of municipal finance. Delaverdy's reform was revoked in 1771 by Terray and Maupeou, and their old *tutelle* restored to the *intendants.*

18. His plans for larger towns had to be submitted to the royal council for ratification and were issued as *arrêts du conseil.* The large number of these budgetary *arrêts* to be found in the registers of *Série E* in the *Archives Nationales* indicates that his edict was indeed implemented. *Arrêts du conseil* relating to particular towns can be traced through Augustin Thierry's *fichier,* now deposited in the *Bibliothèque Nationale,* N.A.F. 3432-77.

19. Colbert, perhaps because he received so many, regarded deputations as an outmoded, expensive, and time-consuming method of bringing local needs and grievances to the attention of the government. A letter to the *intendant* of Aix, 6 November 1682, contains the following *cri de cœur:* 'Et pour vous faire connoistre bien positivement que ces députations, qui se font par des intérests particuliers, sont ruineuses pour les villes, c'est que quoyque je donne des audiences tous les jours et qu'il y ayt plus de trois semaines ou un mois que le député de Marseille est à Paris, je ne l'ay point encore vu . . .' Colbert, *Lettres, Instructions, et Mémoires,* vol. IV, p. 165.

20. Colbert to de Bercy, *intendant* of Riom, 15 April 1683: 'Il n'est pas à propos que vous vous chargiez d'examiner les comptes de toutes les villes, parce que ce seroit un travail immense, qui ne produiroit aucun avantage aux peuples.' Colbert, *Lettres, Instructions, et Mémoires,* vol. IV, p. 178.

21. Colbert, *Lettres, Instructions, et Mémoires,* vol. IV, pp. 155–6.

22. Colbert to the *intendant* of Lyon, 21 November 1681, and 28 October 1682. Colbert, *Lettres, Instructions, et Mémoires,* vol. IV, pp. 150, 164.

23. The significance of the campaign to liquidate municipal debts and the *tutelle* of municipal finance in the evolution of the centralized administration of the old regime was noted by G. Pagès, *Essai sur l'Evolution des Institutions Administratives en France du commencement du XVIe siècle à la fin du XVIIe*. Revue d'histoire moderne, 1932, pp. 133–7.

24. *Arrêt du conseil,* 1 January 1760. Arch. dép. de l'Yonne, C 8.

25. Dufour du Villeneuve to the *maire* and *échevins* of Auxerre, 8 January 1763. Arch dép. de l'Yonne, C 8.

26. Arch. dép. de l'Yonne, C 8, C 11, C 14.

27. Arch. dép. de l'Yonne, C 13.

28. Accounts of 1756–89, Arch. mun. Auxerre, GG.

29. Under the edict of 1683, municipal officials could be required to restore all monies spent without due authorization, but this penalty was directed against embezzlement of municipal revenue and was too harsh to be invoked against mere evasion of the *tutelle;* it would anyway involve litigation, the cost of which would probably be greater than the unlawful expenditure it was intended to recover.

30. This point was made in the *Rapport de la commision chargée de l'impôt à l'assemblée provinciale du Berry,* 29 October 1783. Cited by M. Marion, *Les impôts directs sous l'ancien régime* (1910), p. 234.

31. Paris, 'royal' towns such as Versailles, Fontainebleau, Saint-Germain, and several provincial capitals.

32. These were the two main arguments put forward by the *intendant* d'Argouges, in 1687, when, on his initiative, the town of Moulins was persuaded to replace the direct tax that it levied to pay for its *abonnement* of 12,000 *livres* p.a. with an *octroi* on wine entering the town. Arch. mun. Moulins, Reg. 132, fol. 203. It was opposed by the clergy, nobility, officials of the *bureau des finances,* and magistrates of the *présidial* precisely on the ground that those who were exempt from direct tax would pay indirect tax. Arch. dép. Allier, C 150.

33. *Cf.* letters written by the *intendants* of Rouen and Lyon, cited in M. Marion, *Les impôts directs sous l'ancien régime* (1910), pp. 256–8, 264–7.

34. *Ibid.,* pp. 54–5.

35. *Ibid.,* p. 70.

36. At the end of the seventeenth century, Moulins was paying its venal *maire* 1080 *livres* p.a., its *procureur du roi* 400 *livres* p.a., its *greffier* 300 *livres* p.a., and 60 *livres* p.a. each to five *assesseurs*. Accounts for 1695–6, 1697–8, 1699–1700. Arch. mun. Moulins, 164, 166, 167.

37. *Etat présenté par les Maire et Echevins de la ville d'Auxerre aux Elus Généraux,* 6 April 1727. Arch. mun. Auxerre, BB 43.

38. *Mémoire de la Généralité de Moulins par l'intendant Le Vayer,* ed. P. Flament (1906), p. 29.

39. Arch. mun. Auxerre, BB 55.

40. Arch. mun. Auxerre, BB 55.

41. Arch. mun. Auxerre, BB 77, BB 78.

42. Arch. Nat., H * 140 bis, 1. Arch. mun. Auxerre, BB 38, BB 77.

43. Arch. mun. Auxerre, BB 38, BB 77. This so-called *augmentation des* *gages* was in truth nothing more than a forced loan from holders of venal offices on the pretext of providing funds for an increase in their salary: the interest on the capital sum extorted from the venal official constituted his increase in salary. Towns which acquired venal offices were as liable as individuals to pay for *augmentations des gages.*

44. The office of *lieutenant général de police,* created in 1699 for all major towns, and modelled on that established earlier in Paris, was not merely a financial expedient, but also an important administrative reform: it defined and brought under one authority the multifarious responsibilities connected with the police of the towns. *Corps de ville* were eager to acquire this office, not simply because it extended their authority, but also because it made for administrative convenience, since many of the activities which came within the sphere of police overlapped with those belonging to the *corps de ville.*

45. Arch. Nat., H ¹ 144, 1. Arch. mun. Auxerre, BB 77.

46. Arch. Nat., H * 140 bis, 6. Arch. mun. Auxerre, CC 42.

47. Arch. Nat., H * 140 bis, 49, 52. Arch. mun. Auxerre, CC 37, CC 42.

48. Arch. mun. Auxerre, BB 38.

49. Arch. mun. Auxerre, CC 62.

50. Arch. mun. Auxerre, CC 42, CC 62. The farm of these *octrois* eventually ran for nine years, 1706–15, and raised over 87,000 *livres.*

51. Arch. mun. Auxerre, BB 38.

52. Arch. mun. Auxerre, BB 38.

53. Arch. mun. Auxerre, BB 38.

54. *Assemblée générale des habitants,* 2 November 1767. Arch. mun. Moulins, Reg. 134, fol. 26 verso. The *juré mouleur des bois,* whose function was to collect fees on the sale of firewood and charcoal, was one of two venal offices connected with commerce which the royal government unloaded on to the towns; the other was the *inspecteur aux boucheries,* who collected fees on the sale of meat. Auxerre paid 15,400 *livres* in 1696 for the first, 24,750 *livres* in 1704 for the second. Arch. mun. Auxerre, BB 77, BB 75.

55. Arch. mun. Moulins, 225.

56. Edict of September 1714. *Code Municipal ou Le Recueil des Principaux Edits, Reglemens et Ordonnances du Roi, qui intéressent en général et en particulier les Officiers Municipaux et de Police de Villes et Communautés . . .* published in 1760 by André Giroud, Grenoble. vol. II, pp. 118–24.

57. Edict of June 1717. *Code Municipal,* vol. II, pp. 137–46.

58. Edict of August 1722. *Code Municipal,* vol. II, pp. 152–9.

59. Arch. Nat., H ¹ 144, 1. Arch. dép. Côte d'Or, C 696.

60. Edict of July 1724. *Code Municipal,* vol. II, pp. 160–6.

61. Edict of June 1725. *Loix municipales et economiques de Languedoc,* ed. J. Albisson, vol. VII (1787), pp. 344–9.

62. Moulins handed over *assignations* worth 4329 *livres* and 4761 *livres* 18s. in cash (i.e. 4329 *livres* plus the usual treasury tax of 2 *sous* per *livre*). Arch. mun. Moulins, 125, 126. Auxerre paid 7080 *livres* in *assignations* and 7788 *livres* in cash, the money being raised by means of an *octroi* levied for twelve years on *pain mollet* sold by the bakers of the town. Arch. dép. Côte d'Or, C 696. Arch. mun. Auxerre, CC 47.

63. Edict of November 1733. *Code Municipal,* vol. II, pp. 167–75.

64. It paid 820,000 *livres,* to which Auxerre contributed 16,000 *livres* raised by *octrois* on wood, charcoal and hay. Arch. Nat., H ¹ 144, 1. Arch. mun. Auxerre, BB 38.

65. *Arrêt* 9 March 1734. *Code Municipal,* vol. II, pp. 198–202. *Arrêt* 13 September 1735. *Code Municipal,* vol. II, pp. 217–220.

66. *Arrêt* 4 December 1737. *Code Municipal,* vol. II, pp. 227–32.

67. *Arrêt* 23 January 1742. *Code Municipal,* vol. II, pp. 261–3. *Arrêt* 13 March 1742. *Code Municipal,* vol. II, pp. 264–6.

68. *Arrêt* 22 December 1744 reduced the price of all unsold offices to two-fifths of the original valuation. *Code Municipal,* vol. II, pp. 271–81.

69. *Arrêt* 22 March 1746. *Code Municipal,* vol. II, pp. 297–300.

70. *Assemblée générale des habitants* 21 March 1777. Arch. mun. Moulins, Reg. 135, fol. 16. *Cf.* A. Dupuy, *Etudes sur l'administration municipale en Bretagne au XVIII* ͤ *siècle* (1891), pp. 313–15.

71. Edict of November 1771. *Loix municipales et economiques de Languedoc,* ed. J. Albisson, vol. VII (1787), pp. 448–52.

72. *Arrêt* 24 July 1745. Arch. Nat., E 1223 B. *Arrêt* 7 March 1780. Arch. Nat., E 1571 A.

73. Arch. Nat., H ¹ 144, 10, 11.

74. Arch. mun. Moulins, Reg. 134, fol. 110; Reg. 135, fol. 15 verso–18, fol. 29, fol. 115.

75. A. M. de Boislisle, *Correspondance des Contrôleurs Généraux des Finances avec les intendants des provinces,* vol. 1 (1874), no. 686, p. 179.

76. In the province of Champagne, Troyes and Reims paid 50,000 *livres* each, and Chalons 30,000 *livres. Mémoire concernant la generalité de Champagne par M. De Pommereu, intendant* (1699). Bib. Nat., A.F.F. 4285. In the province of Brittany, Rennes and Nantes paid 500,000 *livres* and 150,000 *livres* respectively. A. Dupuy, *Etudes sur l'administration municipale en Bretagne au XVIII* ͤ *siècle* (1891), p. 273. The provincial estates of Burgundy voted the king 250,000 *livres,* to which Auxerre contributed 33,000 *livres.* Arch. mun. Auxerre, BB 38.

77. Edict of September 1710. Bib. Nat., A.F.F. 11063, fol. 153.

78. Burgundy paid 200,000 *livres,* Auxerre's share being fixed at 15,750 *livres.* Arch. mun. Auxerre, BB 38. In the province of Brittany, Nantes paid 170,000 *livres,* Rennes 120,000 *livres,* and Brest 70,000 *livres.* A. Dupuy, *Etudes sur l'administration municipale en Bretagne au XVIII* ͤ *siècle* (1891), p. 273.

79. Edict of August 1758. Arch. Nat., AD IX 401, 136.

80. Although many towns claimed that they were over-assessed and insisted on reductions: Joigny got its *don gratuit* cut from 10,000 *livres* p.a. to 8,000 *livres* p.a., Chablis from 3,000 *livres* p.a. to 2,000 *livres* p.a. *Déclaration* 3 January 1759. Arch. Nat., AD IX 401, 143. A few towns were influential and wealthy enough to secure special treatment: Troyes offered 140,000 *livres* cash down in lieu of 40,000 *livres* p.a. for six years, which the government, always in need of ready cash, accepted. *Lettres patentes* 29 March 1759. Arch. Nat., AD IX 401, 144.

81. Auxerre's *don gratuit* was cut from 8000 *livres* p.a. to 2666 *livres* in 1768, 2000 *livres* in 1769. Arch. Nat., H ¹ 144, 30.

82. Edict of April 1768. Arch. Nat., AD IX 401, 207.

83. *Arrêt* 15 May 1768. Arch. dép. Côte d'Or, C 696.

84. *Parlement* of Paris, Edict of August 1758. Arch. Nat., AD IX 401, 136.

85. *Arrêt* 20 February 1761. Arch. Nat., AD IX 401, 189. *Arrêt* 3 November 1762. Arch. Nat., AD IX 401, 196. Avallon was one of these towns, and received many impatient, exhortatory letters on this score. Arch. mun. Avallon, CC 50.

86. Except in certain *pays d'états*, where the local *parlement* refused to register the decree authorizing the *ferme générale* to collect these *octrois*. According to figures in the *Recueil des pièces sur l'administration provinciale formé par le Marquis de Castries*, 1777, *dons gratuits* from towns in *pays d'états*, except Brittany, were worth 1,537,400 *livres* p.a. Bib. Nat., A.F.F. 7509, fol. 10, 13, 19, 25, 34, 42, 51.

87. Arch. mun. Moulins, Reg., 133, fol. 387.

88. *Arrêt* 3 January 1759. Arch. mun. Moulins, 383.

89. *Lettres patentes* 22 April 1759. Arch. mun. Moulins, 383.

90. *Lettres patentes* 15 July 1759. Arch. mun. Moulins, 383.

91. *Corps de ville* of Moulins to the *contrôleur général,* 14 August 1768. Arch. mun. Moulins, C 384.

92. *Lettres patentes* 22 April 1759. Arch. Nat., AD IX 401, 153.

93. Arch. Nat., H ¹ 144, 30.

94. Terray to *intendant* Amelot, 31 July 1770. Arch. dép. Côte d'Or, C 696.

95. Arch. dép. Côte d'Or, C 696.

2

RESISTANCE TO ABSOLUTISM

If the state appeared in the provinces mainly in the guise of the fisc, so too were acts of resistance against the state characterized by an antifiscal motivation. But to establish the immediate cause of revolts against the crown is not to explain the profound reasons that drove men and women to defy the absolute monarchy. The problem of revolts is the problem of the nature of seventeenth-century society. Clearly the two case studies of revolts before the Fronde that are presented here challenge a simple class analysis of French society and emphasize the utter complexity of local circumstances. Varying combinations of economic distress, social fears, and local loyalties came together to produce the combustible situation that a particular exaction of the crown finally ignited. Nor, as Leon Bernard argues about the later seventeenth century, should we underestimate the deep currents of humiliation and resentment that moved the popular classes to strike out against the state, and also, when the opportunity arose, against the privileged as well. But in the end, the course of resistance tended to depend on the active or passive cooperation of these elites. The privileged did connive in violence against the state, but, as Loirette shows, they more often used a wide range of legal and political stratagems to defend their rights against the monarchy's encroachments. Such a society could not be dominated by the crown. The liberties of provincial Frenchmen were still a significant political factor in this age of absolutism.

The *Cascaveoux:* The Insurrection at Aix of the Autumn of 1630

BY RENÉ PILLORGET

In September 1630 troubles broke out at Aix and lasted there until December. In fact, the city was in revolt for three months against the central power, and then it was divided by internal battles. The uprising did not extend beyond the immediate environs of Aix, but it culminated a dangerous series of seditions. At least a part of the Parlement supported it, and the governor of the province, the Duke of Guise, remained inactive, or expectant. For 1630 was for Louis XIII the year of the great choice, and the revolt at Aix broke out while he was ill at Lyon, less than two months before the Day of the Dupes.[1]

This insurrection cannot be explained only in terms of the personal quarrel between the Cardinal and the Duke of Guise, studied by Gabriel Hanotaux.[2] Nor can it be explained only as a simple conflict of fiscal origin that united all classes of society in opposition to the establishment of the *Elus,* as M. Porchnev has argued.[3] Beyond the exaltation of the liberties of Provence and the selfishness of notables defending a fiscal system that was advantageous for the best people, one cannot hope to simplify it. An explanation of the movement at Aix should not settle for one of these partial views, nor even for any juxtaposition of them. It was a more complex phenomenon, stemming from numerous and diverse factors, as M. Roland Mousnier maintains.

1
Backgrounds

First, the political and military situation, which was a major preoccupation of contemporaries. Provence was a frontier province. It happened that Spanish or English ships—the siege of La Rochelle occurred in 1627 and 1628—came to cruise on its coasts. The Protestants of Nîmes and of the Cévennes sometimes threatened the lower Rhone region—in August 1628, the Duke of Rohan and his troops pushed as far as the Camargue.[4] The same year, on the frontier with Savoy, there was the affair of the Mantuan succession and the siege of Casal. It had been necessary to allow the troops to pass and to let them buy grain.[5] In the spring of 1629, there was the affair of the Pas de Suse— an operation that was marked in Provence by new passages of troops and new purchases of provisions.[6] In 1630 the province had to furnish seven hundred mules with their muleteers for the siege of Pignerol.[7] Some communities had to borrow in order to satisfy this demand. And if on August 5, 1630, letters patent forbade the exporting of "wheat, oats, vegetables," they pointed out that it was because of the "passage of the military in Savoy and Piedmont," who must not lack supplies.[8] These burdens were heavy, and they were aggravated by plundering and the habitual violence—"great devastation, extortion, and brutality." [9] We must not underestimate these burdens. They helped to plunge into misery a region that, since the harvest of 1627, had known a very serious subsistence crisis.

The dramatic character of this last constituted one of the essential traits of the economic situation in Provence during the years 1628–31. Evidence of it is abundant.

From January 1628, various consuls (municipal officials in Provence) began to express to Parlement their fear of famine.[10] They began to arrest monopolists—the "dardanaires." In 1629, the consuls of several communities, with the authorization of Parlement, proceeded to requisitions and to price controls.[11] The price curve for the region's wheat on the market at Aix, calculated for the months of October and November, passed from 12 livres the measure in 1625 to 12.09 in 1626 to 13.20 in 1627 to 15.15 in 1628. It remained at 15.20 in 1629, and it reached 20.40 livres at the beginning of autumn 1630. Wheat still cost more than 20 livres in 1631. Since 1593, no similar rise had been registered. It was the same for the price of bread, with a slightly different curve.[12] Rye and oats registered equally strong increases and then too lowered in 1632 and 1633.[13]

The epidemics were inseparable from a series of bad harvests. The great economic crisis of 1628–31 was marked not only by famine, but by "contagion"—more violent it seemed, than any Provence had known in the seventeenth century. The plague was terribly feared, and the passage of troops was held responsible for it. Now, as early as July 1628, it was reported in the Rouergue and in Quercy; in August, it was in Burgundy and Dauphiné; then it was at Lyon.[14] That was sufficient to alarm Aix.[15] In October, Toulouse and Grenoble were judged contaminated, then first one and soon several villages of Comtat.[16] The classic precautions were taken. Bureaus of health were established everywhere. Each village reduced to a minimum its relations with its neighbors. Aix refused entry to travelers and to merchandise originating in plague-infested places. "We are presently deprived of commerce with the neighboring provinces," wrote the great scholar, Peiresc, a councillor of the Parlement. Economic difficulties were aggravated. Even the administrative mail was received with extreme caution; they passed it over a flame, and they "perfumed" it—even the receipts for the annual tax on offices.[17] But they could not prevent the army from circulating, and it did not take into account the ordinances.

In June 1629, the plague struck Digne and spread throughout Provence. From July, Aix was in a state of alert. In October, it was necessary to recognize the truth—the city was infected. On the twenty-fifth, Parlement left town.

The plague raged in Aix for some ten months, striking at Marseilles, Arles, and numerous villages as well. The inhabitants lived in fear and under nervous tension. Like the famine, the plague poisoned social relations and stimulated antagonisms. The rich citizens of Aix, who were rural landowners, were able to procure provisions more easily than other inhabitants. When the epidemic came, there was an exodus to the country houses. Only the very poor remained in the city, along with a few devoted notables.[18] Thus the assessor, Martelli, cut out for himself a certain popularity at the expense of the first

consul, Gaspard de Forbin La Barben. Still, a certain number
of poor, suspected of being infected, were expelled and forced
to build huts between the walls and the sanitary cordon that
guarded [the city].[19] Inevitably, hatreds were born and nourished.

Another effect of the plague was to unleash a crisis inside
the Parlement of Provence. It was logical that it should sit, altogether, in a neighboring city, Salon. But within [the Parle-
ment] there existed factions. One of them, opposed to the first
president, d'Oppède—a relative of the first consul of Aix—had
at its head a member of the Chambre Tournelle, Laurent de
Coriolis, aged, nearly blind, but singularly enterprising. Invoking a precedent, he obtained a ruling that the Parlement
should be divided into two chambers—one sitting at Salon
under the first president; the other at Pertuis under him. Each
of the two factions dominated one of the two chambers. And
very quickly, the one at Pertuis tried to set up an independent
Parlement: the Parlement de Outre Durance, having for its jurisdiction the whole northern part of the province.[20] Indignation broke out at Salon, when they learned that Coriolis had
dared to put on the red robe of a first president in order to go
from his residence to the court session of March 19, 1630. His
ambitions, previously disappointed, were not a mystery to anyone. From Paris Oppède obtained letters patent ordering the
reunification of the two chambers at Salon.[21] The one at Pertuis did not submit, and it sent a deputation to the king.[22] Its
failure was certain. The end of the plague happened at the
right time. On September 8, the two parts of Parlement returned to Aix. But the antagonism between Oppède and Coriolis, and their partisans, continued ominously.

If the *parlementaires* were divided among themselves, there
was one point on which they were, it seemed, agreed, but which
did not serve to calm them down. From 1625, Richelieu had
considered the suppression of the *droit annuel*—the precious tax
that assured the officers of the heritability of their offices, or its
value when the holder had no son old enough to be provided
with it. At the beginning of 1629, he wrote about ". . . not re-
establishing the Paulette when it expired in a year. . . ." Effec-

tively, on December 31, the concession of the *annuel* had expired, and they did not speak of renewing it.[23]

Anxiety was great among the officers. The oldest resigned their charges. But in a country ravaged by the "contagion," everyone feared a sudden death and the ruin of their children. Peiresc wrote on June 27, 1630, "The dangers of the plague in this region have put the poor officers in such a state of alarm, that there are hardly any who would not prefer to be held for ransom, than to run the risk of losing all and of seeing their families ruined, the best part [of whose fortunes] often consisted of funds from offices." [24] At Paris, alarm led to invective and to a clear hint about ministers who "disappear after a little while." [25] At Aix, after the return of the chambers, the center of agitation was President de Coriolis. He tried to arouse the common people against the royal fisc and its agents. They listened all the more favorably, because they suffered from famine.

For several years, the king had presented to the Estates or to the Assembly of Communities—which was composed only of representatives from the Third Estate—increasing demands for financial aid. Beginning in 1628, they took the most diverse forms: an increase of the *taillon* and of the price of salt; but also the creation of new offices in the Cour des Comptes; and [the creation] of new treasurers general, of auditors and assessors, and of clerks of court. In May 1628, there was a "great row," [26] and a delegation was sent to the court. It obtained nothing, except that the *superintendant,* d'Effiat, spoke of changing "the forms of the province." [27] Spirits were "moved and greatly changed." The Parlement, and then the Cour des Comptes, feeling the rumbles of sedition, "almost as if besieging the palace," issued decrees that postponed the increase in the salt tax. Certainly, "the forms did not permit these companies to do this sort of thing," but the people threatened. Parlement feared, "some great excess might have been possible, indeed some disorder, and God knows if we could have remedied it," wrote the prudent Peiresc to Paris.[28]

Not only the officers, but all the notables of Provence, began in 1628 and 1629 to fear another calamity—the establishment of new officers, the *élus,* and the transformation of Provence into a *pays d'élection.* D'Effiat had spoken seriously. In order to sell offices, to unify the kingdom, and to obtain a better return from taxes, the king tried to impose this reform on Dauphiné, Languedoc, and Burgundy. Troubles broke out in 1629 and, above all, at Dijon in February 1630 with the revolt of the "lanturlu." [29] The general crisis of subsistence favored them.

The decision was equally taken for Provence, and the intendant, d'Aubray, was charged with having the edict establishing the *élus* verified. Now, the notables of Provence did not at all support a modification of the way that taxes were assessed. Masters of the Estates, and of the councils of the communities, the "most apparent" knew how to distribute this burden for the good of their own interests. [30] They could also mobilize a clientele and stir up troubles. D'Aubray went to Aix on July 30, 1629, and, prudently, had the Duke of Guise accompany him. "Quite conveniently," the plague took its first victims the preceding night. Neither the governor nor the intendant dared to go into the city. D'Aubray, when the epidemic proved to be real, left the province. [31] In April 1630, he reappeared. People were upset. Stormy assemblies were held. That at Valensole decided to send a deputation to the king that was led by a certain Du Loubet. [32] It reached him at Moutiers, in Tarentaise, and was dismissed. In July, d'Aubray thought to profit from the division of the Parlement. He could count on President Oppède, as well as on Séguiran, president of the Chambre des Comptes. He had the Estates of Provence meet at Brignoles, so that he could proceed to the verification of the edict.

The affair turned out badly. A strike of the consuls, a strike of the officers of the *sénéchaussée,* a strike of the artisans, the closing of shops—d'Aubray, "astonished," had the assembly adjourned. [33] At the end of August, he prepared to return to Aix. The epidemic had stopped; a Parlement was reinstalled there.

Now, like all of the Parlements, that of Provence was profoundly hostile to the intendants. For several years, in some of the regions of France, it was the Parlements that had stirred up incidents against them, and even riots.[34] The one in Provence listened all the more readily to Coriolis, because Oppède belonged to a family that was traditionally devoted to the royal power. It saw in d'Aubray the commissioner who was going to lay his hands on its authority, and the founder of a new fiscal regime and a galaxy of new officers, prejudicial to the interests of its members. D'Aubray was going to confront it all the more directly, as he was going to arrive alone. The governor had left on a trip. It was to Parlement that the authority in the province had been restored.

At the beginning of September 1630, it authorized the meeting of an asembly of the provençal nobility at Pertuis. It took place. The president de la Rocque, a member of the illustrious Forbin family, like the Oppèdes and the La Barbens, presided. It opened on September 15 and was emotionally hostile to the establishment of the *élus*.[35]

The Parlement feared for its *droit annuel* and was hostile to the establishment of new officers and to the reform they represented; it was irritated by the coming of an intendant; it was divided into two factions, certainly, but it united under the influence of Coriolis and his friends against the innovations and against the first president. It was informed of what happened in the kingdom and at the court—perhaps by the governor. The latter was involved in a legal action with Richelieu. The superintendant and grand master of navigation wanted to dispossess him of his charge as admiral of Provence. He sent process servers to him.[36] Guise looked for support from Marillac [Richelieu's rival at court] and from the queen mother. Having been in the province for thirty years, this son of Henri le Balafré exercised influence, and he had been assured of the loyalty of the gentlemen. Without doubt, the assembly at Pertuis had been brought together with at least his tacit consent.

As for the population of Aix, it too found itself dissatisfied with the present and anxious for the future. The Parlement supported it in these sentiments. A manuscript text circulated—a copy, or alleged to be such, of the speech that Du Loubet had delivered at Moutiers in Tarentaise.[37] It depicted

102

in pathetic terms the ills that the province was going to suffer because of the establishment of the *élus*. At the end appeared the brief, sharp response attributed to the king and to Superintendant d'Effiat: "Get out of here. . . ."

Food supplies were deficient, and bread was expensive. And at the moment when the plague came to an end, and when a truce had been concluded at Casal, a sinister prospect came into view—the establishment of particularly effective financial officers. "Everywhere in public, one heard only talk about the great prejudice that the *élection* would bring." [38] It sufficed to read Du Loubet's speech. The *élus* were going "to put on the tax rolls our daughters at the age of fifteen and our sons at twenty, along with valets and servants because of the wages and salaries they receive from their masters." In short, there would be no one "so miserable as to be exempted from it." [39] It would mean the suppression of the Estates and the transformation of the province into a *pays d'élection,* and the change from the *taille réelle* to the *taille personnelle.* [40] The weight of fiscal burdens would fall not only on the land, but also on urban activities. Spirits were violently moved. At Aix, in September 1630, Coriolis, La Roque, and some other officers had no trouble in recruiting demonstrators to hoot at their adversaries and to prevent d'Aubray from staying in the city.

2
"The Madness of the City of Aix"

At this time, Aix numbered about twenty thousand inhabitants.[41] The principal image that it suggests to the mind is that of an administrative and judicial city. In reality, it had several characters. First off, it was an aristocratic and bourgeois city. One encountered gentlemen there, but they were, however, less numerous than the officers and the merchants. There were financial officers, certainly, but mainly officers of justice, followed by the inevitable notaries, *procureurs,* and lawyers. Probably all were landowners, who knew how to invest their money,[42] and, together with their families, they composed a well-to-do society—a clientele for the different trades, including luxury trades. In this merchant class, then, from which the officers were most often drawn, there existed very great fortunes. Certain of its members participated, through second parties, in the bidding on the contracts for the collection of various municipal taxes.[43]

Facing the gentlemen and the bourgeois, there were many artisans. Besides the trades providing for the nourishment of the city, the butchers and bakers, there were numerous wood and leather workers, as well as clothes makers. The heads of households worked with their families and their "valets." Their principal quarter, that of the Cordeliers, was the most extensive in the city.[44] One would think that they composed the great majority of the population living inside the walls. This artisanal character of the city helps to explain the number and occasional violence of the riots that shook it.

Finally, because of its vast territory and its rural market, it appeared deeply marked by country life. The surrounding areas, devoted to the classic and varied Mediterranean cultivation—wheat, vineyards, and fruit trees—was noted for its richness.[45] They were well populated, with some country houses belonging to the urban notables, but also with the houses of vine-growers and small proprietors. If the tanners seem to have been the most turbulent, the peasants were sometimes able to equal them. Thus it had happened that they came to the market to provoke disorders on such occasions as the staking of the grapes.[46] The bourgeois, mainly in the period of crisis, also feared the farmer laborers, of whom there were many on the surrounding lands.[47]

Still more, they feared the beggars who flooded in, even from far away, as soon as a difficult year occurred.[48]

These appear to have been the general characteristics of Aix in 1630: a parliamentary city; a bourgeois city; an artisanal center; and an agricultural market—the central point for all of the fertile basin. Each of these aspects shaped the troubles. Three phases can be distinguished. Until the beginning of November, there was an apparent unanimity of the population directed against the edict on the *élus*. The Parlement, led by members of the former "Chambre de Pertuis," had the essential role, the mass of artisans furnishing it with docile troops. Then, a second episode, short but important, during the days of November 3 and 4: [this was] the provocative intervention of the peasants—an intervention heavy with consequences. Next, up to December, there were factional battles, and an attempt at reaction led by the Baron de Bras—the son of a *parlementaire,* but apparently rather detached from his milieu, having become something of a gentleman.

These few months were feverish and full of disturbances, assemblies, decisions, and projects. From the beginning of September until mid-October, one fact emerged: "the heat of the populace that had scarcely recovered from the contagion." [49] The distress due to expensive bread was skillfully focused on a few persons whom they chased out of the city.

First, the leading consul, Forbin La Barben. On Sunday, September 1, while Parlement entered Aix in procession, this relative of the first president was hooted at by the crowd. "Those of the Chambre de Pertuis had done much to fan the hatred." Encouraged, they stirred up a second demonstration the following Sunday, while the return of the Cour des Comptes was being celebrated. Some "younger sons" wanted to throw Forbin La Barben into the celebration fire that had been lighted on the Place des Prêcheurs. He left the city.

A second personage, the target on September 19, was the intendant, d'Aubray. The preceding incidents had only been rehearsals. The action taken against him was striking in its resemblance to one that was launched at Amiens, in 1628, against "royal commissioners for the execution of the edicts." The scenario was the same. D'Aubray had just arrived. They knew what he had come to do. It was noontime. The toscin sounded. Some "wise and clever" persons "ran through the streets arousing the artians." [50] A "multitude appeared without leaders—but it was not long deprived of them"—that was on the point of doing d'Aubray harm.[51] It was necessary, however, that things did not go too far. Some magistrates happened to be there to protect him and had him flee over the rooftops. His baggage was burned in the streets. This time, given the position of d'Aubray, the affair took on serious proportions. It was scandalous. Aix had rebelled against royal authority. It was found to be in a state of "disobedience."

The third personage, who was apparently a target, was an absentee, the Superintendant d'Effiat. They held him responsible for the edict concerning the *élus*. Additional bad news arrived: the Cour des Comptes was to be transferred to Toulon. Under the direction of its president, Séguiran, it prepared to obey: the crowd prevented it. Then the false news of the superintendent's death having arrived on October 13, he was burned in effigy. This demonstration was no more spontaneous than the preceding ones.[52] It turned into protests and gatherings before the residences of the presidents, Séguiran and Oppède. The anticipated result was accomplished: the two magistrates left the city.

Having eliminated their adversaries and hierarchical superiors, Coriolis, La Roque, and the assessor, Martelli, had become the masters. One fact characterized this early autumn—the union of different social groups against the edict concerning the *élus* and against those who accepted it. The action had been decided within the Parlement. On August 5, it had protested. In September, it refused to permit La Roque to obey an order, that he had just received, to appear at the royal court.[53] On October 18, it prohibited anyone from accepting or from exercising any office of *élu* in the province.[54] This language pleased the citizens of Aix. The nobility, gathered at Pertuis, did not insist on any other. As for the governor, returned from the court and settled at Marseilles, he let it happen. Later, Coriolis declared that he had received a gentleman, who came to tell him, "that they might do what they wanted at Aix, and that he [Guise] would be blind and deaf." [55] The king was ill at Lyon; the Parlement ordered a novena for him; the Duke of Guise waited.

The agreement among the social groups manifested itself in the city by a common participation in the riots. Some *parlementaires,* bourgeois, *consulaires,* and lawyers descended into the streets in order to incite the people to act. On October 17, it was under their impetus that the agitation became more serious. That day, the house of the councillor, de Paule, was ransacked by "two hundred persons, mainly above the lowest orders," and by "some artisans." [56] At their head was found the nephew of Coriolis, Paul de Joannis, lord of Chateauneuf. The artisans, seeing that they were given an example, grew bolder. The poorest elements of the city, "lured by petty thievery," joined them. They no longer confined themselves to shouting and singing. They pillaged; they burned—not the houses, but the furniture piled high on the Place des Prêcheurs. Still it was a matter of organized expeditions. "A few black masks followed by a great number of people:" because certain of the notables did not want to be seen on these occasions.[57] An order from one among them was sufficient for this apartment or that house to be spared.[58] But on October 26, they did not spare that of the *prévôt,* Dumas. They even charged into his vineyard, tore up the roots and burned them.

Larger efforts at united action were attempted. Both on the military level—the raising of insurrectionary troops; and on the political level—the creation of a faction.

The will of part of the nobility was expressed by the decisions of the assembly at Pertuis. The most serious was to charge six gentlemen—three from north of the Durance, three from the south—to "assemble their compatriots and oppose with arms" the edict of the *élus.*[59] In order to raise funds, a more restricted "conference" decided, on October 11, to tax the nobility. A messenger went from chateau to chateau to collect the money.[60] It is difficult to imagine that all this happened without at least the tacit approval of the Duke of Guise.

As for the Third Estate, its preoccupations were the same—to raise troops and to buy arms. Moreover, the Parlement served as an intermediary between the two orders. At Pertuis, President de La Roque had been moderator of the assembly. In the city hall at Aix, there was a representative of Parlement who, on October 25, presided over the assembly of the communities, grouping the deputies of the principal cities of Provence. Its tone was revolutionary—mainly in the speech of the assessor, Martelli.[61] Unanimously, it was decided to acquire four thousand muskets and two thousand pikes. These

arms would be "distributed to the cities that belong to the Estates and assemblies, according to the number of households."
They would be "distributed among the gentlemen, bourgeois,
merchants and inhabitants after." [62] The communities voted a
tax to make this purchase, but the terms were diverse and
generous—it had to be done quickly. In order not to alarm
those who might be hesitant, these decisions were hedged in
with prudent statements and with the formula, "under the
good pleasure of the king." Moreover, they carried the battle
on the ground of principles. The assembly decided to search in
the archives for "all the privileges of the province" and to have
them printed.

It seems that the sentiment of regional liberties, and of the
autonomy of Provence in face of the centralizing power, had
contributed to cementing the union of the different social
classes. Everywhere, they repeated that it was necessary "to take
up arms for the defense of the *pays*," and they spoke of "dying
for the fatherland." [63]

A group of men—Chateauneuf and his friends—drew
profit from this state of mind and organized public meetings.
Then they formed a party.[64] This last had for its rallying cry,
fouero élus. When one came to sign the register of adherents,
one received as an insignia, a *cascaveou*—a small round bell attached to a leather strap or to a white ribbon. Promoted chancellor of the party, a lawyer affixed to it Chateauneuf's seal in
wax. For several days he was buried in work. "A great number
of people of all sorts of conditions, and, above all, artisans,"
came to join.[65] They jingled the little bell when they heard
mention of the edict of the *élus*, or when some officers that they
judged to be favorable to it passed by.[66] By extension, they stig-
matized these last with the name of *élus*, while the partisans of
Chateauneuf were called *cascaveoux*.

In the minds of the artisans, an assimilation took place.
Someone who accepted the edict became an *élu;* then someone
who was rich enough to buy the office of *élu*. There "was no one
of any means who did not pass forthwith as an *élu*." [67] Soon
there appeared posted on certain houses threats and orders to
their occupants to leave the city. Bread remained expensive;

unemployment persisted. The enthusiasm stirred up in favor of "regional liberties" had not erased a certain animosity in regard to the prosperous class. Some writings, which circulated then, gave evidence of this. A prayer in pseudo-Latin demanded of God, "that the rich die and be buried in hell." [68] Chateauneuf did not seem to be alarmed by this state of mind. He played a demagogic game, organized popular banquets, and increased the recruitment of his adherents. Residents of the plain came to give their names and to receive the *cascaveou*. Antifiscal, political, and, more and more, social agitation increased in the city and overflowed into the countryside.[69] This was the origin of the days of November 3 and 4—the second phase of the insurrection and its principal turning point.

The movement started in the countryside, and in villages relatively far from Aix.[70] November 3 was a Sunday. The grape harvest had ended. Perhaps convened by Chateauneuf and his friends, deputies left Pelissanne, Saint-Canat, Lambesc, Eguilles, Ventabren, and Rians. With the exception of the latter, these places shared the common characteristic of being closest to the chateau of La Barben.[71] Now on November 1, following custom, the first consul of Aix, Forbin La Barben—already having fled—had been replaced, along with his colleagues, by a new consular list. For a long time, these communities neighboring his chateau had quarreled with him. He oversaw rigorously "the supervision of his woods and the hunting on his land." [72] On their side, the citizens of Aix found themselves in difficulty both with him and with all of the villages surrounding them. For more than four centuries, they had received rights of pasturage and of wood cutting within a radius of five leagues around their city.[73] The exercise of these rights entailed numerous lawsuits.[74] The right of wood gathering particularly interested the lower class of Aix. They encountered great difficulties in procuring wood; the more years that passed, the farther it was necessary to go. Forbin La Barben, the first consul, appears to have profited from his office to prevent the residents of Aix from going to gather or cut wood on his lands. This time, there was no union of the *seigneur* of La Barben and the villagers, his neighbors, against the invaders from Aix. On the contrary, there was a union between the common people of Aix and the villagers near the chateau against Forbin La Barben—at one and the same time, *seigneur,* proprietor, first consul of Aix, and, finally, traitor to the *pays.* Chateauneuf seems to have had the idea of encouraging the *cascaveoux* to undertake a plundering expedition on the lands of his enemy, but he did not succeed in convincing them. After that, he proposed the same to his followers from the plains region. His appeal appears to have had greater effect than he had hoped. Departing after mass, the delegations comprised several hundred people, if not more. They arrived at Aix in the late afternoon and went into the city. "Soon after" there was an assembly of "all sorts of persons" on the Place des Prêcheurs which "was filled." [75] "Every rebellious person in the city" agitated, reproached his neighbor for "sluggishness," and said "that he found more courage and ardor in the weak villages than in the capital of the province." The throng and the cries became such, that the Parlement assembled in haste, "nearly as a full body." [76] With the consuls, it tried to disperse the crowd and to calm it. In vain.

Parlement, the notables, and all of the prosperous classes seem to have passed a night of terror. They dreaded the agricultural workers, the "laborers," "the people who plunder the city in times of great misfortune," or if it [the city] was found "deprived of its magistrates." [77] That evening, along with the peasants, "there slipped into the city of Aix vagabonds and other unknown people," who circulated mainly in the popular quarter of the Cordeliers, among the artisans and their journeymen.[78] Neither the Parlement nor the consuls, recorded a witness, "were able to be the masters." The disorder lasted the whole night.[79] They feared still more "a general disorder." [80] The crowd pillaged, among others, the houses of two officers—those of the auditor, Chaix, and of the *greffier,* Menc. It did more than during the preceding days; it set about to demolish them. "They believed," the proprietors "had an interest in the edicts." [81]

In the morning, the consuls and other notables met at the

city hall. "Riots" occurred. One of them wrote, "We did not see any use in talking, because we were not the strongest." [82] The consuls were content to dispatch emissaries to the Duke of Guise, and they tried to stop the destruction of houses. They received some respect, but no obedience at all. "As we appeared, all of the workers left, but as we left, they went back to their task, at which the women worked harder than the men."

Chateauneuf, who had unleashed the tempest, saved the situation. They beat the drum. Flags were unfurled. A crowd, composed of peasants and townsmen, several thousand strong, left the city. It marched for half a day. Arriving at La Barben, it did not do much to the chateau; it was content to pillage a few out-buildings and to burn a few small houses. Above all, it fell upon the neighboring pine forest. The inhabitants of Aix had come to provide themselves with firewood. When the peasants regained their villages, they returned heavily loaded down, triumphantly exhibiting furniture, doors torn from their hinges, and sacks of salt and wheat. Night came. A surprise awaited the artisans of Aix. The bourgeois militia had been mobilized, and the gates closed. "They came very close to finding nobody at home and to being left completely outside." [83] But no one dared do this, given the number of their friends that remained inside the walls. Parlement ordered, "that they return to the city without drums and flags, and clustered together in small goups, which [order] they obeyed." [84]

The events of November 3 and 4, and the fear of certain of the popular forces, provoked a breach between the rebels and the party of Chateauneuf, the *cascaveoux,* and inflamed a factional struggle. Until then, the rebels had followed Coriolis, La Roque, and Chateauneuf—the group of the Chambre de Pertuis. In face of all the disorders, Parlement had investigated only feebly in order "to keep the appearances of judicial control." No one was fooled. Baron de Bras, the new first consul designated by the notables, was no less on good terms with the *cascaveoux.* He banqueted with them. The common enemy was the potential *élus,* or those who accepted them. But on November 3 and 4, the bourgeois of Aix were frightened by the invasion of their city; frightened by the arrival of agricultural workers and vagabonds from the plains country; and frightened by this union of inferior social groups, rural and urban.

A few hours after Chateauneuf had led the crowd outside the city, the first measures directed against his party were taken. Thus opened the last phase of the insurrectional period. First, there was a defensive action. Parlement, the Cour des Comptes, and the consuls met at the law courts with the officials and the captains of the quarters. The mobilization of the bourgeois guard was decided upon. Fifty men were placed at each of the city's gates; fifty at the city hall; and one hundred on the Place des Prêcheurs. The enemy was to be found more within the city, than outside of it. A large body of the guard was organized. Despite all, the artisans were not calmed. The captains drew up lists "of all persons of quality," who had something "to lose in the city—that is gentlemen, lawyers, bourgeois, prosecutors, notaries, merchants, sollicitors, houseowners, and other similar people." [85] On November 6, they composed a "legitimate force" with "a part of the weapons that were in the city hall." [86] On November 8, Parlement prohibited, under penalty of death, all assemblies, by day or night, and all violence against persons and property. Some councillors, accompanied by armed bourgeois, went through the different quarters, but mainly that of the Cordeliers, to forbid [people] to follow "those who carry bells," and to expel vagabonds and tramps from the city. With the fears of some, and the fury of others, social tensions mounted. A violent polemic of the time expressed the disapproval of many over the expulsion of the very poor: "it is an act against God and Nature. Why is the city less the home of the poor, than your home, Rich Gentlemen? Where did you learn that your wealth gives you more powerful rights in the city than they have?" It expressed hostility to the captains of the quarters: "you see only poor people in the city, and that is a bad sign." And in regard to the rich: "bankrupters, scum, who drink the sweat of the people and fatten on its flesh." And in regard to the municipal authorities who were accused of failing to avert unemployment among the artisans: they ought to have "given them [the artisans], while they worked, enough to support themselves during the harsh season." Purification: "first it is necessary to cleanse the city of this vermin (the *élus* and others) through our care and our vigilance, and then they must make us the guardians of the public order." And the *cascaveoux* wanted all the more to wield "the belled whip," because they were certain of going unpunished: "there are many of us in the city, and, if only for reason of state, they will pardon the multitude." [87]

On Sunday, November 10, there were seditious rumblings among certain of the *cascaveoux* artisans, their "journeymen from the shops and apprentices." Under penalty of death, the Parlement prohibited them from having any weapon and from obeying the cry of "close the shops" that the *cascaveoux* urged.[88] The city was in a stir—"all in arms." Artisans, with the small bell attached to their sleeve, passed through the streets and among the houses, "most of which were still marked with white crosses on the doors"—souvenirs of the plague. Improbable rumors circulated—Monsieur, brother of the king, was coming to besiege the city—and they discoursed and made grand gestures.[89] The next day, Parlement asked "members of the consulate and people of honor" remaining in their country houses after the end of the plague to return all the more quickly, "in order that the people of property be strong enough to resist the rebels." [90] On November 14, it ordered the consuls to name for each street two overseers, "heads of households who have something to lose." [91] The break between the Parlement and consuls, on the one hand, and the *cascaveoux,* on the other, was striking. On the one side were the comfortable classes of the city; on the other, the artisans and their possible allies on the outside.[92] In reaction, the notables began to draw close to the central power. To the Duke of Guise, they sent the assessor and the second consul to ask for his mediation and to obtain an amnesty from the king, and perhaps the suppression of the edict concerning the *élus*. Above all, they decided to pass to the offensive against the *cascaveoux*. A factional struggle was going to begin. The first consul, the Baron de Bras, enjoyed a certain popularity. The development of events gave him the idea of creating a new party—"the blue ribbon." In order not to affront the citizens of Aix—and besides, this corresponded to the ideas of its members—he declared his hostility both to the *élus* and to the *cascaveoux.* His insignia was also a small round bell. But to the cry, *fouero élus,* he added *vive le Roi.* On November 10, had not some fanatics declared that, if necessary, Aix would be defended against the king himself? [93] They had used "the liberties of the region" to stir up the artisans against an edict; Baron de Bras called for loyalty to the king, who was Count of Provence, in order to rally around him as many of his compatriots as possible. He recruited mainly people "of quality or high condition," clearly "above the lower class." However, some prosperous artisans, from among those that they dared put on guard at the Place des Prêcheurs, were sometimes to be found at his side.[94] His party wanted to combine a defense of the liberties of Provence (against the *élus*) and a social defense (against the *cascaveoux*). His followers wore the small round bell attached to their sleeve by a blue ribbon. "The bell was to show that he agreed with the plan to defend the liberty of the homeland, and the ribbon distinguished those of his party, people of quality who had only honor for their object, from those with the leather strap, who were said to act only out of sordid and mercenary motives." [95]

At the end of November, under leaders who were all city notables, both of the two opposing parties brought together people from all social levels—with a larger popular participation undoubtedly on the side of the *cascaveoux.* Personal enmities and the fact that everyone moved about armed could only have increased the tension. At the beginning of December, a spark ignited the explosion. It was the "tumult of the blue ribbon"—a struggle between groups of noble ringleaders, and involving in turn some of the artisans.[96]

On the evening of December 3, the first consul, making his rounds, encountered a rather animated meeting. The two groups exchanged insults. During the two following days, the atmosphere was very tense. Bras promised to expel from the city, at the first opportunity, the principal *cascaveoux,* President Coriolis and his nephew, Chateauneuf. Two parties, or better, two clans of ringleaders, jostled one another for the domination of Parlement and of the city.

It was on December 6 that there unfolded the most violent scenes that Aix had known since the beginning of the rebellion. Rather foolishly, Baron de Bras initiated action. But the essential participants, and the victors, were the artisans of the Cordeliers quarter. At the beginning of the afternoon, a minor incident—a quarrel between two "insignificant individuals" —sufficed to arouse them. They closed their shops, and they ran about, armed. Fearing lest the affair turn to pillaging, Baron de Bras came with the men of his bodyguard. He dispersed the mob without trouble. But he did not want to rest there and undertook to exploit his success. He ran through the streets, wearing the hood that was the insignia of the *consulat,* and he tried to rally to him the artisans, crying that it was necessary to drive out "the seditious thieves." As soon as his following was sufficiently strong, it went to the residence of Coriolis. The door was smashed down. The president, his nephew, Chateauneuf, and some friends were expelled from the city. The prestige of the magistrates remained so great—and the future so unsure—that the prudent bourgeois respectfully saluted those whom they were driving out, and they indicated, by gestures, that they were only obeying orders. Coriolis and his followers did not go far; a nearby convent took them in. This expulsion did not take place without violence; before the residence of Coriolis, two men lay wounded, and one dead. It had succeeded only through surprise. Excitement mounted in the city. Bras, who had overestimated his popularity, tried to calm things down. He increased the watch at the gates—mainly at the one that allowed entry directly into the Cordeliers quarter. But agitation became such that Parlement, two hours after the departure of Coriolis, met and decided to recall him. Furthermore, it had been deeply shocked by the deed of Baron de Bras. Coriolis remained a judge, a president, and he was old and infirm to boot. Parlement could only admit that they treated him cavalierly, and they had created a precedent. Coriolis returned and came to the court amidst an extraordi-

nary uproar. The two parties shook their bells—some with enthusiasm, others with fury. A very timely rumor restored calm:
the governor, and some horsemen, were approaching the city.

The night was spent in setting up watches and increasing
the number of guards.[97] Indeed, more than to repel an eventual attack coming from outside, they prepared themselves for
an internal battle. Parlement had recalled Coriolis under pressure from certain artisans, and because it had been shocked by
the action of the first consul. But it abstained from taking a
similar measure with regard to Chateauneuf and others, whom
it considered to be dangerous agitators. The *cascaveoux* wanted
not only to reinstate the latter in Aix, but to expel Bras and his
followers.

Parlement was no more on the side of the "blue ribbon,"
than on the side of the *cascaveoux*. It appeared to be a sort of
arbiter, on this morning of December 7. Between the two parties, and claiming to obey Parlement alone, was a captain of the
quarter who was named Fabre. He refused to execute an order
that the Baron de Bras had given him. The quarrel degen-
erated into a brawl, and two men fell dead on the Place des
Prêcheurs. Fabre, soon followed by the bourgeois guard, assaulted the Baron de Bras's guard. He won the day. In the
middle of a discharge of muskets and pistols, the first consul,
two of his valets, and a certain cloth merchant, Perrin, managed to get clear and to find refuge in the belfry of the church.
. . . Their adversaries did not dare climb the staircase. Then
Parlement intervened. Certain gentlemen recalled that the first
consul "was the son of a first president and former head of the
company." [98] Five courageous magistrates, "in robes, hoods,
and caps," went to the church with two bailiffs.[99] The crowd
"everywhere made way for them." Acting as mediators, they
led Bras and his companions away, under pretext of interrogat-
ing them, and then, at the end of the afternoon, had them dis-
cretely leave the city. By another gate, Chateauneuf and
his followers returned and were wildly acclaimed—"almost
unbelievably, the walls and streets were overflowing." They received command posts in the bourgeois guard, for it, like Parlement, appeared to be in agreement with the *cascaveoux*. Una-

nimity appeared to return. Calm also. They reopened the shops. "Many people put aside their weapons and withdrew to their houses, except for those who were in the guard." However, the family of the Baron de Bras, an attorney general, and some others were expelled or left themselves. But, of these exciting days, the citizens of Aix retained only an impression of lassitude and confusion. "The people were unsettled and did not know which way to turn." On the whole, "the gentlemen" thought only of making "an inquiry about the dead and wounded."

3
The Conclusion

Only Coriolis, Chateauneuf, and their friends continued to agitate. They had members of the Parlement sign an agreement and brought out a polemical satire, the "Laophile"—the friend of the people. It was a violent discourse to the people of Aix, designed to rekindle their declining ardor. "Generous citizens . . . Citizens without fear . . ." Coriolis was characterized as "the father of the people." The Laophile raised the bogy of the *élus* and warned about treason inside the city. "The party of the *élus* are more powerful than you think." From there, the necessity for a "list of suspects." It protested the loyalty of the *cascaveoux* and, on the other hand, pictured the "blue ribbons" as seditious enemies of the king—an indication that the accusation brought against the first had found some hearing. It announced false news and news already old: the solidarity of Marseilles and Arles with Aix, the revolt of the Parlements of Toulouse and Grenoble, the support of the queen mother. It invoked God and the Blessed Marys.[100] Parlement suppressed this pamphlet "on penalty of whipping and for the printers a penalty of life." [101] Its violence was revealing of the distress of the party that inspired it. For several days, Aix had lived in fear. The least band of children and peasants, seen passing in the distance, was a cause for alarm. On December 12, news of the court came from the Duke of Guise. They could not count on the queen mother, nor on anyone. The Prince of Condé, accompanied by five thousand men and with five hundred horses, approached; two intendants, Aubray and La Potherie, were with him.[102] Aix, so feverish a few days previously, seemed frozen with fright. The end approached.

From November, the citizens of Aix knew that they would not succeed in drawing all of Provence into the rebellion. They had indeed dispatched messengers to different communities to exhort them to remain in the union signed on October 25, and to raise troops and equip them.[103] The results were very meager. Only one city, Apt, seems to have stood by Aix and to have procured arms.[104] In truth, the communities could have made these purchases only with difficulty. There were no dis- banded troops to run about the province and to sell their equipment, as had been hoped.[105] To buy at Genoa was long and costly.[106] Above all, the essentially partisan character that had overtaken the agitation at Aix was bound to make the nota- bles of each city reflect. Moreover, a wave of fear seemed to emanate from the capital. Nine days after the expedition of La Barben, they believed at Toulon that, "four hundred men had come to cut the olive trees in the vicinity," in order to punish the inhabitants, "because they were not rebels." [107]

And Toulon prepared its defenses. For their part, Arles and Marseilles refused to listen to the emissaries of the Parle- ment.[108] Without doubt, they feared seeing sedition spread among their urban and rural commoners. Besides, these two cities, like others less important, were not exactly part of Pro- vence, but of the adjacent territories. Because of this, they were taxed separately, and they did not seem to fear the establish- ment of the *élus*. They tried to preserve their privilege and to carry as little as possible of the burdens that were going to fall on the province. Thus Aix found itself the only insurgent city. And it knew itself to be strategically indefensible, above all before the army, very large for the times, that was marching toward it under the command of Condé.

The council had acted without haste. As long as Marseilles remained faithful, the insurrection did not constitute too serious a danger. It clearly saw where the responsibilities lay. It exiled the Parlement to Brignoles.[109] In January 1631, it pro- hibited the meeting of an assembly of the nobility.[110] The order

118

arrived too late, and it was held at the Abbey Saint-Victoire, but was harmless. Less than sixty persons attended. It seems that disorder reigned. It voted to send a delegation to Condé to protest its loyalty and to ask for the suppression of the edict of the *élus*.[111]

During this time, at Aix, fear grew more marked. The notables, returned after the plague, went back to their country houses. "The fear of the poor people," noted Peiresc, "is so great that the city of Aix is deprived of its most notable citizens, or nearly so." [112] Those who could not leave were indignant and posted threats on the squares and the church doors. They would destroy the residences of those who were absent, and there would be new uprisings. In fact, those threats could not be carried out—the army of Condé approached. In February, the Parlement and the consuls sent delegations. The prince had just arrived in Avignon, accompanied by the first president, Oppède, intendants, and the principal exiles from Aix. On February 13, President de Monier delivered a remonstrance. It was a protest of loyalty. Never, as an intendant had dared to suggest, had they in the city government used the sword, nor, above all, burned the portrait of the king. He went further: never had the officers "authorized the movements that arose in the city." [113] Condé's response was benevolent. "They were not after blood, but money," said a contemporary.[114] Nonetheless, the prince put into execution letters patent that ordered the transfer of Parlement to Brignoles. Just as he exiled the Cour des Comptes to Saint-Maximin, the *trésoriers généraux* to Pertuis, and the seneschal's court to Lambesc. Then he summoned the Estates of Provence to Tarascon on March 8 and negotiated with them.

In one week, the fiscal problem was settled. Condé had received sufficiently flexible instructions.[115] In exchange for a sum of one and a half million livres, payable in four years, the king renounced the edict on the *élus*—as he had done in Burgundy—and the diverse "increases" and extraordinary taxes.[116] From a certain point of view, the insurrection had not been useless. The customs and privileges of the province were safe, and the "notables" were satisfied. The citizens of Aix could think they had escaped from particularly oppressive fiscal agents. The king would receive no less than the amount that the sale of the offices of the *élus* would have provided him. As for the adjacent territories, they retained their privilege of being taxed separately.

On March 18, the troops of Condé occupied Aix. The next day, the prince made his entry, accompanied by the intendants. A few magistrates were prosecuted and, although not immediately, others were suspended; but, on the whole, he was rather benevolent in regard to the Parlement. Besides, that institution had other reasons to be reassured: "They say that the king has put the Paulette back to the eighth *denier* [12.5 percent] for those who have not paid. And that those who have paid the fourth *denier* [25 percent] will have the surplus applied to the first resignation," wrote Valavez to Peiresc.[117] An accommodation in this domain also seemed possible. Moreover, in April the Parlement was authorized to return to Aix. Whereas in regard to the city, the prince and the intendants were rather severe. Compensation for the victims of the troubles was charged to it, and it lost, at least temporarily, the right to elect its consuls. Above all, troops remained there several months, ravaging the surrounding areas. Thus they chastized the communities that had participated in the expedition of La Barben, but also many others—the majority—that had not participated. This punishment was all the more difficult, because economic problems persisted.[118]

Beyond this, the intendants wanted a few examples. "We know how to proceed on such occasions, after the execution the trial takes place," Aubray wrote in October 1630.[119] There was a condemnation to the galleys, and only one condemnation to death—that of a conjurer, a poor fellow named Rostan. During his interrogation, the unfortunate had accused Coriolis, La Roque, and others, in turn for a promise to save his life and even of liberty. He became mad with fury, when they came to take him to his execution. It was necessary to kill him in his prison.[120] La Potherie sought other victims, but did not find any.[121]

This repression took place not far from Marseilles, the residence of the governor. He could hardly express his ill humor. This prince of Lorraine had, in his own jurisdiction, to face a Bourbon prince. He distrusted Condé and feared being arrested. He would only go to convey his respects at Tarascon accompanied by an imposing guard.[122] He felt under suspicion and threatened. Above all, he was conscious of belonging in the kingdom's affairs, to a party. In the spring of 1631, he joined in the intrigues that were led by Marie de Medicis and Gaston d'Orléans. After their failure, he left for Italy and did not return. The question of the admiralty of Provence was *ipso facto* resolved to the advantage of the cardinal [Richelieu].[123] The fact that the principal parlementary leaders belonged to one of the kingdom's factions was a most important feature of the insurrection of 1630. In December, the Laophile tried to make the citizens of Aix aware of the real connection between the *cascaveoux* and the party of the queen mother—"this Marie who works only to secure for us the repose that is so much desired." Coriolis and his friends, remaining at Aix until the arrival of Condé, fled next to Baux, a fortress the governor of which "was strongly attached to the party of the Duke of Orléans." [124] And it was after having participated in the revolt of Montmorency, that Coriolis was captured and thrown into prison. The other members of Parlement, even those who had nothing to do with the *cascaveoux*, kept informed as much as possible about what happened at the court and in other parlements. The messages, ciphered or not, from Valavez to Peiresc, concerned Monsieur [the king's brother], the queen mother, and the cardinal. "Now that they assure great changes at court and, above all, in the person of the superintendant (d'Effiat) . . ." wrote Peiresc on November 18, 1630.[125] But the Day of the Dupes—badly understood moreover—had counted for nothing in the reversal of Parlement's attitude in face of the *cascaveoux* movement. It had clearly taken place before.

The sedition was favored by the sequence of epidemic and a state of nervous tension. But no one, neither Abel Servien [a royal secretary], nor Aubray, nor the traveler, Jacques Bouchard, expressed any doubt as to its real origins—the action of certain magistrates.[126] No insurrectionary movement was, at the beginning, less spontaneous. Among the artisans of the Cordeliers quarter, or the workers in the surrounding fields, there was no sense of belonging to one of the kingdom's parties. But there was a latent feeling, that it was easy to arouse—the hatred toward a new fiscal agent. Then there was indignation against Superintendant d'Effiat, against his executive agents, and finally against the king. He came to Provence in 1622, and he had solemnly confirmed the privileges of the region. He could not, they wrote—and probably proclaimed—"violate the conventions under which this province has been reunited to the crown of France." Well, by the edict on the *élus* did he not attempt this? He perjured himself, and was not "atheism less of crime than perjury"? [127]

Very quickly the insurrection against the king and his council—instigators of innovations and unifiers of the kingdom—was compromised by personal battles among the leaders of the rebels. Groups, based on family and clientage and ambitious to control the Parlement and the city for their own profit, clashed. One and the other attracted artisans and peasants and formed parties that fought each other. We might have studied more closely the social connections—the links of clientage between certain groups of artisans and peasants and the leaders of the revolt. In any case, probably some popular elements escaped from the control of those who were using them and created the fear of a social revolt. "Vagabonds," "vagrants," they were the ones who earned their living day by day, doing occasional work, without any permanent security—street porters, agricultural workers, etc.—[who stood] in contrast to those who were part of a statutory group and who, if they did not themselves have a shop, belonged in some permanent way to a workshop, a household, and had a master.[128] A sort of proletariat emerged and created fear. This is probable; it is not certain. For did the workers, who, on November 4, demolished the houses and refused to obey the magistrates, act for themselves and for their own interests, or on the orders of their party chiefs—nobles and notables? And did those who denounced the risks of an uprising by the poorest people truly believe it, or did they see this as a means of separating a

number of artisans and householders from Coriolis and Chateauneuf? Whatever the answer, it was one of the reasons for
the set back of the *cascaveoux,* who set in motion certain prole-
tarian elements, and for a lessening of the influence of Coriolis
and Chateauneuf. But the divisions among the rival leaders
and the weariness that they engendered were one of the principal causes for the failure of the revolt. Yet let us not forget
what was probably the essential condition: the highly local nature of a movement, interested only in the privileges of province and city, and therefore the weakness of this movement,
easily conquered once the king was able to provide a few
troops.

NOTES

1. This work was inspired by the article of Roland Mousnier, "Recherches sur les soulèvements populaires en France avant la Fronde," *Revue d'histoire moderne et contemporaine,* V (1958), 81–113.

2. Gabriel Hanotaux and the Duc de la Force, *Histoire du Cardinal Richelieu* (Paris, 1893–1947), IV, 182.

3. Boris Porchnev, *Die Volkaufstände in Frankreich vor der Fronde, 1623–1648* (Leipzig, 1954), 110. But the Séguier papers at Leningrad can only be truly useful for the period after 1633. Moreover, Porchnev does not seem to have been acquainted with two *Histoires de la ville d'Aix* that were written in the seventeenth century. One is that of J. S. Pitton—in manuscript (1666); and the other, P. J. de Haitze, *Histoire de la ville d'Aix* (Aix, 1880–1889), 5 vols. Finally, we do not understand why, Porchnev dates this rebellion in 1631.

For the point of view that the rebellion was in defense of the liberties and fiscal privileges of the notables, see René Baehrel, *Une croissance: La Basse-Provence rurale depuis la fin du XVIe siècle jusqu'à la veille de la Révolution* (Paris, 1961).

4. Nicolas Fabri de Peiresc, *Lettres,* Tamizey de Laroque ed., (Paris, 1888–1898), 7 vols., I, 699.

5. *Archives départementales des Bouches-du-Rhone,* C 986; B 3348, fol. 29. [Henceforth cited as A.D. B.-du-R.]

6. Peiresc, *Lettres,* II, 25–27, 50, 59, 81–87; VI, 629–631. A.D. B.-du-R., B 3348, fol. 240. *Bibliothèque Inguimbertine* (Carpentras), Ms. 1841, fol. 352.

7. A.D. B.-du-R., *Abregé des délibérations de l'assemblée des communautés,* February 13, 1630.

8. A.D. B.-du-R., B 3348, fol. 384. Also see Georges d'Avenel, *Lettres, instructions diplomatiques et papiers d'état du Cardinal de Richelieu* (Paris, 1853–1877), 8 vols., III, 809–810, 859.

9. Peiresc, *Lettres,* II, 46–47.

10. *Bibliothèque Méjanes* (Aix), Ms. 972, *Déliberations du Parlement,* V, fol. 195.

11. A.D. B.-du-R., B 3348, fol. 244. Lancon F. Guichard, *Souvenirs historiques sur Digne* (Digne, 1847), 104.

12. Baehrel, *Basse-Provence,* 533, 547, 558.

13. *Ibid.,* 30–31.

14. *Bibliothèque Méjanes,* Ms. 972, fols. 227, 236. Peiresc, *Lettres,* I, 717.

15. *Bibliothèque Méjanes,* Ms. 972, fol. 238.

16. Peiresc, *Lettres,* I, 717.

17. *Ibid.,* 742.

18. Such as the canon, de Mimata, future member of the Company of the Holy Sacrament.

19. Peiresc, *Lettres,* II, 145.

20. *Archives départementales des Basses-Alpes,* Sub-series IE: the numerous seigneuries held by Coriolis, the Arnaud, Leydet, Joannis, Cheilan, etc., all of whom chose to serve at Pertuis, and not at Salon, in order to have their properties in their jurisdiction.

21. *Bibliothèque Méjanes,* Ms. 936, 471.

22. *Ibid.,* Ms. 794, 216.

23. Roland Mousnier, *La vénalité des offices sous Henri IV et Louis XIII* (Rouen, 1946), 605.

24. Peiresc, *Lettres,* II, 253.

25. Mousnier, *La vénalité,* 605.

26. Honoré Bouche, *Chorographie de la Provence,* (Aix, 1674), 2 vols., II, 873–874.

27. "Mémoires du président de Gaufridi," in *Mémoires pour servir à l'histoire de la Fronde en Provence* (Aix, 1870), 220.

28. *Lettres,* I, 759.

29. Porchnev, *Volkaufstände,* 103.

30. Baehrel, *Basse-Provence,* II, 756–774.

31. Peiresc, *Lettres,* II, 142–149.

32. *Bibliothèque Inguimbertine,* Ms. 1841, fol. 420.

33. Haitze, *Histoire d'Aix,* V, 73–74. Also see the justification of Sieur de Périer, councillor in the Parlement of Provence (*Bibliothèque Méjanes,* Ms. 955).

34. Mousnier, *La vénalité,* 606–607.

35. *Bibliothèque Méjanes,* Ms. 736, 730–736. A.D. B.-du-R., C 108, fol. 36.

36. *Bibliothèque Inguimbertine,* Ms. 1841, fol. 464.

37. *Ibid.,* fol. 459v.

38. Bouche, *Chorographie,* II, 881.

39. Speech of Du Loubet (*Bibliothèque Inguimbertine,* Ms. 1841, fol. 446.)

40. They do not seem to have imagined at Aix the possibility of the *élus* assessing the taxes consented to by the Estates.

41. Jacqueline Carrière, *La population d'Aix-en-Provence à la fin du XVIIIe siècle* (Aix, 1958), estimates, on the basis of the head tax registers of 1695, the population of Aix, including the surrounding country, at thirty thousand. From 1630 to 1695, the city had grown.

42. "Mémoires de Regusse," in *Mémoires pour servir à l'histoire de la Fronde en Provence,* 4.

43. A.D. B.-du-R., B 3343, fol. 190.

44. Justification of Perier (*Bibliothèque Méjanes,* Ms. 955).

45. J. J. Bouchard, *Les confessions de Jean Jacques Bouchard, Parisien, suivies de son voyage de Paris à Rome en 1630* (Paris, 1881), 113.

46. *Bibliothèque Méjanes,* Ms. 971, fol. 15.

47. Peiresc, *Lettres,* II, 145.

48. *Bibliothèque Méjanes,* Ms. 972, fols. 11 and 157v.

49. Haitze, *Histoire d'Aix,* IV, 180.

50. *Ibid.,* 178.

51. *Bibliothèque Nationale,* Dupuy 154, fols. 111–115. On this uprising, see also the following: *Bibliothèque Méjanes,* Ms. 946; Pierre Louvet, *Histoire du Parlement de Provence,* 364–367; Bouche, *Chorographie,* II, 882; Gaufridi, *Mémoires,* 106–107, 212–213; and Haitze, *Histoire d'Aix,* IV, 177–178.

52. Haitze, *Histoire d'Aix,* 182–184.

53. *Bibliothèque Méjanes,* Ms. 794, 280.

54. *Ibid.,* 243–249.

55. Cited by Hanotaux, *Cardinal Richelieu,* IV, 191.

56. Haitze, *Histoire d'Aix,* IV, 184–185.

57. *Bibliothèque Méjanes,* Ms. 946, 367.

58. To take two examples, the residence of Councillor de Paule (Haitze, *Histoire d'Aix,* IV, 185), and the residence of Peiresc (see his letter to his printer of October 28, 1630, published in the *Annuaire-Bulletin de la Société de l'Histoire de France,* XXVI (1890), 121–126).

59. Haitze, *Histoire d'Aix,* IV, 176; *Bibliothèque Méjanes,* Ms. 736, 730–736; *Bibliothèque Inguimbertine,* Ms. 1841, fol. 456.

60. *Bibliothèque Inguimbertine,* Ms. 1841, fol. 382. A certain number of nobles evaded payment. Far from all of them went to Pertuis.

61. A.D. B.-du-R., C 16, fol. 91.

62. A.D. B.-du-R., *Déliberations de l'assemblée génerale des Communautés du pays de Provence, tenue en la ville d'Aix, au mois d'octobre mil six cens trente* (Aix, 1630). This was the first time that these deliberations were printed. Two copies were to be circulated in the province to incite the communities to execute the decisions of the assembly.

63. Haitze, *Histoire d'Aix,* IV, 183.

64. Bouche, *Chorographie,* II, 881–882.

65. Haitze, *Histoire d'Aix,* 183.

66. *Bibliothèque Méjanes,* Ms. 955, 2 (Périer).

67. Pieresc, *Lettres,* II, 262.

68. *Bibliothèque Méjanes,* Ms. 794, 225–226. This prayer—*Alia oratio*—constituted in reality . . . a curse upon the rich. It invoked the parable of Lazarus and the rich man. It alluded to the number of beggars and poor in the city.

69. On November 1, the canons of the cathedral were menaced by a crowd, following an incident between them and the consuls.

70. From 20 to 25 kilometers.

71. None was more than 18 kilometers from the chateau. Pelissanne, the nearest, was 5 kilometers away.

72. Haitze, *Histoire d'Aix,* IV, 189.

73. That is 35 kilometers.

74. *Archives communales d'Aix,* AA 2, fol. 79 (right accorded in 1202); AA 13, Cartulary called the "Liber Corneti." Almost exclusively devoted to the numerous conflicts on this matter.

75. Haitze, *Histoire d'Aix,* IV, 189.

76. *Bibliothèque Méjanes,* Ms. 946, 369.

77. Peiresc, *Lettres,* II, 145.

78. *Bibliothèque Méjanes,* Ms. 955, 4 (Périer).

79. Gaufridi, *Mémoires*, 109. *Archives communales d'Aix*, BB 100, fol. 153v.

80. Haitze, *Histoire d'Aix*, IV, 189.

81. *Ibid.*, 190. *Archives communales d'Aix*, BB 100, fol. 153v.

82. Gaufridi, *Mémoires*, 109.

83. Peiresc, *Lettres*, II, 261–262.

84. *Bibliothèque Méjanes*, Ms. 946, 370.

85. Gaufridi, *Mémoires*, 110.

86. *Bibliothèque Méjanes*, Ms. 955, 3–4 (Périer).

87. *Bibliothèque Inguimbertine*, Ms. 1841, fols. 348–350. *Bibliothèque Méjanes*, Ms. 794, fols. 159–162. We have published this text in the *Revue de la Méditeranée*, No. 101 (1961).

88. *Bibliothèque Méjanes*, Ms. 955, 4 (Périer).

89. J. J. Bouchard, *Confessions*, 114–118.

90. *Bibliothèque Méjanes*, Ms. 955, 4 (Périer).

91. *Bibliothèque Méjanes*, Ms. 946, 370.

92. Moreover, this preoccupation was common among the notables of Aix. Peiresc expressed satisfaction that the *Parlement* had, "driven out all these vagabonds and people who had no known business there, who flocked there from all over the province, as to the sacking of a city, and who were going to pillage it little by little, if God had not intervened" (*Lettres*, II, 262). Pierre Louvet noted that if, "The gentlemen of *Parlement* had left the city, it would have been lost and completely sacked" (*Bibliothèque Méjanes*, Ms. 946, 370).

93. They asked J. J. Bouchard, "at the gate, if he had met the troops of Monsieur, brother of the king, who, they said, was coming to besiege the city, against whom they were resolved to close the gates, and against the king too, if he came to install the *élus*. And passing through the streets, he was stopped by a large number of poor people (who held the bridle), who asked him if the king continued to desire the *élus*, and who swore, while tearing their hair and stomping on their hats, that they would rather let their throats be cut, than receive them" (*Confessions*, 116). Note that this scene took place on November 10, a day when there were rumblings of revolt, although none broke out.

94. *Bibliothèque Méjanes*, Ms. 955, 5 (Périer).

95. Haitze, *Histoire d'Aix*, IV, 194.

96. Accounts of these days are to be found in the following: Bouche, *Chorographie*, II, 884; Pitton, *Histoire d'Aix*, 387; Haitze, *Histoire d'Aix*, IV, 194; and Pierre Louvet, *Bibliothèque Méjanes*, Ms. 946, 371. The most interesting is that of an anonymous author, *Bibliothèque Inguimbertine*, Ms. 1841, fols. 385–391.

97. Bouche, *Chorographie*, II, 884.

98. *Bibliothèque Inguimbertine*, Ms. 1841, fol. 389. *Bibliothèque Méjanes*, Ms. 946, fol. 373.

99. "After several of these gentlemen refused to join the delegation, in order to avoid the danger. . . ." (*Bibliothèque Méjanes*, Ms. 955, 5 [Périer]).

100. "La Remontrance de Laophile à Messieurs d'Aix," *Bibliothèque Méjanes*, Ms. 794, 163–170.

101. *Bibliothèque Méjanes,* Ms. 955, 6 (Périer).

102. *Bibliothèque Inguimbertine,* Ms. 1841, fol. 391.

103. The councillor, Flotte, to Arles, and Gaufridi, although he denied it, to the region of Sisteron (*Mémoires,* 215–216).

104. *Musée Arbaud,* Ms. M O 136, 113, "Extraits de l'histoire de la ville d'Apt par Remerville de Saint-Quentin."

105. A.D. B.-du-R., *Déliberations de l'assemblée,* 11.

106. The representative of the king at Genoa, however, was not able to overcome certain arms trade between Genoa and Fréjus (*Bibliothèque Nationale,* Ms. fr. 4133, fol. 192).

107. Bouchard, *Confessions,* 125–126.

108. *Bibliothèque Méjanes,* Ms. 909, 73; Ms. 794, 234–235. Note that the history of Arles, the most aristocratic of cities in Provence, and of Marseilles, was, at least until 1660, marked by often violent partisan struggles.

109. *Bibliothèque Méjanes,* Ms. 909, 77; A.D. B.-du-R., B 3348, fol. 493.

110. *Bibliothèque Méjanes,* Ms. 909, 76.

111. *Bibliothèque Inguimbertine,* Ms. 1941, fol. 484.

112. *Lettres,* II, 268.

113. *Remontrance faite à Mgr. le Prince dans la ville d'Avignon, par les Deputez de la Cour de Parlement de Provence* (Aix, 1631).

114. Pitton, *Histoire d'Aix,* 388.

115. *Bibliothèque Méjanes,* Ms. 794, 240–243.

116. A.D. B.-du-R., B 3349, fol. 590. These 1,500,000 livres were probably destined to reimburse a tax farmer for sums he had advanced.

117. *Bibliothèque Inguimbertine,* Ms. 1841, fol. 484.

118. A.D. B.-du-R., B 3348, fol. 506. Moreover, the plague reappeared in May at Salon, and it raged there in July.

119. *Bibliothèque Inguimbertine,* Ms. 1841, fol. 436.

120. *Ibid.,* fol. 470; *Bibliothèque Méjanes,* Ms. 953, no. 38.

121. *Bibliothèque Inguimbertine,* Ms. 1841, fol. 479 (a coded message from Valavez to Peiresc).

122. Composed of 200 gentlemen (*Bibliothèque Méjanes,* Ms. 909, 78).

123. The authoritarian Maréchal de Vitry—the man who had killed Concini—succeeded him as governor (A.D. B.-du-R., C 986; B 3348, fol. 593).

124. Bouche, *Chorographie,* II, 888.

125. *Lettres,* II, 263.

126. Servien: "The evil has been contained almost entirely in that [city] of Aix and in a few surrounding villages, which shows rather clearly who the authors of these disorders are" (*Bibliothèque Méjanes,* Ms. 909, 77). Aubray: "The farm worker, the wine grower, the artisan does not incite these revolts. They are led to it by their superiors" (*Bibliothèque Inguimbertine,* Ms. 1841, fol. 435). Bouchard: ". . . the nobility, having a great interest in it, and the Estates being controlled by their order—which, consequently brought them great gain and power—, had made the *élus* so detested and so horrible to the populace. . . ." (*Confessions,* 114).

RESISTANCE TO ABSOLUTISM

127. *Bibliothèque Méjanes,* Ms. 953, no. 39, 681–696: "La verité provençale au Roi," by L.S.D.N.G.P. (The Sieur de Nibles, a gentleman of Provence). Should one interpret Richelieu's letter, cited by Hanotaux and Porchnev, which speaks of rebels "on the point of beating priests who prayed to God for him [the king?]," as evidence of the antimonarchical character of the uprising (D'Avenel, *Lettres du Cardinal de Richelieu,* IX, 171)? On November 1, 1630, the crowd violently took the side of the consuls, following one among dozens of confrontations between consuls and canons concerning which gate to take to enter the cathedral. The crowd threatened not to pay the ecclesiastical tithe and even to empty the canons' cellar. The prayers said for the king on this occasion do not appear to have had anything to do with this incident. Besides, it is possible that the "Oratio," cited above (*Bibliothèque Méjanes,* Ms. 704, 225–226), as well as the "Dialogue of the Two Cats," were, partially at least, written by ecclesiastics. Moreover, we do not see, as Porchnev contends, that the clergy supported the "blue ribbon."

128. Porchnev, *Volkaufstände,* 253.

Research on the Popular Movements at Amiens in 1635 and 1636

BY J. GALLET

At the beginning of the seventeenth century, the city of Amiens was the scene of several popular movements. These movements assumed different forms—mobs composed largely of women; pillaging of wheat shipments, of shops and of bourgeois at the time of famine; a strike by artisans and an attack upon officials come to impose a tax on their craft; a riot against the soldiers from the fortress.

Official and private sources tell us very little about these movements. In the accounts of judges and chroniclers, the revolts received little attention, and preference was given to "noble subjects"—receptions, monuments, and the histories of great families. Moreover, when a revolt was mentioned, it was invariably presented in the same fashion. It was never an act of hostility against the king, but it was always touched off by misery, by the act of a petty official, a tax agent, a governor, a garrison (and these were always carefully distinguished from royal power), or by a concern to maintain privileges. It was always the act of "the populace," "commoners," "lowly working people," "unemployed drifters," and "the ignorant." The judges, bourgeois, and ecclesiastics who evoked these facts all agreed that they had nothing to do with any attack on the king, that the city fathers were innocent and sought to prevent wrongdoing, and that the responsibility for the incidents lay with the common people. Only a few satires make us suspect that there was a reality different from the official story.

These movements have been little studied and have always

been considered very simple phenomena that encompassed different events under a single theme or explanation and that included participants and victims who belonged to well-defined social groups. The case is particularly clear for a series of popular disturbances from July 1635 to November 1636, which were incited by a tax on textiles and were called the "wool carder riots."

For G. Lecocq, it was a conflict that opposed the bourgeoisie and the artisans to the nobility and the king: "The victory rests with the bourgoisie and the artisans over the humbled nobility and over the monarchy forced to renounce an unfair and vexatious tax." H. de Montbas saw in this revolt an episode of the Thirty Years War in which the people opposed Richelieu's European policy. B. Porchnev considered it an uprising of the wool carders against the owners.[1]

The study of the documents that concern this revolt and the years that surrounded it does not confirm these interpretations. The revolt was not a simple thing, unless one isolates it from the totality of circumstances within which it took place.

1

The City of Amiens
at the Beginning of the Seventeenth Century

Set on the left bank of the Somme, Amiens in the seventeenth century included a high city—centered on the market, the belfry, city hall, and the cathedral—and, to the north, the low city—the Saint-Leu and Minimes quarters whose winding and narrow streets intermingled with the numerous branches of the river.[2]

The population varied: in normal times between thirty-five and forty thousand, it could fall to twenty-five thousand during epidemics.

Despite the sack by the Spaniards in 1597, Amiens was a rich and active city. A frontier city—middle distant between the Parisian basin and Flanders—it constituted a great market for the most diverse goods—wheat, wine, butter, cheese, herring, iron, wool, and, above all, textiles. It was a market that had relations with the countries to the north—Danzig for wheat and

Flanders for textiles—with Paris, Limoges, Chartres, Lyon, Toulouse, where the city's merchants sold their products.

The basis of this richness and of this activity was not banking, but the textile industry, and especially the manufacture of serge cloth—a mixture of different materials that included wool, flax, silk, and goat's hair—which had been in fashion since the fifteenth century. Amiens was "certainly the major textile manufacturing city in the kingdom." The bulk of its production was exported. Thus the fortune of Amiens—the livelihood of a good third of the population and mercantile profits—depended on the serge cloth industry.

This wealth was certainly menaced in 1635, after several years of the plague, and at the beginning of a war that interrupted all commerce and threatened an imminent invasion along a frontier stripped of troops. Nevertheless, it continued to leave its mark on the city, and its influence was clearly apparent on the social structures.

In daily life, one seldom encounters the traditional hierarchical divisions according to "estates." Certain documents—accounts of receptions, inventories, charters—sometimes picture society organized by "churchmen, nobles, bourgeois, and simple commoners," [3] but these documents are exceptional. The great majority of documents—chronicles, satires, archival sources—leave the impression of another form of organization and of another hierarchy.

The clergy constituted an important group. Numerous and rich—religious houses and churches comprised nearly half of the buildings in the city— [4] it intervened in and played a role in the life of the city—a role always accentuated in times of distress. However, it was distinguished from other groups by its function and thus occupied a place apart. Moreover [the clergy] did not form a homogeneous and unified block. Its recruitment varied; regular and secular clergy opposed one another; the bishop and canons were distinguished from the parish clergy by their wealth and outlook; certain monks, particularly the Augustinians, were very turbulent and readily brutal; the Catholic Reformation and theological controversies brought divisions; the bishop did not enjoy uncontested authority. Thus members of the clergy, depending on the circumstances, might join up with other social groups.

Unlike the clergy, the nobility seldom appeared in everyday life, and little was said about them. Certainly, they still remained numerous. Adrien de la Morlière dwelled at length on "the great houses" and composed a "Heraldic Treasury" in 1627.[5] Petitions to obtain nobility were frequent. But overall, chronicles and archival sources devoted little place to them, and they do not appear to have been active in the life of the city. Only the great names crop up—de Chaulnes, de Créqui, de Soyecourt, de Caumartin—and the others seem to have been absorbed into the category of bourgeois. The links between nobles and bourgeois were many [and included] marriages and the purchase of fiefs—"most fiefs in Picardy were held by residents of Amiens who were exempted from vassal military obligations."[6] The distinction between noble and bourgeois was less and less clear; and it was the bourgeois who occupied the preeminent place in the social hierarchy.

From a juridical point of view, the bourgeois was a resident who received this title after having taken an oath; but what characterized him above all was his wealth. In truth, the society of Amiens was divided into groups more or less rich, and not into estates. The archival documents and the chronicles constantly summon up a group of wealthy people who were clearly differentiated from the rest of the population—the "bourgeois," the "bourgeois and privileged," the "decent people of quality." Among them the most important were the merchants, and, above all, wholesale merchants and those who dealt in fabrics and serge. They directed all of the city's textile industry. They imported wool, sold it to master carders, bought the finished material from them, had it dyed, and assured the flow of production. It was, then, upon the merchants that all of the craft activity in the city depended. These merchants had connections everywhere and commanded huge fortunes, comparable to those of "the richest Spanish merchants of the time." They formed powerful dynasties, allied to the nobility—the de Sanchy, Mouret, Revillon, de Villiers, du Croquet, Pingré. They ran the city: they were the city councillors and the colonels and captains of the militia. Certain of them were royal officers, such as Guillaume Pingré [who was] "lord of Fournier, counsellor to the king, receiver general of the salt tax, keeper of the royal seal in the city and in the *baillage* and *siège présidial* of Amiens." [7] Between these royal officers and the town councillors there were frequent conflicts. And it was often from among these officers that the king selected the first councillor.

So, rich, ennobled, holding diverse administrative functions, the merchants occupied the principal place in the city. Such appears to have been the nature of that category of wealthy men into which the nobility was absorbed.

To this group the same texts oppose the poor. In face of the rich, they appeared to form a block; in fact, they too were divided into several "estates and qualities." [8] First, there were thirty-six craft guilds, of which the most important were the carders, the combers, and the weavers. In normal times, fourteen to fifteen hundred master carders each possessed five or six machines that were worked by five or six helpers—that was nearly fifteen to twenty thousand inhabitants, if one includes the women. But in 1636, there were only two hundred masters [who employed] twenty-five hundred to three thousand persons. In any case, this was the most numerous group of artisans. The salaries of artisans were miserable, and they were often forced into debt.[9]

Beyond this group of people who had a craft or a regular job and a home, swarmed the world of the destitute—"good-for-nothings, rogues, vagabonds," "without work or shelter," "of bad habits"—who were sometimes supported at the city's expense, but who were often driven out of the city. How many of them there were, it is difficult to say, but certainly they numbered several thousands. In any case, [their numbers] increased in 1635 owing to the influx of refugees from the countryside and the neighboring cities—an influx that had already in 1634 disturbed the governor of Amiens, the Duke of Chaulnes.

Were these different social groups antagonistic to one another?

One grouping was arranged according to quarters—the carders in the low city and to the northwest; the merchants in the city center and to the southeast where the most splendid mansions were. But this was neither a strict nor a general rule. Carders and merchants lived on the same street.

Except for the special case of the governor, the Duke of Chaulnes, there was no evident hostility between bourgeois and nobles. Nor, indeed, within the bourgeoisie. Of course, the wealthiest commanded the city guard, and they alone could become city councillors (retail merchants were excluded), but we have not encountered signs of hostility or any closing of groups.

On the other hand, the demarcation line between the bourgeois and the rest of the population was far more clear. The bourgeois scorned the artisans and the poor. However, this attitude came through almost exclusively at the time of riots.

Among the artisans, there were no particular signs of opposition between journeymen and masters. At this time, masterships were not closed, and two thirds of the new masters were former journeymen, and not the sons of masters.[10]

There does not seem to have been an atmosphere of habitual hostility among the social groups, and, generally, the social structure was not called into question—at least according to the texts that we have consulted. These texts derived from the same social group. They do not necessarily reveal what the reality was, but perhaps simply the idea of society that this group had and wished to convey. We should confront them with other documents that come from different social groups. It would be very interesting to know what artisans thought of the bourgeois, and what they thought of the unemployed below them.

If there were no characteristic social struggles, the population was, nonetheless, turbulent, and this characteristic can help us better to understand the popular movements. Customs were brutal. Take, for example, the game of *mahon* which consisted of hitting with fists. People assembled and attacked—street against street, quarter against quarter, and even respectable people plunged into the *melée*. Magistrates multiplied their prohibitions against playing *mahon,* but to no avail. Brawling was endemic. Faith was general, and spirits were easily aroused. Controversies (such as one over the *illuminati* of Roye in 1634), processions, the cult of relics, and witchcraft accusations violently agitated the whole population.

Instability was easily aggravated by material insecurity. The interception of wheat from Danzig by Abbeville, the depreciation of currency, a raid by soldiers, epidemics—all the scourges, as the communal archives bear witness, were common during this period when the events of 1635 and 1636 occurred.

2
The Preparation for the Revolt

The troubles that broke out in 1636, over a tax on finished fabrics, had older and more complex origins. From the beginning of the century, the citizens of Amiens had been fighting the central power and its representative in order to regain lost privileges. For several years the plague had ravaged the city and brought with it dissension and a very particular atmosphere. And since 1635 the Spanish menace to the unfortified city had weakened loyalty to the king.

The struggle to maintain privileges

"To obtain some choice privileges for the city," "to maintain and conserve privileges"—that had been the traditional program of the city government and the notables whose policy aimed at maintaining and strengthening municipal independence.

In 1597 Henry IV ended this dream. As a consequence of the "surprise" of Amiens by the Spaniards, he suppressed the greater part of the privileges. He reduced the number of councillors, suppressed the office of mayor, limited the judicial and military attributes of the city council, and built a citadel. Municipal independence no longer existed. Henceforth, the citizens of Amiens were inconsolable. De Court and Pagès exonerated the inhabitants who, decimated by the plague, were not responsible for the disaster.[11] Adrien de la Morlière spoke emphatically of the "city's great privileges," of "the splendor of the old mayors," and even in 1642 hoped for a return of this past.[12]

A satire of 1616 protested the establishment of the citadel. Since the city of Amiens now had at its disposal "twelve thousand men bearing arms," this citadel was useless; it was even harmful, because it was vulnerable to the north and could be turned against the city; it was filled with strangers, which the citizens of Amiens regarded as an affront; finally, it was only an instrument of oppression directed against the city, and even contrary to the interests of the king. The violence and riots of the early seventeenth century, which turned all of the city's inhabitants against the soldiers, suggested the deep hatred that the citizens of Amiens had for the citadel.

The situation grew worse with the arrival of the Duke of Chaulnes, an ostentatious and authoritarian great lord. The councillors were "continued" without any elections in 1628 or 1630; despite the council's protests, the duke imposed an outsider as first councillor.[13] Later, in regard to a quarrel between the inhabitants and the citadel, the governor upheld one of his lieutenants against the council; in May 1634, a quarrel began over military affairs, any control of which the duke wanted to remove from the councillors.[14]

Thus the regret for lost privileges, the wish for independence, the desire to secure the guard and to eliminate the soldiers, and hostility in regard to the Duke of Chaulnes combined with a feeling of insecurity in face of the Spanish menace and created a general discontent.

The plague

"Contagion" embittered spirits and contributed to dissensions. From 1632 it regularly devastated the city each year during the warm spell. It left the city only intermittently—rare moments "when one can attend to one's business" (the Duke of Chaulnes), and which the populace rejoiced over while maintaining measures to avoid the scourge that everyone knew to be ready to return. In truth the plague would come back in July 1635 and during the first days of April 1636. It touched all of the city's quarters, above all the poor quarters on the outskirts. Repeated over several years, it upset the life of the city: the population diminished; the bourgeois left the city for the country; the poor who stayed behind lived in a kind of permanent state of siege. It was necessary to make the disease known, to put marks on the houses, to wear recognizable clothes, to remove the sick to the city hospital, in the unhealthy quarters of the low city to carry out *airiements* (the cleansing of houses struck by the plague), and to bury the dead or even to throw them into the river (bodies floated right up to the doors of houses, many of which opened directly on the river). All sorts of constraints had to be accepted: quarantines were established, and public assembly, games, the frequenting of taverns and public places, and commerce with neighboring cities—even Calais, Saint-Quentin, and Flanders where wool came from—were prohibited. The constant presence of death, the sermons and processions—that of 1633 for example—and the stringent measures forced people to live in a doom-laden atmosphere calculated to depress nervous systems.

At the same time, murmurs of discontent appeared, as the plague divided the population and created germs of conflict. First off, the rigorous character of the measures that were taken turned the population against the authorities. It was the city councillors who took exceptional measures and made them respected—multiple decrees, inspections, sanctions, demands for money—and the Duke of Chaulnes intervened for the same ends. Contraventions were numerous: M. de Sachy himself refused to be evacuated. The hatefulness of the measures that it was necessary to take fell back on the authorities. These authorities were divided: the city council opposed the Duke of Chaulnes. The councillors proved to be less rigorous than the governor, who often reproached them for this. He was an advocate of extreme measures—"the most violent remedies are the best." Whereas the councillors were satisfied with removal to the city hospital, the duke recommended expulsion from the city and even a general expulsion to "air out all of the houses in the city." "You do not obey me," he said, "your administration is poor, all of the sick are not removed; use violence, knock down houses, set them on fire, and if you do not do it, I shall send for one or two regiments that shall. . . ." The violence of the conflict, the threats raised, and the measures recommended forced a hardening of positions among the population, among the doctors, and in the city government itself.[15]

The clergy was also concerned by the epidemic, and, in this connection, they collided with the town council and divided. In 1632 the parish priests resisted the councillors, who confided to them the sick in the city hospital, but who refused to pay them. These parish priests convoked the bishop and the chapter "to which they were bound to release them from any judgment that might be made against them for the percentage of profits, rights, and emoluments that they [the bishop and chapter] levied on the parish priests." On the other hand, priests neglected the parishes to which they were assigned. Father Jean Conchie intervened, summoned those responsible, and decided to administer the sacraments for the dead himself.[16]

All of these discontents crystallized in the *affaire des airiements*. Every house touched by the contagion had to be cleansed, and all sorts of objects were burned. *Airieurs* [those who did the cleansing] specialized in this work and were accused of enriching themselves from it.

On May 3, 1633, the Duke of Chaulnes recommended to the first councillor "an individual named De la Cointe, who was said to have a remedy." [17] The councillors accepted him; he alone would be charged with the cleansings, and that would cure both the contagion and the disorders caused by the *airieurs*.

Henceforth, the affair grew worse. Doctors intervened for or against the new cleansings. The Sieur de Ponthieu wrote a polemic against M. de la Cointe; the Sieur de Fresnes replied to him. Doctors in the city signed one or another manifesto. The quarrel was lively. Polemics were printed and distributed throughout 1635. Everyone felt concerned. The polemics claimed that "the new nostrum of *airiements* will destroy the entire city." The two factions accused one another—"certain people maintain and stir up the contagious evil"—and turned away "thousands of innocents whom the cleansings have killed." They had recourse to theological arguments: De Ponthieu imputed the plague to the will of God who wished to chastise the people. M. de la Cointe, who boasted of destroying the scourge, was guilty of seeking to surpass God; he was only a wizard "who used little animals that he carried in his pocket, by means of which he spread the plague." They contested signatures; they insulted one another; they prepared retorts; they appealed to the doctors of Paris and to the king's men; they came to the point of committing violence against M. de la Cointe.

The authorities entered the conflict. The Duke of Chaulnes hotly defended M. de la Cointe—"La Cointe will be under my protection"—and restored him to office when, in December 1634, the councillors dismissed him.[18] Here again appeared the opposition between the governor and the city council. But the councillors were divided. "The Sieur de Correur and others in your institution," wrote the Duke of Chaulnes, declared themselves hostile to M. de la Cointe, and the governor accused these adversaries of seeking to lose the city and of being "bad servants of the king." The inhabitants also took sides. Some resisted the new cleansings, mistreated the surgeon, and felt supported by the doctors and the councillors. The Duke of Chaulnes feared a rebellion (October 9, 1634) and began legal action against the guilty ones and, in particular, against Correur, whose case was several times brought before the council and who was obliged to appear before the king at the beginning of 1635.

By means of this affair, an opposition group was established that kept up the agitation. The *airieurs* formed the principal nucleus of it—"sixty to eighty, both men and women . . . low working types." As was frequently the case, they were probably carders. When there was an inquiry in 1638 concerning access to the mastership, some journeymen carders boasted of having been *airieurs* for three or four years.[19] There were other artisans among these "working people" and some without a craft, such as the monks, Augustinians—"who were called the fathers of death"—Franciscans, and Capucines.[20]

In normal times, these *airieurs* formed an unstable group, a center of agitation. They were characterized as "of bad habits." De Fresnes accused them of stealing, of enriching themselves with high wages, of carousing day and night. But there were undoubtedly two categories: "There will be no general register of *airieurs* . . . [they] will be chosen from among the most loyal and respectable people." [21] Accustomed to perilous missions—sometimes outside of Amiens [22]—intimates of danger, one can easily imagine them closely united and, without doubt, exuberant at times.

Regarding the affair of M. de la Cointe, they adopted a rebellious attitude. Beyond their attachment to the old ways of cleansing—and to what degree was superstition responsible for the energy behind these revolts?—they were driven by the desire to preserve this source of revenue "to continue the evil in order to earn their living." [23] According to the Sieur de Fresnes, "Night and day they assembled by a mutual agreement they had with one another, provoked grumbling against M. de la Cointe, passed him off as a wizard, opposed the new cleansings by force, and raised their chins to their political leaders."

These *airieurs* were not alone. Equally part of the opposition were some of the doctors: Ponthieu, de Moulin, Roussel, Pecquet, Sallen, Ducrocq, and Martin who signed the "declaration of censure against M. de la Cointe." There were also councillors, Correur in particular. This group of rebels, then, included elements belonging to very diverse social categories; all social classes were represented. And it was this entire group that revolted. The Sieur de Fresnes accused Ponthieu of demagoguery and of opposition to the councillors; the Duke of Chaulnes accused some councillors of being the authors of all of the unrest inspired by the de la Cointe affair.[24] This agitation over the cleansings would not end in 1635. It would continue in 1636, mixed up with the affair over the *sol pour livre* [a supplementary tax on sales].[25]

It is impossible to separate the revolts of 1635 and 1636 from the contagion that struck at morale and tested the nerves and turned one part of the population against the magistrates and governor.

The threat from the outside

While people feared the plague that might return, the peril from outside became more pressing. War against the Spaniards was declared on May 19, 1635, and Amiens was threatened. In April, an alarm kept the inhabitants under arms from ten o'clock to midnight. It was a false rumor, but the inhabitants believed it all the more easily, because their city was poorly defended—"the fortifications were falling into ruins, and there were neither artillery pieces nor munitions in the store-houses." [26] Not even the citadel was well-guarded; "they said that the garrison had been reduced to sixty men, and that it had been pulled from its place to be sent to the Duke of Chaul-nes." [27] This feeling of insecurity gave birth to a spirit of revolt that rested upon the traditional claims of the citizens of Amiens. "Since Henry IV recaptured this city from the Span-iards, those who have been its governors have always worked, not only to destroy the few privileges that this prince accorded it, but also to render it helpless, as if one depended only on the citadel." [28]

Loyalties wavered. "The most rebellious did not hide that it made no difference to them who their master was, because they could not be worse treated." "The rebels proclaimed that if their security was not attended to, they would be forced to search out someone who would treat them better and who would consider them more." [29] At court, they feared very much for the city of Amiens.

It was under these difficult circumstances, which created anxieties, that there arrived the news of the tax of the *sol pour livre* that touched off the disturbances and riots of 1635 and 1636.

3
Popular Movements from
July 1635 to November 1636

All of these movements have been subsumed under the revolt of April 1 and 2, 1636, and summarized under the title of the "carders' revolt over the tax of the *sol pour livre.*"

In fact, the agitation began before this. Altogether the re-volt had three distinct phases: from July 1635 to March 1636, opposition was, above all, the act of merchants and city coun-cillors; in March and April 1636, the carders' rebellion broke out; and, from April 1636 to October 1636, the merchants and the councillors again confronted the central power.

The revolt of the notables

It was on July 14, 1635, that a letter from Bullion [one of Richelieu's secretaries of state] informed the councillors of an edict that raised the tax on wool and linen cloth, and that asked them, "to see to it that the execution of the edict encountered no difficulty." [30]

This was a useful precaution, because the affair came at a bad time. Beyond the strained atmosphere of the time, the economic conjuncture was hardly favorable. There were difficulties with the currency. On August 14, 1635, an edict closed the Cour des Monnaies for six months "in order to relieve the people and to stop the disorders." [31]

Some people manipulated the changing currency rates. "During the eight or ten days since the edict concerning currency was published, the city's merchants have refused and still refuse to buy camlets [a kind of cloth] and wares of any kind, and this refusal causes total ruin and forces the workers to be sacrificed." [32]

On the other hand, the new tax was not the only one. There was already a tax on gunpowders of France against which the city council had protested in March.[33]

Currency depreciation, unemployment, misery, and again the plague at the end of July. The councillors wrote to obtain relief from the *sol pour livre* and "opposed the levying of the said charge." [34]

For all that, the usual conflicts were not extinguished. The Duke of Chaulnes was discontented that the plague had reoccurred; he blamed the councillors; and he protested that de Sachy had not been expelled. "You have preferred the satisfaction of one individual to the public good, which will oblige me to write about it to the king." [35]

In August 1635, a rebellion broke out. "Some individuals have contravened orders concerning the guard and have sought to arouse the people to action that could have impaired the king's service." "Doctor Martin was involved in this rebellion over the guard. The duke congratulates the councillors for their diligence in repressing the revolt." [36]

This good feeling did not last long. The conflict relating to the guard and fortifications resumed, when the Duke of Chaulnes tried to remove from the councillors what remained of their privileges in regard to military matters. On October 6, 1635, a councillor made a call on a guardpost by the Noyon gate; he noticed absences, but the Sieur de Bocourt, sergeant-major of the citadel, disputed his right to inspect. The councillors complained to the Duke of Chaulnes. The affair remained suspended. Because the city was not well-protected, the council sent protests to the governor—one in September 1635 to "point out to him the bad state of the fortifications and gates," and another, in November, suggesting that he "advance the hour for the closing of the gates, dredge the moats, employ youth in the guard, and force ecclesiastics and wealthy widows to contribute funds." But a deputation to the governor met a clear and haughty refusal—"this affair concerns only him, and the councillors should attend to their own business." This case was not settled at all; the city's security was not assured; spirits were aroused; and the authorities confronted one another on this very important question of privileges.

The affair of the *sol pour livre* would not be the only one that was involved, even though, at the beginning of 1636, it held all of the attention. Indeed, the councillors, who were for the most part, merchants, sent a deputation to Paris. It failed. Delegated to Paris, M. de Mons, Boullenger, and de Sachy intervened with Bullion and with Sublet de Noyers. They were, more or less politely, shown the door, and the Sieur Bryois, the contractor charged with levying the tax of the *sol pour livre,* thwarted their action and menaced the councillors. M. de Mons and Boullenger left. M. de Sachy remained at Paris and had the Sieur de Villiers—of a merchant family of Amiens—intervene to influence his brother-in-law, the Sieur Bordier, secretary to the council. All this was in vain. "It was necessary to drain the cup of bitterness."

The diplomatic maneuvers of the merchants had failed. De Sachy concluded his intervention by warning Bullion, de

Chaulnes, and de Noyers, "so that they will not blame us for what might come" (February 21, 1636).

Consequently, the Duke of Chaulnes entered the scene. Up to this time, he had not favored the tax. He supported the councillors at Paris; he spoke on their behalf; he regretted the hasty departure of de Mons and Boullenger—"their departure, or rather their flight, will prejudice your affairs and give the advantage to the contractor." But now he was responsible for levying the tax. He convoked the councillors to communicate the king's will to them and to call upon them to take all useful measures. Likewise, he convoked the most notable merchants to command them to buy, and he convoked the overseers of the serge workshops to see to it that the masters continued to have work done. These meetings took place in March, and the Duke of Chaulnes left Amiens for Corbie.

What would the attitude of the merchants be? Sieurs Thierry Nicolas de Fresnes, Gabriel de Sachy, Etienne Feuguel, Adrien Cornet, and others among the notables, to whom the governor had given his orders, showed their discontent. They cited the stock of merchandise which they had not sold because of the war and the disasters of the times.

Since the duke ordered them to continue to buy in order to provide for the needs of the poor and to see that the poor had no cause for disturbances, they promised to do what their resources would allow. When the Duke of Chaulnes insinuated to the overseers that the weight of the tax would fall not on them, but on the merchants, the latter protested vigorously. Finally, they did not accept the new tax. They attempted a last approach to Bryois and to the Duke of Chaulnes. The failure of these final parleys led them to a decisive act: they ceased their purchase of camlets from the master carders. This merchants' strike did not, in any case, begin in March 1636; we have seen that it went back to September of the preceding year. But in March, it became general.

As for the city councillors, they simply took refuge behind the Duke of Chaulnes whom they asked to take steps, and to whom they protested several times their loyalty to the king, "in order that they would not be blamed for what might happen."

At the moment when the notables appeared to quit the stage, each of them knew very well what was to happen among the carders deprived of work. More especially, because an agent of the Sieur Bryois [the tax contractor] had been in the city since May 20.

From the end of 1635, the carders had been touched by the crisis. In November 1635—and then in February and March 1636—there had been dismissals of "serge workers and others discharged by their masters who had no work to offer them." [37] Correspondence addressed to Chancellor Seguier spoke of three thousand unemployed in January 1636. The figure would appear high, and most likely it included refugees and artisans other than carders. The condition of the unemployed was miserable, and "a number were reduced to begging and to death." [38] Already some disturbances had broken out. On February 6, "workers had assembled and done insolent things leading to an uproar and sedition." On March 20, twelve to fifteen people assembled on the Rue Saint-Leu in front of a house where the agent of the Sieur Bryois had come. But—and this fact is important—there was no general movement.

The revolt of the carders and the lower classes

At the time when the agents of the Sieur Bryois came to reside, foreign troops unleashed their first attacks. The first hostile acts occurred on March 22, 1636, when the garrisons of Bapaume, Lens, Arras, and Hesdin came to burn the villages of Contay, Vadencourt, Bertancourt, Acheu, Belle-Eglise, Baizieu, and Lealvilliers. They came within twenty kilometers of Amiens.[39]

This event, joined to the arrival of the agents, aroused terror, rekindled old quarrels, and unsettled the nerves of the population. All of the accumulated discontent, added to the misery and fear, was to explode in the revolt of this early April 1636.

The troubles began early in the morning of April 1, around eight o'clock, in the Minimes quarter at the very end of the Rue Saint-Leu, in the twists and turns of the alleys and canals of the lower city.

A number of carders gathered and formed groups, "that joined eight or ten together with fifteen or twenty young men," who were employed as wool finishers. They hid their faces and attacked the workshops where they were employed. They struck at the windows, broke into the houses, molested the workers and the masters, and cut all craft ties. The masters were no more the target than the workers. It was Lieutenant Cornillon of the citadel who gave the alarm. The councillors met at the city hall at nine o'clock, and they decided to send a delegation to the carders, urging them to go back to work, and to the masters to whom they hinted at the possibility of an arrangement with Bryois.

The councillors, Castelet and de Mons, accompanied by the *greffier*, de Bailly, and the *procureur fiscal*, Jean Boullenger, and five policemen, went out to search for the rebels and returned without having detected any agitation. But toward ten o'clock, four master carders, combers, and weavers arrived at the city hall and complained that, when some of the masters dismissed part of their workers, these unemployed workers attacked the others. The four masters demanded punitive sanctions. Six overseers were summoned to the city hall, and the usual orders were repeated to them. The bourgeoisie was called to arms, and a letter was sent to the Duke of Chaulnes to inform him of the situation and to request his intervention.

The disturbance of the morning of April 1 was, then, the act of workers who were unemployed or discontented with reductions in their wages. Likewise, some masters, who had stopped work, rose up against the orders they had received. The victims were master carders and their journeymen who continued to work, as they were ordered to do. It was a movement within the corporation of carders, workshop against workshop. However, a letter sent to the Duke of Chaulnes expressed the fears of the city council: "The bourgeoisie has been called to arms; there is no one here yet; we fear that the evil is becoming great." It seems that the strike of the carders, following that of the merchants, was integrated into a larger movement that concerned the whole city.

On the afternoon of April 1, the disturbance began again.

But it had changed; it was much more violent. Grumbling discontent became a rebellion. It spread elsewhere—to the Rue des Rabuissons, quite opposite from the Minimes quarter, at the other end of the city in the quarter of the monasteries and great noble town houses. The governor had his town house there, as did the Pingré family. The demonstrators were no longer just carders as during the morning. "These carders stir up strong feelings among the humble people." Other artisans, the crowd of vagabonds, "people of no account" joined the carders. "We have neither work nor bread; we prefer to die." Their entire program was contained in these few words in response to the councillors. There were none of those joyous chaps—imagined by H. de Montbas—who, between two demonstrations, refreshed themselves in the cabaret. They presented an altogether more desperate face. The rebellion took on a more tragic aspect than the morning's disturbance. It was a riot caused by hunger and misery.

The victims also changed. And, from this point of view, there were two periods during the afternoon. First, the rioters attacked houses to pillage them (we do not know which ones). Next, the anger turned against the houses inhabited by the tax agents—the house of the Sieur de Vauchelles, agent of Bryois, and, far from the Rue des Rabuissons, the lodgings called the Elephant and the Red Bull . . . where other agents had put up. But this was only in the second instance, and in an entirely different quarter from that where the afternoon disturbances had begun. The rioters attacked houses with stones and tried to force the gate with a wagon.[40] No document tells us what happened to the tax agents. It seems that the rioters did not succeed in forcing the gate. However, the resistance was not strong. The rioters first ran into four soldiers from the citadel, who guarded the house. These soldiers did not hesitate to fire and wounded three or four persons. They disappeared without doubt, because the rioters managed to reach the gate. Then two councillors intervened—Castelet and Mouret. They were jostled and struck, and Castelet had to take refuge in the belfry. And only at the end of the day did the bourgeois companies appear. Summoned toward noon, they gathered together around five o'clock, and not all were there. There were twelve companies of militia and three chartered companies. The plague had reduced the total by two thirds.[41] There remained nearly five companies at least. But only two assembled—that of de Vauchelles (a relative of the agent of the Sieur Bryois, or the agent himself?) and that of Pingré, merchant and officer of the king. We do not see Correur, councillor and colonel of the bourgeois guard.

The bourgeois companies thus arrived very slowly; they were not at full strength; their action was insignificant (different from that of the soldiers from the citadel). These two companies did not charge nor fire upon the crowd. They were content to rescue the councillors and to fire a few shots with their arquebuses that wounded nobody. The rioters dispersed. It was six o'clock in the evening. No arrests were made; it had been impossible to discover the instigators of the riot.

When the Duke of Chaulnes arrived from Corbie, with eighty soldiers, he found the bourgeois under arms and, despite all, he carried out the rounds and patrols with trumpets sounding.

Next morning, April 2, the disturbances began again. The lower orders—it was not a question of carders—assembled in the public square. The Duke of Chaulnes, accompanied by de Soyecourt and de Messieurs, undertook to disperse the rioters. "The angered populace violently threw stones"; the duke received one on his head. He had three or four people imprisoned. A few days later eight hundred Swiss guards entered the city, manned the guard at all of the gates—leaving only one to the bourgeois. The rebellion was over.

How to turn the revolt to good account?

The rioters returned home, but the affair did not rest there. It was continued by will of the councillors, of the merchants, and of the governor.

The Duke of Chaulnes demanded money to compensate him for the displacement of his troops. The councillors and the treasurer refused—using as a pretext, the city's debts and its numerous problems—and they transferred the expenses to the tax contractor for whom the duke had come. The duke lost his temper, cursed, and threatened with his baton; the councillors remained steadfast. The duke reminded them of their conduct during the riot. He accused them of hesitation, of weakness, and of complicity. Because they had managed no captures, nor undertaken any legal action, "he said to them that he had reason to believe that they had connived with those who committed the disturbance, because most of the councillors were merchants." [42] He insulted them before the king's officers and wanted to remove them from all control over the police, guard, and fortifications of the city.

It was a position directed against municipal independence that coincided with the precautions taken by the soldiers upon their arrival in the city on April 4 and the four days following. The councillors responded with a delegation to the king. The duke raged against this deputation, which was sent without his consent, and, because the plague had returned, he supported Henri de la Cointe to be in charge of the cleansings.

For his part, M. de Sachy wrote from Paris that he had spoken to the council about the carders' riot. Also he spoke about it to M. de Noyers who was responsible for the fortifications. The Cardinal [Richelieu] knew that, "the councillors had done what they could." It seems that each group wished to exploit the uprising for its own ends and usual interests. The revolt was only one element in a much larger conflict.

However, outside circumstances were to modify the situation. The Spaniards lay siege to Corbie, which fell on August 15, while Soyecourt, who directed the defense, was accused of treason. The enemy attacks in this month of August became very disturbing to Amiens: Longueau, Saleux, Salouel, Rivery, Longueau again, the suburbs of Noyon.[43] The enemies were at the gates of Amiens, and this threat, and the fear of treason, gave rise to panic. "The capture of Corbie alarmed the city of Amiens: there was not a soldier in the garrison; no fortification in a state of readiness; the city was deserted by the bourgeois because of the plague. . . ." [44]

This new situation inclined the central power to indulgence:

> Cardinal Richelieu, following new warnings he received of this sickness of spirit, urged the Duke of Chaulnes to forestall the evil that might come, to look after equally the security of the place and the satisfaction of the inhabitants, and to bring in five hundred extra men for the citadel, with sufficient munitions to defend against the enemy and the rabble of this city that they believed to be poorly disposed. In a word, it is very certain that after the capture of Corbie, they were afraid at court for Amiens, and that they dreaded certain unfortunate results from the misunderstanding between the inhabitants and the governor.[45]

Consequently, a series of decisions would bring all opposition to an end. On August 22, 1636, the king granted relief from the *sol pour livre;* a regulation of November 1636 satisfied other demands—there would be twelve councillors instead of seven, from among whom the king would choose the mayor. The city council would oversee the fortifications and the police at the gates—the conflict unleashed by the Duke of Chaulnes in 1634 ended here. Of course not all conflicts were settled—the affair of the cleansings and the conflicts with the garrison troops. The residents refused to provide subsistence, and on September 17, 1636, there were again barricades and the taking up of arms. The councillors had no illusions about the degree of independence left to them—at the end of September, the king organized the elections as he wished. However, the circumstances that had created the revolts of March and April 1636 no longer existed. The tax was suppressed, and the external threat was temporarily averted. At the end of the year 1636, the popular movements ceased.

Conclusion

Many points remain very obscure. What had been the role of certain important persons—Pingré, Mouret, Castelet, Correur, Martin, de Cornillon, de Bocourt, Maurepas? Did the opposition group formed around the *airieurs* in 1635—a well-organized and involved group—intervene in April 1636? Who were the seditious artisans of the morning of April 1, and who directed them? And there are many other questions which the scarcity of documents prevents us from answering.

Nonetheless, it does appear possible to draw some conclusions.

The revolt of April 1 and 2 had not been a compact and homogeneous thing that revealed from beginning to end the same characteristics. On the contrary, there were four successive "moments" of the revolt, each quite different from the others. These were the following: on April 1, in the Minimes quarter; on April 1, at the beginning of the afternoon, on the Rue des Rabuissons; on April 1, toward the end of the afternoon, around the belfry; and, finally, on April 2, again in the morning, and around the belfry. Each of these moments had its original features; there was one movement of discontent, but it was manifested in various ways.

A multiplicity of events, then, and also a multiplicity of motives. These riots cannot be understood, if one separates them from the events that preceded them or from those that followed. Thus placed in the life of the city, they convey its complexity. There were several motives for the hostility to the Duke of Chaulnes, the tax agents, and the magistrates—the desire to avoid a new tax, certainly; but also a reaction against hunger, fear before the enemy and the desire for protection, a wish for municipal independence, hostility to the policies and the person of the Duke of Chaulnes, and a wish to avoid the measures taken against the plague (fears that were justified, because these measures would be applied in part in May 1636). When the agents arrived under orders to levy the tax, Amiens was in a very particular situation: an exhausted city, ravaged by the plague for several years, haunted by famine, and without protection against the approaching enemy. Under these conditions, the arrival of the agents had been the decisive shock that focused all of the causes of discontent. The new tax of the *sol pour livre* had been a cause of the revolt, but it was not the only one. The battle against the tax was mixed up in an inextricable fashion with the battle against all of the other dangers by which the inhabitants felt menaced.

The actors in this battle were numerous, and it is not easy to distinguish the revolting faction from the well-behaved faction. Who revolted? In turn, merchants, some councillors, some masters and their artisans, the lowly people, the bourgeois militia—all had participated, from near or far, openly or secretly. Who were the victims and, more or less, opposed to the revolt? Some artisans and their masters, residents of the Rue des Rabuissons, the agents of the tax contractor, some councillors, the troops in the citadel, some elements of the bourgeois militia, some royal officers, and the Swiss. But, outside of the Duke of Chaulnes and his soldiers, attitudes were equivocal. Did these rebels and these law-abiding types belong to rigid and well-defined social groups: workers against owners, merchants and artisans against nobles? Such groupings do not take into account the complexity of the events. Never did the movement take on the aspect of a battle between workers and owners, or of workers against masters, or of workers against merchants. Rather, one has the impression, on the contrary, of an alliance between artisans and bourgeois. Merchants led the affair; they had anticipated the riot; they stirred it up by systematically organizing the buyer's strike; they repressed it lightly and sought to draw some advantages from it. The Duke of Chaulnes was not deceived: from the beginning to the end, the movement developed with the complicity and the support of certain merchants, councillors, and members of the militia. However, the alliance was not total: other merchants and magistrates, other masters and artisans, were much more reserved. In any case, one can say, at a minimum, that the revolt did not turn against the merchants and masters. Nor was the nobility a target. The attack on the person of the Duke of Chaulnes was not an attack on it. The documents leave no trace of any animosity whatever against the nobles. Nor were there allusions to the clergy.

These riots do not give the impression of an opposition between coherent and unified social groups. Those who revolted and those who remained passive belonged to many social categories. If there was a union of the rebels or a rebel faction, what form did it take? The comparison with the agitation provoked in 1634 and 1635 by the affair of the *airiements* suggests a grouping along the lines of cabals similar to the one that formed around the *airieurs*. Bound together by many interests (personal sympathies, family ties, economic solidarity, the solidarity of the workshop, the solidarity of a quarter, an identity of views on problems of the moment), people who belonged to all conditions of society, from the humble to the councillors, got together and opposed similar groups. In April 1636, the population would be divided as it was some months before—into cabals, heterogeneous in nature and recruited variously according to the rhythm of the revolt.

In sum, the official sources that oversimplify the popular movements of April 1636 at Amiens and that put responsibility on one or another social group must not deceive us. They were written to put us off the scent. The reality, which remains in part to be discovered, seems to have been very different and much more original.

NOTES

1. G. Lecocq, *Lutte entre la ville d'Amiens et le duc de Chaulnes, gouverneur de Picardie en 1636* (Amiens, 1881); H. de Montbas, *Episodes de la guerre de trente ans: une émeute gréviste des sayeteurs d'Amiens* (Paris, 1914); Boris Porchnev, *Les soulèvements populaires en France de 1623 à 1648* (Paris, 1963).

2. J. Pagès, *Manuscrits de Pagès, marchand d'Amiens, écrites à la fin du XVIIe siècle et au début du XVIIIe siècle sur Amiens et la Picardie,* ed. L. Douchet (5 vols; Amiens, 1856–1864), II.

3. *Archives communales de la ville d'Amiens,* AA 12, fol. 171v [Henceforth, all sources from the city's archives will be cited by series and folio numbers only].

4. The capital of certain ecclesiastics was invested in the city's commerce.

5. Adrien de La Morlière was a contemporary nobleman and author of *Les antiquités, histoires et choses plus remarquables de la ville d'Amiens* (Paris, 1642).

6. AA 13, fol. 322, March 26, 1630.

7. *Ibid.*

8. BB 51, fol. 84.

9. BB 63, fol. 77 and Series FF.

10. Pierre Logié, "Requêtes d'admission à la maîtrise du métier de saieteur, Amiens, au début du XVIIe siècle," *Bulletin de la Société des Antiquaires de Picardie,* L (1964), 293–302.

11. Jean-Joseph de Court, *Mémoires chronologiques qui peuvent servir à l'histoire ecclésiastique et civile de la ville d'Amiens* (Amiens, n.d.); Pagès, *Manuscrits,* V, 112.

12. De La Morlière, *Antiquités,* 80.

13. BB 61, fol. 90v; Pagès, *Manuscrits,* II, 295.

14. AA 60; Pagès, *Manuscrits,* II, 295.

15. AA 60.

16. H. Macqueron, "Un incident au sujet de la maladie contagieuse de 1632," *Bulletin de la Société des Antiquaires de Picardie,* XXXII (1928), 610–16; De Court, *Mémoires,* 104.

17. AA 59.

18. AA 60.

19. Logié, "Requêtes d'admission."

20. AA 51, 63.

21. BB 63, fol. 2.

22. FF 1300, fol. 41.

23. BB 63, fol. 2.

24. AA 60.

25. BB 63, fol. 66; BB 36, fol. 73.

26. De Court, *Mémoires,* 652.

27. Pagès, *Manuscrits,* II, 280.

28. De Court, *Mémoires,* 652.

29. Pagès, *Manuscrits,* II, 280.

30. AA 61.

31. 1B 22.

32. 1B 21, fol. 133.

33. BB 63.

34. AA 51.

35. AA 61.

36. *Ibid.*

37. EE 51.

38. Roland Mousnier, *Lettres et mémoires adressés au Chancelier Séguier* (2 vols; Paris, 1963), I, 340.

39. FF 1119; BB 63; AA 62.

40. It was a wagon, and not a cannon as is suggested in the inventory of series BB—"a hand-wagon on two wheels" (FF 1119, fol. 24). Also, Pagès, *Manuscrits,* II, 283.

41. BB 63, fol. 77.

42. BB 63, fol. 64.

43. Pagès, *Manuscrits,* II.

44. De Court, *Mémoires,* 650.

45. Pagès, *Manuscrits,* II, 281.

French Society and Popular Uprisings Under Louis XIV

BY LEON BERNARD

After decades of neglect, historians are renewing their interest in the popular revolts of seventeenth-century France. Credit goes principally to the Soviet historian, B. Porchnev, professor at the University of Moscow, who in 1949 published a work on popular uprisings in France from 1623 to the Fronde based on a large cache of Chancellor Séguier's correspondence discovered in a Leningrad library. In the original Russian, Porchnev's book went unnoticed among Western scholars, but in 1954 an East German translation appeared which badly ruffled some French sensibilities.[1] The most notable reaction was the long article published by Roland Mousnier in the *Revue d'Histoire moderne et contemporaine.*[2] Since Mousnier, more than any other living French historian, served as Porchnev's target,[3] he was the logical man to reply. In a larger sense, however, Mousnier defended not only himself but all non-Marxist French historians, for Porchnev implied the existence of a sort of conspiracy among "bourgeois" historians to suppress objective inquiry into seventeenth-century popular revolts. The Russian scholar credited only one French historian, Pierre Boissonnade,[4] with a proper view of these revolts, but his work, Porchnev charged, was "a scandal in the eyes of academic circles and he quit."[5]

Since the publication of Mousnier's rebuttal of Porchnev, interest in seventeenth-century popular revolts has grown impressively, as Mousnier, lamenting the insufficiency of knowledge on the subject, hoped it would.[6] A French translation of Porchnev's book has appeared along with a number of articles in scholarly journals.[7] Very promising, too, is the work of the

Centre de Recherches sur la Civilisation de l'Europe moderne founded in 1958 at the Sorbonne, which now includes a specific section headed by Roland Mousnier for the study of the *émeutes* in modern French history. One of the many services rendered by this organization is the preparation of a "Questionnaire" which spells out in great detail the problems awaiting historical investigation.[8] In the offing is a large volume containing the researches carried on under Mousnier's direction at the *Centre de recherches*.

At the heart of the historians' new look at the seventeenth-century popular revolts, and ranked in the "Questionnaire" of the Centre de Recherches as the "question peut-être la plus importante," [9] is the thorny problem of the involvement of the various social groups, the principal issue in the Porchnev-Mousnier controversy. Predictably, the Moscow scholar attributes the revolts of the pre-Fronde decades to the grinding oppression of the popular classes—both urban and rural—by the "dominant classes." The revolts are popular in origin and spontaneous. The concept of social "fronts" is basic to his thinking: the "front" of the peasants and urban workers arrayed against one comprising seigneurs, bourgeoisie, and even clergy. The true social and economic reality is the landed aristocracy, whose domination of the seventeenth-century scene would appear as complete as in the palmy days of feudalism. The bourgeoisie are acknowledged to have made considerable progress since the High Middle Ages, thanks largely to the institution of the venality of office, but what has really taken place, in Porchnev's opnion, is, not the "embourgeoisement du pouvoir" so dear to Mousnier's heart, but rather the feudalization of the office-acquiring bourgeoisie. As for the monarchy, it is simply the pliant tool of the feudal nobility, as is the clergy. Porchnev concedes that occasionally the "fronts" break down, that the nobility may side with the populace, for example, but this is sheer opportunism and for short-term, limited objectives only.

For Porchnev's thesis of class warfare and the spontaneity of the popular revolts, Mousnier [10] would substitute a much more optimistic analysis of seventeenth-century French society

based on amicable social interrelationships and class cooperation in the face of the common enemy—the centralized government. Mousnier emphatically rejects the notion of "fronts"—
both the front of the upper and middle classes and that of the
peasants and urban lower classes. He insists on the "liens de
fidélité qui unissaient ces nobles à toutes les classes sociales et
aux paysans eux-mêmes, en général les liens qui unissaient les
paysans à leurs seigneurs, même si ceux-ci étaient des officiers
ou des bourgeois." [11] The occasional peasant revolt which *seems*
spontaneous must perforce have some seigneurs lurking behind the scenes. For Mousnier, even an act as unfriendly as the
invasion of a château by a mob of peasants is subject to misinterpretation, being perhaps simply a matter of "tactique" rather
than a manifestation of hostility towards the unfortunate
owner. Moreover, Mousnier cautions his readers, "des nobles
. . . mettaient leurs châteaux à la disposition des paysans." [12]

In the towns, Mousnier asserts, it is the officials of the *hôtels
de ville,* the magistrates, and rich bourgeois who foment popular sedition in order to defend local liberties or to protest some
new tax. Such worthies are either directly involved in fomenting rebellion or they are morally responsible because of their
constant anti-government agitation and their failure to preserve order once the "canaille" had taken to the streets. In
short, Mousnier insists on a "vertical" social organization in
seventeenth-century France in which the component elements
"sont unis par des relations mutuelles de protection et de service"—in contrast to "la stratification horizontale" of Porchnev. [13]

This study aims to examine the major post-Fronde uprisings—Boulonnais, 1662; Gascony, 1664–65; Vivarais, 1670;
Bordeaux, 1675; Brittany, 1675—in the light of these opposing
theories. [14] There is a practical consideration for choosing the
uprisings of the reign of Louis XIV rather than the earlier
ones: The printed primary sources on which this article relies
are far more extensive for the former. However, no pretense is
made of arriving at definitive judgements. Perhaps at this point
questions can be posed more effectively than they can be an-
swered. Still, we do not think it suffices to dismiss Porchnev

with the flat statement that "Mousnier has demonstrated the shallow nature of Porchnev's thesis of aristocracy versus the lower classes." [15]

The first rebellion of note Louis XIV had to face after the death of Mazarin came from an unlikely quarter. Boulonnais in 1662 was highly favored politically and economically. Still *pays d'état,* governed by the easy-going Duc d'Aumont, it enjoyed enviable exemption from most forms of royal taxation, a condition Colbert was bent on changing forthwith. At first glance, the uprising of 1662 appears a classic example of the union of the classes to defend local privileges against the encroachments of the Crown. It coincided with the demand for a *don volontaire* of 30,000 *livres,* which itself followed hard on the heels of a request for 40,000 *livres* in 1661. An official deputation of the province had first been sent to Paris to protest the latest demands.[16] When it returned home without achieving its objective, a revolt broke out. Some 6000 peasants from the countryside around Boulogne took arms in the summer of 1662, chased out some royal cavalry units, occupied a number of châteaux and small towns, and began a systematic campaign to recruit followers from the surrounding region. Their leader was a seigneur, later hanged for his crime. The *Gazette de France* announced that the peasants of Boulonnais had taken arms "à la suscitation de quelques particuliers"; Bussy-Rabutin wrote that the King saw the nobility behind the uprising.[17] Eight bourgeois of Boulogne were exiled to Troyes on *lettres-de-cachet* after order had been restored, "reliable" judges imported, and 400 prisoners sent off in irons on a tragic trek to Toulon.[18] The pattern seems complete: nobility, bourgeoisie, peasantry all joining forces in common protest against a despotic central power.

But, in reality, this cooperation among the various classes was an illusion. When the peasantry resorted to arms, they were concerned with their own economic interests rather than with those of their seigneurs or province. At the trials presided over by Machault in the summer of 1662, it became apparent that the real complaint of the rebels was not the *don volontaire* in principle but rather the exemption therefrom of both the nobility and their *fermiers*. As a consequence of this exemption, the burden fell entirely on the "moyen et le menu peuple." Machault, intendant of Picardy, wrote Colbert that the people were not revolting against the King but solely in order to force payment by the "fermiers des nobles qui s'en disoient exempts." [19] The reaction of Boulogne was further evidence of the purely rural, antiseignorial character of the 1662 rebellion. No inhabitant of that town of any class felt the need to rise to the defense of provincial liberties. No troops were sent into the city. Nor was there any evidence of urban sympathy for the rural rebels. The revolting peasants, in their turn, seemed unconcerned with Boulogne. Their quarrel, until the arrival of the military, was with the country seigneurs and the better-off *fermiers*. Eyewitnesses tell of the pillage of many of the châteaux and "fortes maisons." [20] Machault wrote Colbert of interviewing noblemen "lesquels ont été pillés et maltraictez par les paysans." [21]

The leader of the movement was a certain Bertrand Postel, Sieur du Clivet, who before being sentenced to the wheel was stricken, along with his descendants, from the ranks of the nobility.[22] However, the appearance of a seigneur at the head of the uprising can lead to misinterpretation of the event. Clivet's relationship with the rebellion in no sense implicates the nobility of the province. He was a man of no standing, "abandonné au vin, au libertinage, et à toute sorte de débauche," a poverty-stricken soldier of fortune of the type so frequently encountered among the provincial nobility of the time. Moreover, the intendant's letters to Colbert state that Clivet had put himself at the head of the peasant bands *after* the rebellion had been launched, so he cannot be credited with instigating the troubles. Even under torture, Clivet failed to reveal any noble accomplices—"que des gueux qui n'ayant pas chez eux de quoy vivre, le suivoient pour en piller et voler par tout." [23]

The bourgeoisie of the province were viewed by the government with great suspicion, despite the assurance of local royal officials that this class had not participated in the revolt. When the repression of the sedition seemed about over, the governor of the province received eight blank *lettres-de-cachet* to be filled in with the names of some of the principal bourgeois of Boulogne. Nonplussed, he obediently exiled eight men he knew to be innocent to Troyes.[24] The *exemple* so dear to the hearts of King and minister had been made. Equally revealing of the manner Colbert used such revolts as this for his own ends is his secret letter to Machault stressing the "très grande conséquence" of directing the official investigation of the affair so that the King would be fully justified in abrogating the privileges of Boulonnais.[25]

Two years later, in 1664, another serious uprising took place, this one in the Chalosse-Labourd-Béarn area in southwest France. The immediate cause was the attempt by the state to impose the *gabelle* on a region hitherto exempt. In late May, in the small town of Hagetmeau, the agents of the tax farmer were attacked by a mob of inhabitants and fatalities suffered on both sides. The intendant, Pellot, was given a couple of companies of dragoons, and proceded to make the customary "justice exemplaire" of the seditionaries.[26] Nevertheless, the revolt spread. Some "thirty or forty parishes" around Hagetmeau joined the townspeople. By August the intendant informed Colbert that "on ne peut pas voir une rébellion plus complète ni plus ouverte." [27] A colorful *gentilhomme* by the name of Bernard Audijos appeared as leader and converted the undisciplined popular resistance into a skillful guerrilla campaign against the *gabeleurs,* with such success that the intendant sent urgent requests to Paris for reinforcements to cope with the rebels, who by the end of the year numbered as many as 6000 men. The following spring Pellot's troubles were compounded when the rebellion spread to Bayonne.

The intendant viewed the uprising as a conspiracy on the part of the local nobility, magistrates and principal inhabitants, who had stirred up "les paysans et la canaille." [28] But, again, the intendant could do no more than point the finger of suspicion at the upper classes. The leader of the rebellion, Audijos, was a man of noble birth, it is true, but, like Postel in Boulonnais, had all the earmarks of an adventurer rather than a representative member of the local nobility. The intendant referred to him as a "désespéré." [29] Son of an impoverished country nobleman, after almost a decade of army service, he had at the age of thirty returned to the very modest family manor. When the rebellion at Hagetmeau broke out, he appeared at the head of a band of peasants, small town artisans, butchers (such was the occupation of the first of his lieutenants captured and executed) and the like, proclaiming himself and his followers "martyrs for the public good." [30] Throughout the uprising, he remained the only nobleman in evidence on the side of the rebels. Furthermore, Audijos is at no time credited in the intendant's published correspondence as the organizer of the revolt of May 1664. Not until five months after the outbreak in Hagetmeau is Audijos' name mentioned by Pellot, namely in his letter of October 3, 1664. The presumption is that he, too, joined a movement already well established.

When Bayonne joined the rebellion in the spring of 1665, the essentially lower class nature of the movement was further evidenced. The town fathers of Bayonne were convinced that Audijos had his headquarters in the town and that money was being collected among the working classes for the support of his guerrilla bands. The frightened bourgeoisie of Bayonne pleaded for troops to ensure that the local magistrates would remain the masters and the "canaille" punished.[31] Furthermore, they asked that changes be made in the organization of the *Hôtel de Ville* "afin que le peuple n'y ayt pas d'entrée." [32] Such a request to the King, not only for troops but for the reform of the town government, is surely extraordinary for the reign of Louis XIV and is good measure of upper class fear of the populace. The most common reason cited for bourgeois participation in such rebellions as these is the safeguarding of local (i.e., bourgeois) liberties, but in this instance the bourgeoisie engineered the destruction of town liberties out of fear of the *peuple*.

Judging from the information Pellot obtained later in the summer of 1665, the upper classes were justified in their fear of the "canaille." Several men arrested in Bayonne confessed to the intendant that the "artisans et les principaux de la populace" had sent a deputation to Audijos to enlist support for a mass rebellion in Bayonne. The principal inhabitants were to be assassinated, royal châteaux seized, and negotiations entered into with England or Spain.[33] Pellot informed Colbert that "les meilleurs et principaux habitans" praised God that this dangerous conspiracy had been uncovered since they were not "maistres de la populace" and the plot would probably have succeeded.

Except for perennial nationalist outbreaks in Roussillon, France enjoyed internal tranquility for the next five years or so. But the spring of 1670 brought another major uprising, this one in Vivarais, in northern Languedoc. The immediate cause was the fiscal exactions of the Crown, made all the more pressing by the need for money for the nearby Languedoc Canal then in construction.[34] When a tax agent arrived in Aubenas on April 30 to arrange for the collection of a new tax, "plusieurs femmes . . . assistées de quelques manœuvres" attacked his lodgings and put him to flight.[35] The authorities restored order and made some arrests, but the following day a mob, consisting mainly of women, broke down the jail doors and freed the prisoners.

The *émeute* spread from town to country and a certain Antoine Roure appeared as "généralissime des peuples oppressez." [36] In mid-May Roure appeared before Aubenas with some 300 peasants. According to a bourgeois Aubenas chronicler, the town fathers wanted to close the gates in his face, but the unruly inhabitants of the lower-class St. Antoine quarter dictated otherwise. Once inside the walls, Roure's men got out of hand. Several upper-class residences were broken into and pillaged, causing the Aubenas bourgeois to take arms and chase Roure out of the town.[37] This set-back did not diminish Roure's popularity in the countryside. In May a popular assembly was held with more than fifty parishes represented. The delegates resolved to send a deputation to the King complaining of the depredations of the privileged classes in the province. (The central government, the target of the initial rioting in Aubenas, seems to have been viewed in a more favorable light by the country people.) Roure's supporters multiplied rapidly. The rebel cry—"Haro sur les élus! Mort aux sangsues du peuple!"—echoed through the countryside. Roure's followers declared ominously that the time had come when "les pots de terre casseront les pots de fer." [38] In urging mayhem on the "élus," the rebels were not limiting their vengeance simply to the officials of that name; by "élus" they meant nobles, officialdom, and virtually all men of property.[39] Roure's peasants had apparently declared a primitive type of class war.

By mid-June, Roure, now at the head of a still-growing force of 5000 peasants, reappeared in Aubenas, joining forces with a popular rebellion in that town. Two newly-arrived army companies, one French and the other Swiss, were attacked and forced to beat a humiliating retreat into the château, the Jesuit college, and town church, along with groups of terrorized town councillors and bourgeois. They remained under seige until the dramatic arrival, on July 26, of 4600 regulars, including a detachment of the King's own household musketeers. The rebels were routed and the following day six of the more obvious ringleaders were hanged. By trade they were a *cordonnier, chapelier, chaudronnier, brasseur,* and *cardeur.*[40] Roure was apprehended in his flight to the Spanish border, and before the end of 1670 his butchered remains served as grisly warning to passersby of the perils of sedition. In this rebellion there are not even the usual hints and insinuations of upper-class involvement.

The year 1675 marked both climax and end of the long series of popular disturbances dating back to the start of Richelieu's ministry. Two areas were primarily affected: Bordeaux and Brittany, both traditional trouble spots. Together, these rebellions were probably more worrisome to the Crown than any that had occurred in the century, with the exception of the Fronde. Like the latter, the rebellions of 1675 occurred while France was at war. Once again, rebellious Frenchmen made overtures to their country's enemies, but for one reason or another Holland and her allies failed to capitalize on their opportunity.[41]

Bordeaux was reputed a "difficult" city. Louis XIV and his ministers were much aware of the ill-feeling between populace and bourgeoisie. In 1661 one of the councillors of Louis XIV, in discussing the strengthening of the local fortress, Château-

Trompette, in order to hold in check the turbulent population, remarked hopefully that the Bordeaux bourgeoisie itself saw in this fortress a means "de se sauvegarder de la canaille." [42] In a letter to a Bordeaux parlementarian in the summer of 1674, Colbert recognized the danger of social disturbances in a city like Bordeaux, but urged the bourgeoisie, "qui ont quelque bien," to bestir themselves to maintain public authority. [43]

But, acting in a manner which showed little political sense and pressed by the financial demands of the Dutch War, the government adopted a fiscal program calculated to arouse and even unite populace and bourgeoisie. In March 1673, the *taxe du papier timbré* was adopted, forcing the legal class to employ a special kind of paper marked with a *fleur de lis* and the name of the *généralité* in which it was to be used. In early 1675, new taxes were decreed on pewter utensils and on tobacco, items of everyday use among the poorer classes. The different social reactions to these taxes are noteworthy. The tax on legal paper created the usual mutterings among court officials, lawyers, notaries, and the like, but, at least in Bordeaux, there were no repercussions worthy of note, no threat of sedition. [44] The excise taxes on pewter and tobacco were another matter. While the popular classes had paid little attention over a space of two years to the new excise taxes affecting members of the upper classes, their reaction to the levies on pewter and tobacco was swift and violent. On March 26, just a few days after the introduction of the new taxes, a large crowd of women (*femmes regretières*) stoned and cursed the agents who were attempting to affix the *marque de l'étain* in the shops. For three days, mob rule prevailed in Bordeaux as the populace took to the streets in "sédition sans exemple," drums rolling, shrill-voiced hoydens in the van in true revolutionary style. The city gates were captured by the populace and thrown open to onrushing peasantry. Several men, including a parlementarian, a couple of young students, and the servant of the subdelegate were killed and their bodies mutilated in open view. The governor of the province, Marshal d'Albret, finding himself hopelessly outnumbered, surrendered to the mob's demands, granted amnesty to the insurgents, freed their prisoners, and promised to obtain the suspension of the new taxes which had provoked the trouble. In the words of Pierre Clément, "Jamais, depuis la Fronde, le gouvernement n'avait subi pareil échec." [45]

For more than four months Bordeaux was under the domination of the populace, the King having been compelled to confirm d'Albret's decree of amnesty in view of his involvement on the Rhine with the Dutch. Disorder was rife among the town artisans. The *compagnons* of the masons and shoemakers went on strike and tried to "seduce" other workers to do likewise. In May, the "canaille" threatened to burn the town bakers in their own ovens if a bread shortage was not remedied. Submissively, the town fathers ordered an increase in bread production. But in mid-August, Governor d'Albret finally seized the initiative and at the head of 300 men from the garrison plus some stout-hearted noblemen and bourgeois inflicted the first defeat on the rebels. In November sixteen regiments of troops arrived by ship from Spain, moving into the city in battle array. After a winter of playing unwelcome host to several thousand undisciplined troops, Bordeaux became virtually a ghost town, its commerce ruined.

As might be expected, the government promptly perceived in the rebellion the long arm of the bourgeoisie. From d'Albret it received complaints of the failure of the bourgeois militia to rise to the defense of established order. Such inactivity the government equated with complicity. The bourgeoisie were accused of egging on the populace.[46] When reprisals began, both groups were punished with equal severity. Nevertheless, the evidence indicates that populace and bourgeoisie each went its own way, occasionally led by circumstances to seeming cooperation but distrusting one another with such intensity as to make effective cooperation impossible. Their sharply divergent reactions to the new paper and pewter taxes have been noted. The intendant De Sève had the political subtlety to recognize this split and to attempt to exploit it: A few weeks after the troubles began, he wrote Colbert that the lower classes were willing to accept the stamp tax if the King lifted the levies specifically affecting them.[47]

The inactivity of the bourgeoisie in the spring and summer

of 1675 in the face of serious social disorder cannot be considered prima-facie evidence of the involvement of this class in the disturbances. Such inactivity is also explainable in terms of their natural, elemental fear of the lower classes. The rolling of mob drums on the pavements of Bordeaux; public murders and the desecration of bodies in plain view; town councillors besieged in the *Hôtel de Ville;* wine-laden peasantry rushing into the city through open gates—all this must have been a traumatic experience for the orderly, peace-loving bourgeoisie. At the height of the rebellion, the municipal council estimated the number of armed urban rebels at four or five thousand and their peasant allies at about the same number, a frightening superiority over the forces of constituted authority even if one allows for the inevitable exaggeration.[48] As might be expected, the only local police force available, the *milice bourgeoise,* failed to rally to the cause of law and order. No one in seventeenth-century France took the untrained and undisciplined urban militia very seriously. One member of the town council at this time, a nobleman by the name of Fonteneil, was particularly harsh in his indictment of the bourgeoisie. He maintained that they were completely intimidated by the populace and fearful of stepping out of their locked houses. A royal official, Lombart, writing to Colbert, alluded to the "grande timidité" of the bourgeoisie. The intendant in his turn intimated to Colbert that bourgeois dislike of the State was matched by fears for their property.[49]

The role of the Parlement of Bordeaux during the uprising is worthy of note since the government later charged it with a major share of the responsibility. There can be no gainsaying that the paper edicts caused much discontent among the parlementarians, for the burden of the impost fell squarely on their shoulders. If any members of the upper classes were involved in the Bordeaux sedition, it would be the parlementarians. But the facts do not bear out the suspicion. The rebellion was but a few hours old when the Parlement ordered the bourgeoisie of the city to arms "pour empescher que les séditieux ne se rendent les maistres." [50] This, perhaps, was simply window-dressing, but what followed could not be. One of the first victims of the mob was a councillor of the Parlement who was killed while trying to talk reason to the mutineers. His body was thrown into the street and trampled upon. When a compassionate streetporter tried to intervene, he met the same fate. A president of the Parlement and his wife, arriving on the scene, were lucky to escape with a simple beating.[51] Another president, M. Lalanne, was taken prisoner and, in peril of his life, forced to order the release of some "gens du peuple" held captive in the Château. A few weeks later, the intendant wrote Colbert that the Parlement during the first crisis had done "tout ce qu'on pouvait souhaiter du zèle de cette Compagnie." [52] So, at least in the opening weeks of the troubles, the behavior of the Parlement was apparently above suspicion.

Nevertheless, at the end of the summer, when government troops had taken control of Bordeaux, the Parlement was harshly sentenced to indefinite exile to the little provincial town of Condom. Whether its actions during the summer months had been such as to warrant the punishment we are not in a position to judge, but considering the physical mistreatment of its highest officers at the start of the rioting, we would find it illogical that the parlementarians had quickly forgotten the fate of their colleagues and had joined forces with the populace against the King. More likely, Louis XIV and Colbert found another opportunity to discipline a provincial parlement, a course of action they generally relished.

The March 27 rising in Bordeaux touched off an even more extensive rebellion in Brittany. As in Bordeaux, the rioters had things pretty much their own way during most of the summer. No strong counter-measures were employed simply because the government, preoccupied with the Dutch War (this was the summer of Turenne's death on the Rhine), could not find the necessary troops to maintain its authority at home. Brittany, too, sent deputies to the Hague to request assistance, and the belief was strong among the Dutch that France was ripe for a general revolt.[53]

Rennes was the first city affected. Three outbreaks occurred in the spring and summer, the first on April 18. The offices of the tobacco, pewter, and paper tax farmers were put out of commission by mobs numbering several thousand. On May 3, Nantes experienced a popular outbreak described as the worst in the history of that turbulent city.[54] Later that same month, the contagion spread to rural Lower Brittany. In mid-July, the castle of Kergoet, reputed one of the strongest in the province, fell to a surprisingly disciplined band of 6000 peasants, who marched along the country roads in orderly ranks, drums beating, ensign flying.[55] The destruction of Kergoet led to a panicky flight of the nobility from the country to the comparative safety of the cities.[56] More than 200 manors in this area alone were said to have been pillaged.[57] But the inevitable soon followed: In late August 6000 regular troops arrived, soon reenforced by 10,000 veterans of the Rhine. Mme de Sévigné now penned her gruesome and strangely unemotional description of the roadside trees weighed by the bodies of hundreds of wretched victims of the repression.

When one considers social involvement in the uprising in Brittany, the same pattern emerges that we have discerned in earlier insurrections. Among the royal officials and ministers we find the familiar insinuations against the bourgeoisie and particularly the parlementarians, the usual allegations of inciting the "canaille" and deserting the *milice bourgeoise*.[58] When repression began at the end of the summer, the bourgeoisie were held collectively responsible along with the *menu peuple:* the burden of troop quarterings and heavy financial indemnities fell principally on the former. Furthermore—and this was the punishment which apparently hurt the most—the Parlement of Rennes was peremptorily exiled to the small town of Vannes, remaining there for fifteen years, to the great financial loss of the people of Rennes. Clearly, Colbert would not agree with the conclusion reached by one of the most reputable modern historians of Brittany, namely, that the Rennes outbreak was "une émeute sans chef, sans plan arrêté et sans préméditation," and that the riots in Nantes were exclusively lower-class in origin.[59]

But, again, one suspects Colbert's almost paranoiac distrust of the parlements. When the spring outbreaks began in Rennes, parlementarians joined with members of the nobility and the pitifully inadequate *milice bourgeoise* in restoring order and closing the town gates to prevent incursions from the faubourgs.[60] The Parlement acted with dispatch in ordering severe punishment for falsely spreading rumours of new impositions[61] and harboring vagabonds. It also reestablished the *bureaux* destroyed by the mob in April. At no time did the Parlement show any collective resistance to the governor or to any royal official. No specific parlementarian was charged with any crime. At least one historian who studied the documents closely concluded that the court, individually and collectively, was free of involvement in the sedition and showed no lack of energy in its repression.[62]

Once he had a few regiments behind him, the Governor made wholesale arrests among the Rennes bourgeoisie. On October 30, 1675, Mme de Sévigné wrote "qu'on a pris soixante bourgeois." As in the Boulogne rising, the bourgeoisie seems to have been arrested for the sake of form rather than guilt. The phrase Mme de Sévigné employed to describe the manner of arrest was, "à l'aventure."[63] A dozen *procureurs* of the Parlement and *Présidial* were arrested in the middle of the night. The flimsiness of this procedure is evidenced by the prompt release of these same men after interrogation.[64] On the other hand, those acutally executed were all from the lower class. Six men hanged at the end of October and beginning of November were all residents of the faubourgs or of the rue Haute, the working-class district. The residents of this particular street were so heavily implicated in the Rennes rebellion that the entire street was ordered razed.

The peasant phase of the rebellion in Brittany offers little support for the thesis of amicable social interrelationships in these seventeenth-century revolts. It is true that the outstanding leader in the countryside was a middle-class notary by the name of Sébastien Le Balp, who, considering his prosaic background, did a remarkable job of terrorization and intimidation, until he met his match in a certain redoubtable Marquis de Montgaillard. But like so many other bourgeois or noble leaders of the populace, Le Balp was an apostate to his class. When the 1675 rebellion began, he had just completed a prison sentence for forgery and theft.[65] Such conduct hardly qualifies one as a member of good bourgeois society.

The overwhelming evidence is that the peasants of lower Brittany rose up in 1675 spontaneously and on their own behalf. It has been asserted that the Breton peasants had arrived at the truly revolutionary notion that the privileges enjoyed by the nobility were no longer proportionate to the services they rendered to society, that the revolt was social at least as much as it was a protest against the new tax edicts.[66] The governor of the province in his report to Colbert was also of this opinion; the peasants, he wrote, were as much interested in shaking off the yoke of their lords as they were in protesting the new financial edicts.[67] Eyewitnesses to the pillage of the châteaux later testified unanimously that the prime object was the destruction of the manorial records.[68] The peasant manifesto ("Code Paysan") issued by the "nobles habitanz des quatorze parouesses unies du pays Amorique" rang out against the privileges of the seigneurs, demanding among other things intermarriage between peasants and nobility, the abolition of the *champart,* the *corvée,* seignorial hunting rights, and other feudal privileges.[69] Nor did the peasants show any love for the bourgeoisie of adjacent towns; these were commanded to accept the "Code Paysan" on pain of being declared "ennemies de la liberté armorique," and until they did accept it they were to be provided with no foodstuffs (Article 13).

In nearly all the uprisings we have examined, the Crown, at least at the outset, was the common enemy for all social groups. (Boulonnais in 1662 is a possible exception.) But the mere existence of a common foe does not permit the conclusion that the uprisings of the lower classes were somehow initiated, masterminded and directed from above. As we have seen, what started out as lower-class protests against royal tax-gatherers often quickly developed into movements against the local privileged classes. The impoverished urban worker or peasant was more inclined to regard the local parlementarian, municipal oligarch or seigneur as an enemy than he was to link arms, even symbolically, with him in common battle against royal tyranny. In his turn, the magistrate or seigneur tended to rally—often slowly and reluctantly—to the cause of law and order rather than to fan the passions of the "canaille."

But such was not the analysis made of the revolts by the King and his ministers. It is well known that Colbert, for example, labored under a constant fear of the conspiratorial union of the upper and lower classes. To our mind, he probably lost much unnecessary sleep on this account, simply because contemporary class divisions were so great as to minimize the chances of any effective working agreement among the classes. The lower classes were not somehow persuaded by their social betters to imperil their lives repeatedly in order to help the latter achieve their own ends. Leaving aside the question of whether the upper classes were endowed with the Machiavellian cunning to carry out such a policy, we do not believe that they would have had the naiveté to do so. They were relatively well-educated people, undoubtedly versed in the frightful history of the medieval *jacqueries,* and knew, some of them at first hand, of the risings of the *croquants,* the *va-nu-pieds,* and the like in Richelieu's ministry. The atrocities and property damages which had occurred in these pre-Fronde uprisings, the intervention of thousands of troops, their quartering in bourgeois homes (nothing worse could befall a seventeenth-century household)—these were not memories quickly forgotten. Reason questions whether these *bons bourgeois* and seigneurs would encourage the *lie du peuple* to march around their cities and countryside in riotous and drunken demonstrations, burning and pillaging. The seventeenth-century bourgeois had a very healthy distrust of the "canaille" and was far more conservative than his counterpart of 1789; if not, a good deal of the history of 1789 needs rewriting.

To Louis XIV and his ministers, every popular revolt took on the appearance of a general conspiracy against the State. Since no social or professional group had ever been favored by the central government, since parlementarians, municipal officials, seigneurs, business men, artisans, peasants had all been made to feel the weight of royal authority, more or less impartially, it was natural for the ministers to conclude that the challenge to royal authority came from all; parlements which had been guilty of little more than mutterings and footdragging, *hôtels de ville* which had dared no more than send a deputation to Paris, found themselves charged with complicity in the rebellions of the populace. Seventeenth-century ministers of state seemed unable to conceive of a spontaneous uprising of the popular classes. Whenever the peace of town or countryside was disturbed, the first task was to have the intendant or governor uncover the behind-the-scene director. No statesmanlike effort was made to distinguish degrees of guilt. If the artisans of Bordeaux, for example, demonstrated on the streets against high taxes, then everyone, from parlementarians on down, was in some way responsible and punishment must be dealt out accordingly. A governing principle of Louis XIV's state was suspicion of its citizenry. Latent disloyalty was taken for granted, and when it became overt the guilt was collective. A perusal of Colbert's papers or of Boislisle's collection of intendants' correspondence will bring home the obsessive preoccupation of officialdom with this question of "l'état des esprits."

It is a striking fact that while the history of popular rebellions in France can be traced well back into the Middle Ages, the notion of conspiracy, of hidden direction from above, is introduced only in modern times. The medieval *jacqueries* are acknowledged to have been "honest," spontaneous acts of desperation; no one looks for anything deeper. But when we arrive at the seventeenth- and eighteenth-century revolts, this is no longer true. A cloak and dagger atmosphere pervades the scene. The rebellions became much more than they seem to be on the surface. The culmination of this theory of conspiracy is found in the great rural upheavals of the spring and summer of 1789. From the start of the 1789 rebellion, the cry went up that peasants and townsmen were being prodded into action by sinister bourgeois revolutionaries in Paris. The bourgeoisie in turn pointed the finger of suspicion at the aristocrats for "fomenting anarchy in order to prevent [the bourgeoisie] from installing itself in power." [70] Generations of historians took up one position or another according to their social predilections. Georges Lefebvre, whose opinion on the subject would be generally accepted today, discards both these theories. He sees the bourgeoisie embarrassed and compromised by the revolutionary display of the countryside and fearful of "accès de désespoir." [71] The last thing the bourgeoisie wanted was the destruction of the seignorial system, in which they held a very heavy stake. Lefebvre maintains that the rural "révoltés [of 1789] ont un caractère anarchique évident; ni plan, ni chef." [72] Men and women revolted simply because they were hungry, oppressed, and angry enough to risk their lives. Such was the character of the revolts of medieval times, and such, essentially, were those of the seventeenth century. We do not agree with the overall "feudal" view of seventeenth-century society drawn by Porchnev, but do believe that his analysis of the popular rebellions of the times deserves closer examination.

NOTES

1. B. P. Porchnev, *Die Volkaufstände in Frankreich vor der Fronde* (*1623–1648*), tr. M. Brandt (Leipzig, 1954).

2. "Recherches sur les soulèvements populaires en France avant la Fronde," *R.H.M.C.,* V (1958), 81–113.

3. Especially Mousnier's *La vénalité des offices sous Henri IV et Louis XIII* (Rouen, 1946).

4. Notably Boissonnade's article, "L'administration royale et les soulèvements populaires en Angoumois, en Saintonge et en Poitou pendant le ministère de Richelieu (1624–1642)," *Mémoires de la Société des Antiquaires de l'Ouest,* 2ᵉ série, XXVI (1902).

5. Mousnier, "Recherches sur les soulèvements popularies," p. 84.

6. *Ibid.,* p. 112.

7. Boris Porchnev, *Les Soulèvements populaires en France de 1623 à 1648* (Paris, S.E.V.P.E.N., 1963); Robert Mandrou, "Les soulèvements populaires et la société française au XVIIᵉ siècle," *Annales,* no. 4 (1959), 756–765; Pierre Deyon, "Recherches sur les soulèvements populaires en France de 1483 à 1787," *Revue du Nord,* April–June, 1962; Monique Degarne, "Études sur les soulèvements provinciaux en France avant la Fronde: la révolte du Rouergue en 1643," *XVIIᵉ Siècle,* no. 56 (1962), 3–18; Roland Mousnier, "Les mouvements populaires en France au dix-septième siècle," *Revue des Travaux de l'Académie des Sciences morales et politiques,* 4ᵉ serie, 1962, 28–43. For the treatment of 17th century popular revolts on a European rather than French level, see H. R. Trevor-Roper, "The General Crisis of the Seventeenth Century," *Past and Present,* no. 16 (Nov., 1959), 31–64, and E. H. Kossmann, E. J. Hobsbawm, J. H. Hexter, Roland Mousnier, T. H. Elliott, Lawrence Stone, "Trevor-Roper's 'General Crisis'. Symposium," *Past and Present,* no. 18 (Nov., 1960), 8–42.

8. "Recherches sur les soulèvements populaires en France de 1483 à 1787: Questionnaire," (Sorbonne, n.d.), 24 pp. The aims and method of procedure of the *Centre de recherches* are the subject of an article by Roland Mousnier in the *Revue historique* CCXXV (1961), 407–412.

9. "Questionnaire," p. 14.

10. The most detailed expression of Mousnier's views on this subject is to be found in his article in the *R.H.M.C.* An excellent summary of Porchnev's book will also be found here. An emphatic reiteration of Mousnier's views in much briefer form may be found in "Les mouvements populaires en France au dix-septième siècle," *supra.*

11. Mousnier, "Recherches sur les soulèvements populaires," p. 91.

12. *Ibid.,* p. 99.

13. *Ibid.,* p. 106.

14. A good narrative account of these five revolts may be found in Ernest Lavisse, ed., *Histoire de France* (Paris, 1911), VII (1), 345–358.

15. A. Lloyd Moote, "The Parlementary Fronde and Seventeenth-Century Robe Solidarity," *French Historical Studies,* II, no. 3 (Spring, 1962), 349.

16. Pierre Clément, *La Police sous Louis XIV* (Paris, 1866), p. 284.

17. *Ibid.,* p. 286.

18. Poulletier to Colbert, July 31, 1662 in G. B. Depping, ed., *Correspondance administrative sous le règne de Louis XIV* (Paris, 1850–55), II, 897.

19. Nacquart to Colbert, July 12, 1662; Machault to Colbert, July 19, 1662 in Alfred Hamy, *Essai sur les ducs d'Aumont . . . Guerre dite de Lustucru, 1662. Documents inédits* (Boulogne-sur-Mer, 1906–7), pp. 285, 292.

20. E. Dutertre, ed., "Livre de Raison des Frest ou Fret, sieurs d'Imbretun," *Bulletin de la Société Académique de l'Arrondissement de Boulogne-sur-Mer,* VII (1907), p. 596.

21. Machault to Colbert, July 10, 1662 in Hamy, *Essai sur les ducs d'Aumont,* pp. 280–281.

22. "Sentence de du Clivet," *ibid.,* pp. 319–320.

23. Machault to Colbert, August 13, 1662, *Ibid.,* p. 310.

24. Clément, *La Police sous Louis XIV,* p. 289.

25. See the undated letter of Colbert to Machault in Alfred Hamy, *Essai sur les ducs d'Aumont,* pp. 282–283.

26. Pellot to Colbert, July 25, 1664 in A. Communay, *Audijos: La Gabelle en Gascogne* (Paris, 1893), p. 116.

27. Pellot to Colbert, August 13, 1662, *ibid.,* pp. 118–119.

28. Pellot to Colbert, August 6, 13, 20, *ibid.,* pp. 116–118, 119, 120.

29. Pellot to Colbert, Oct. 31, *ibid.,* p. 130.

30. Pellot to Colbert, Nov. 3, *ibid.*

31. Pellot to Colbert, May 10, August 3, 1665, *ibid.,* pp. 208–209, 298.

32. *Ibid.*

33. Pellot to Colbert, Aug. 29, 1665, *ibid.,* pp. 318–321.

34. Colbert to Louis XIV, May 22, 1670 in Pierre Clément, ed., *Lettres, instructions et mémoires de Colbert* (Paris, 1863), II (1), ccxxviii.

35. "Fidèle Relation de la Révolte de Roure," in J. L. de la Boissière, *Les commentaires du soldat du Vivarais* (Privas, 1908), p. 268. The anonymous author, a bourgeois of Aubenas, provides the most detailed contemporary account of the Vivarais revolt.

36. He is so characterized by Charles d'Aigrefeuille in *Histoire de Montpellier jusqu'en 1729* (1875–77), II, 168. Little is known of Roure. The contemporary accounts make him a complete unknown before his brief moment of prominence. His death sentence refers to him only as a "laboureur," although he was known to own some property. See "Fidèle Relation," p. 304.

37. *Ibid.,* pp. 271–272.

38. Dourille de Crest, *Histoire des Guerres Civiles du Vivarais* (Valence, 1846), pp. 342, 349.

39. *Ibid.,* p. 342f.

40. "Fidèle Relation," p. 302.

41. Camille Rousset, *Histoire de Louvois et de son Administration Politique et Militaire* (Paris, 1886–91), II, 136–137.

42. Jean de Boislisle, ed., *Mémoriaux du Conseil de 1661* (Paris, 1905), I, 49f.

43. Colbert to de Pontac, June 15, 1674 in *Lettres, instructions et mémoires de Colbert*, II(1), 342–343.

44. J. Barraud, "La Gabelle à Bordeaux. La révolte de 1675," *Revue philomathique de Bordeaux et du Sud-Ouest*, X (1907), 170.

45. *La Police sous Louis XIV*, p. 297. For detailed descriptions of the March rebellion in Bordeaux, see the letters of Lombart to Colbert, March 27, 28, 29, in Depping, *Correspondance administrative*, III, 248–53 and the procès-verbaux of the Jurade of Bordeaux in J. Barraud, ed., "Documents relatifs a l'émeute de 1675," *Archives historiques de la Gironde, XLI*, 145–258.

46. See the letter of the intendant de Sève to Colbert, April 24, 1677, in Pierre Clément, *Histoire de la vie et de l'administration de Colbert* (Paris, 1846), pp. 365–66, and Lombart to Colbert, March 27, 28, 29 in Depping, *Correspondance Administrative*, III, 248–253.

47. Letter of April 24, Clément, *Colbert*, p. 365.

48. "Procès-verbal de Jurade" (March 29) in Barraud, "Documents," pp. 161–165.

49. De Sève to Colbert, August 22, Depping, *Correspondance administrative*, II, 202.

50. Lombart to Colbert, March 28, 1675, Depping, *Correspondance administrative*, III, 250.

51. Lombart to Colbert, March 28, *ibid.*, 251.

52. de Sève to Colbert, April 24, Clément, *Colbert*, pp. 365–366.

53. Rousset, *Histoire de Louvois*, II, 197.

54. Arthur de la Borderie and Barthélemy Pocquet, *Histoire de Bretagne* (Rennes, 1913), V, 486.

55. D. Tempier, "La révolte du papier timbré en Bretagne. Nouveaux documents." *Mémoires de la Société Archéologique et Historique des Côtes du Nord*, II (1885–86), 133.

56. Bishop of Saint-Malo to Colbert, July 23, 1675 in Depping, *Correspondance Administrative,* III, 264–265.

57. Borderie, *Histoire de Bretagne*, V, 513.

58. See especially the letter of Chaulnes, governor of Brittany, to Colbert, June 12, 1675 in Depping, *Correspondance administrative*, III, 256 and de Lavardin to Colbert, June 14, *ibid.*, p. 269.

59. A. de la Borderie, *La Révolte du papier timbré advenue en Bretagne en 1675,* (Saint-Brieuc and Paris, 1884), pp. 20, 27.

60. Borderie, *Histoire de Bretagne*, V, 483–484.

61. S. Ropartz, "Exil du Parlement du Bretagne à Vannes, 1675–1690," *Bulletin de l'Association Bretonne* (1874), p. 111.

62. *Ibid.*, p. 105.

63. Cited in Borderie, *La Révolte du papier-timbré*, p. 179.

64. *Ibid.*, p. 181.

65. Borderie, *Histoire de Bretagne,* V, 507.

66. *Ibid.,* 496.

67. Chaulnes to Colbert, July 9, 1675 in Depping, *Correspondance Administrative,* III, 262.

68. Tempier, "La révolte du papier timbré," *passim.*

69. The full text of this document may be found in Borderie, *La Révolte du papier-timbré,* pp. 93–98. Its authenticity appears beyond dispute.

70. Georges Lefebvre, *La Grande Peur de 1789.* (Paris, n.d.), p. 246.

71. *Ibid.,* p. 246.

72. *Ibid.,* p. 141.

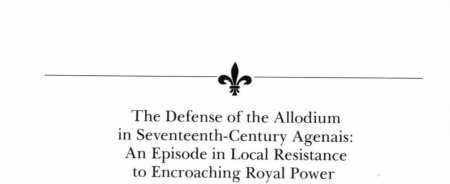

The Defense of the Allodium in Seventeenth-Century Agenais: An Episode in Local Resistance to Encroaching Royal Power

BY FRANÇOIS LOIRETTE

The persistence of the allodium—those noble or common domains free of feudal charges and similar to full ownership of the Roman type—was one of the original legal features of the Midi of France in the seventeenth century.[1] Submitted to public authority, but protected by the written law against seigneurial pretensions, they provided their possessors, in the midst of a society still bound by links of dependence, a sense of liberty that was well expressed in formulae such as the following: "François Falachon, merchant of the city of Agen . . . has said and declared that he holds, enjoys, and possesses in common freehold a house exempt from all seigneurial duties and obligations, for him to enjoy free and clear of all rents." [2] "Raymond Andrieu, bourgeois and merchant (of Agen), declares . . . that he owes no obligation, having no property that owes tax to His Majesty." [3] But this independence exposed them, if not, at this late date, to the application of the celebrated formula, "no land without a lord," [4] at least to the attacks of the royal power, whose lawyers upheld the "directe universelle"— that is, the eminent ownership by the crown of all lands alleged to be free.[5]

Despite the disproportion of the forces facing one another, the freeholders opposed an obstinate resistance—although one that was unequal according to circumstances and place. Studied in the Bordelais and the Bazadais by Boutruche,[6] it has remained nearly ignored in another region of the *généralité* of Bordeaux, the Agenais, though it seems to have been particularly long-lasting there. On this question, the communal archives of Agen offer an abundant documentation that covers more than a century: registers of the city government, letters of deputies and intendants, ordinances of the latter and of their subdelegates, and diverse legal proceedings.[7] With the aid of this documentation, we would like to clarify a few points: why had the resistance of the allodium been so lasting in the Agenais? What had been its adversaries, its means of defense, and the principal episodes in the struggle?

In a memoir prepared in 1746 with a view to defending the *directe universelle* of the king in Agenais, Fretteau, the inspector general of the domain, explained the origins of the allodium in this region as follows: [8]

> *The city of Agen was once charged with the collection of the seigneurial dues for the profit of the king, and from this, it proceeded to suppress the first proofs of ownership; this city, which had always been the capital of the region, had also been a kind of frontier city, as long as the English had been masters of part of Guyenne. That is why the kings of France and of England had been equally concerned to use discretion in its regard, when it passed successively from the hands of one into the hands of the other. . . . They knew that under similar circumstances, the officers of the kings of France or of the kings of England, and their collectors, had not insisted on the payment of lesser dues and fees, the very exact pursuit of which might have produced results very much contrary to the true interests of these princes.*

After the expulsion of the English, "the zeal that the officers of the king had for the reestablishment of his rights . . . had soon been discouraged and suppressed by the new divisions caused by internal troubles, by the quarrels over religion, by the furies of the league, and by other civil wars. . . ." The result had been "the loss to the king and his financial agents of the seigneurial rights attached to his domain." [9] It was a question, then, of simple usurpation that was favored by the position of the region and by the troubles that occurred over the course of the centuries. But the Agenais defended their allodium by arguments which, if they perhaps lacked a solid legal basis, were nonetheless full of interest.

First, it was a question of natural law—an expression that recurred again and again in the texts. "The common freehold is not a privilege, nor a concession, but a natural immunity preserved since the beginning of the centuries by the possessors of allodial property," said a petition of the assembly of the three orders to the intendant, de Sève, in 1673.[10] The city officials in 1676 proclaimed, "We have the privilege of the allodium, which is one of the most beautiful flowers in the garland of the city hall, and one that our predecessors have defended and preserved from time to time, during the two centuries that it has been attacked with full force, without having received any alteration." [11] They held that possession was as good as any title, even against the king. "In the city and jurisdiction of Agen, there has never been a property register made, nor has the king ever taken any quitrent." [12] If homages had once been given,[13] they had the character of personal allegiance, and were not in contradiction to the common freehold, "a natural liberty in a free region like ours that is ruled by the written law." [14]

It was, in fact, as a region of the written law that the Agenais claimed to enjoy the allodium, and, more precisely, as a former dependency of neighboring Languedoc.[15] However, the temporary reunion of the Agenais to Languedoc in the twelfth and thirteenth centuries (1196–1279), on which it depended,[16] was not considered as a valid argument by its adversaries, who even claimed that this region was under customary law since its union with Guyenne. They invoked the work of a judge of the *présidial,* first consul in 1659, Jacques Ducros, entitled, "Réflexions singulières sur l'ancienne coutume d'Agen" (1666), where there was no question either of written law or of the allodium. The consuls of Agen retorted by characterizing this book as "a bunch of sketches and ideas that an individual wanted to have printed," and by opposing to him the authority of Pierre Pithou, who declared that Agen was ruled by the written law.[17] Outside of the legal arguments, more or less solid, they put it in rather touching terms to the king's justice: "Our good cause will always be the same in all times, since our right is a natural right, and there is only the authority of the king

182

that is above all right, and his will alone can silence us, but, since he is very just, there is room to hope that he would like to restore it to us, and if this affair is tried, it is certain that it will end up before the king." [18]

But what realities were there behind these controversies? Do we know the importance, at this time, of allodial property in the *sénéchaussée* of Agen? First, it seems that it was a question of urban domains; [19] no mention of rural freeholds is met with in the texts; in the proceedings, it is only a question of cities.[20] Cities, moreover, that were modest. Agen, honored by the frequent visits of the governor or of the intendants, was often characterized as the "second city of the province." But a roll of households in November 1685 counted, for the four urban parishes, only 1646, corresponding approximately to 8000 inhabitants.[21] This was neither a manufacturing city,[22] nor an important center of commerce—the Lot, and even the Baise, seemed busier than the Garonne—upstream from their confluence. A memoir of 1645 notes, "It is a city of very little commerce"; it has "almost no other resource than that which the *siège présidial* furnishes it." [23] The jurists thus held an important place there and dominated, more and more, the consular elections.[24] But we find alongside them, among the authors of declarations or people sued for nonpayment, some merchants or simple bourgeois. The total is rather significant: on May 5, 1682, 694 declarations of common freehold had been registered,[25] which, by comparison with the number of households, represented roughly a little less than half of the property.

Against this little world of freeholders, an offensive was to develop, conducted for more than a century until the nearly complete disappearance of these islands of independence in the first half of the eighteenth century. "All the land is against us," wrote Lalande, deputy to Paris, in June 1687.[26] In fact they had some powerful enemies—the royal power and its servants, the *trésoriers de France,* intendants, revenue farmers and their agents, without speaking of the great lords—investors in the domain lands.

"We would have nothing to fear if it were a question of no other interest than that of the king," remarked the first consul,

Beaulac.[27] In having the property rolls of the royal domain redone, Colbert certainly thought less of affirming the *directe universelle* of the sovereign, than of extracting the maximum of resources from one of the most fruitful of the "extraordinary affairs" that derived from the lord's share demanded at the time of each change [in ownership].[28] At the beginning of the ministry, a deputy could write to his colleagues from Paris the following: [29]

> *All that can ever so little offend the interest of the king and diminish his revenues is very badly received, and it is to augment them that they work mightily . . . there was never so much severity and exactitude. Judged from the case of the allodium . . . the king does not want to speak of privileges. . . . The minister aims only to fill the coffers of the king, and everything that seems to divert or retard his funds is rejected. . . . Never was there a more difficult ministry to make affairs of this nature succeed.*

But the "great storms" against the allodium coincided with costly wars, and, above all, the one with Holland, "one of worst wars with which the kingdom has ever been burdened." [30] If the war continues, Colbert wrote to the intendant, de Sève, on April 27, 1674, it will be necessary to draw aid from all parts for the armies; it will be necessary to investigate carefully the "extraordinary affairs" that can be imposed in this province, "it being much more advantageous to look for affairs of this nature, than to increase the assessments on those who pay the *taille*." [31] The privileged were furious; at the most, circumstances dictated a certain prudence. "There is perhaps nothing so dangerous, nor which would more incite the hotheads of the region where you are, than these kinds of exemptions, but it is important to conduct these tax collections in such a way that no agitation occurs at one of the ends of the kingdom, when His Majesty is engaged at the head of his armies." [32]

It was a question, above all, of recovering money. To a deputy of Agen, a revenue farmer declared bluntly in 1693, that is to say, right in the middle of the War of the League of Augsburg, that the allodium "is only a pretext for taxing the cities, and that it is really a gift they are asking them for." [33] In spite of the legal controversies and even the absence of titles, the king seemed always ready to confirm the right of the allodium in return for a sum set by the royal council. It is true that the latter, deeply hostile to this privilege, would indefinitely delay the question of right.

The *trésoriers de France,* guardians and natural judges of the domain, were, for their part, quite disposed to prove their zeal by prosecutions, hoping to safeguard their prerogatives that were more and more threatened by the intendants.[34] As early as the beginning of the century, those at Bordeaux declared themselves against the allodium without title. They were eager to have acts of homage, acts of recognition, and inventories required. The consuls in 1661 accused them of finding, "a taste so delicate in this affair [the land register] that they make it the dessert for all their meals; they claim to establish in the province this maxim, no land without a lord, and that all real estate that is not dependent on a lord will henceforth be dependent on the king." In 1662, they went so far as to seize at Bordeaux, under the pretext of default of declaration, the postal boat of Agen, which constituted the principal revenue for the city.[35] But this ardor would be poorly rewarded: in spite of their reproaches, the government gradually diminished their functions. Special commissions of the chamber of the domain were first substituted for the land register. Then a regulation of December 1670, confirming this dispossession, obliged them to hand over documents relating to the domain to the commission, now presided over by the intendant. The latter would appoint some of them as subdelegates—a meager consolation—reserving for himself, moreover, final judgments.[36]

Thus the intendants were called upon to consider the affair of the allodium. Servants of the king, strangers to the province, they looked with little favor upon the pretensions of those who were under their jurisdiction—"people extremely prejudiced and infatuated with their privileges." [37] The opposition of Agen and Condom to the execution of the land register "consists more of the obstinacy of minds, than of pertinent reasons," wrote de Ris to Colbert.[38] Which did not prevent him from recognizing that these privileges were "rather well supported." Fundamentally, the intendants did not intend to prejudge the question of right, which was the business of the council; all that the government demanded of them on this question was, in case of difficulties, to "make a written report, to give advice and send it to the council." [39] The essential thing was to procure money for the king. "The intention of the intendant [Bazin de Bezons] would be that they come to terms by giving a sum of money," even "by way of a free gift." [40] These solicitations were accompanied, according to circumstances, by deference or by threats. De Ris became angry with the convocation by the consuls of the assemblies of the region on the subject of the land register—declaring to the deputies that he will investigate these "gatherings," and bring the guilty to trial.[41] He refused authorization to the first consul, Beaulac, to go defend the interests of the community at Paris. "After that I was most anxious to be away from him," the person concerned confessed, "given the tone he had taken." [42]

The multiple tasks that faced them obliged the intendants to subdelegate—which Colbert recommended for the allodium.[43] They chose local magistrates about whom the subjects sometimes complained: Preissac, a judge of Laparade, subdelegated by de Sève, then by de Ris, was thus the object of recriminations motivated by his investigations "at great expense" and "the great crowd" that he forced upon many communities in the name of the interests of the Duchess of Aiguillon, holder of the domain rights; the intendant had to disavow him.[44] Sallat, *procureur* of the king in the *élection* of Agen, subdelegated by de Ris, was accused of numerous extortions; he imposed heavy penalties for estates possessed in freehold that lacked acts of recognition; he condemned a man who had bought some trees to thirteen hundred livres in lord's due, just as for cutting in the forest; he would end up by being the object of an investigation by the Parlement.[45]

But the people most hateful to the public remained the revenue farmers (*traitants*), whom the government could not do without for the collection of extraordinary exactions. "I have never heard it said that there were as many tax agents as there are presently . . . they solicit and are very powerful, because they have never had so much credit, nor have been so much in vogue, as in our times," wrote a deputy in 1687.[46] These revenue farmers—Vialet, Buisson, Fauconet, La Cour de Beauval—were represented by their subfarmers and agents. Resented by the treasurers, they were protected by the intendants.[47] In their petitions to the latter, they furiously set about attacking the freehold without title, and against it they invoked acts of homage that were more or less old, and they sought to extend to all properties the right of the *franc-fief*.[48] They "trampled hard on the subjects of the king," inspiring in them a "great fear" and a general "consternation" with their summonses, writs, and the misuse of process servers. Their excesses were recognized by the intendants themselves: "In order to fill up their declarations, they have issued writs against many people who do not possess estates nor noble properties—indeed, who have no funds at all—and wrongfully require a tax for the reception and registration of these declarations."[49] De Ris wrote to Colbert in 1681 that the farmer of the domain in Agen was in part responsible for a "tumult and agitation" that was minor, but severely repressed. "In order to keep the fees and profit from them, he will not receive the dues by mutual agreement. He personally issues writs for billeting troops; instead of one constable, he sends five or six; he doubles the taxes on the writs; despite prohibitions, he seizes the livestock; and finally, we are at the point where I would have him arrested, except for my scruples about discrediting the king's affairs in this region, and my not knowing if the council would approve my conduct." The farmer for the land register "has sought by every means to make it a source of profit, instead of promoting it; his clerks and agents, appointed by him, have committed a thousand vexatious acts that he allowed and authorized, because he shared the gains with them."[50] After the copy of a decree of the council returned in favor of the Duchess of Aiguillon, we find this indignant reflection: "In this decree, we find only the clear interest of the revenue farmer, who would like to arouse this great machine of the land register, in order to liquidate his fees. But what kind of justice is it to trouble the repose of a province for the interest of a particular person."[51]

Still opposed to the freehold were the holders of domain rights. These were the Dukes of Aiguillon—more precisely, the two duchesses, Marie-Madeleine de Vignerod de Pontcourlay (1604–75), a niece of Richelieu who had obtained the concession of royal rights in the counties of Agenais and Condomois in 1642, and, after 1675, her niece, Marie-Thérèse (1636–1704).[52] They were capable women, and all the more keen on demanding their due, so that they engaged in a lengthy lawsuit against the consuls of Agen, regarding the subject of the nobility of certain lands for which they refused to pay the *taille*. The second sent a representative when the land register was drawn up, issued writs against residents for the payment of the lord's due, intervened on the side of the revenue farmers, all the while contending against them that she alone could receive the taxes, with the assistance of her own agents.[53]

Against these multiple attacks, what were to be the means of defense used by the threatened community? Basically, it sought to obtain the recognition of its right; first off, disavowing the *trésoriers de France*—"both judges and parties to the affair"—it tried without success to have its case judged by the Parlement of Toulouse—evidently well-disposed.[54] Desperate over its case, it looked to the council, a direct emanation of royal justice. But the latter was hardly favorable to privileges: "However good your means," their lawyer wrote the consuls in 1683, "you must, nevertheless, look upon this business as very difficult, and in which there is danger for you because of the present mood of the council to do away with freeholds."[55] Begun in 1670, with the first serious offensive against the freeholds, the affair dragged on, like so many legal proceedings, without ever being fully judged.[56] Delegations—sent to Paris to follow the case, or to Bordeaux near the intendant—ruined the municipal finances: there were travel expenses, more or less heavy; stays that were sometimes very long;[57] solicitations to influential people—beginning with the court recorder—and accompanied by "some honey" (i.e., bribes); "horrible" expenses of justice, and high fees for the solicitors to the council and the attorneys.[58] The deputies were often obliged to advance their own money. Short of funds, they were, moreover, subjected to many rebukes: one of them was refused admission by a court recorder, because the latter "had a dose of physic in his body." In order to be admitted to the office of another, one had to have, "the ordinary keys, that is to say an écu for the porter and thirty sols for the lackeys, which I was not reluctant to do, because I saw it was necessary, and I was already well-informed about this manner of introduction, which is most useful because, otherwise, you are put off." [59]

Yet the will to defend the allodium asserted itself. The consuls of Agen, who "ordinarily ruled the conduct of others" as syndics of the region,[60] united with those of other cities in the *sénéchaussée*, as well as with those of Condom, in a common action "on a question so important for all of the region of the Agenais, of which our city is the leader." [61] It was a characteristic demonstration of the solidarity of the freeholders in defense of their immunity.[62] But the assemblies, frowned upon by the intendants, were, in the end, forbidden.[63] Then, against the declarations and taxes, to which were added other "extraordinary affairs," without counting heavier and heavier impositions,[64] there was passive resistance: "The magistrates do not apply the orders of the king and the intendant," stated the process servers.[65] They prolonged the declarations, neglected drawing up the tax rolls, and multiplied objections. Seizures and writs fell down upon the indebted, and, behind the dryness of the texts, we perceive distress. The consuls in 1683 deplored "the shocks and the violent and iniquitous exactions that our poor inhabitants suffer each day." But they added, "that it is necessary to understand that it is better to suffer some little distress, than to see them and their descendants subjected to homages and rents that our fathers have never heard of." [66] For their part, the revenue farmers were indignant that "all the cities of the kingdom that have similar privileges to the said city of Agen have not at all resisted providing what has been commanded of them concerning the said rights, in order to contribute their share to the great expenses that His Majesty is obliged to make in the present state of affairs." [67]

The last word in this unequal struggle had to rest with the

monarchy. In the progressive dismantling of the allodium, we can note several stages—at least in the framework of the Agenais, one case in the larger study we would like to have.

Until about 1670, attacks against the allodium remained limited. Article 383 of the Code Michau of 1629 put all lands under the crown's eminent domain, except on proof of their allodial status, but it does not seem to have been applied any more in the Agenais than elsewhere.[68] Above all, the government counted on an increase in direct taxation.[69] Nevertheless, in the period of financial difficulties that preceded the Fronde, the intendant, Lauson, was ordered to collect the tax that confirmed exemptions from the right of *franc-fief*. He encountered some resistance, and, meanwhile, the consuls of Agen, anxious over the pretensions of the farmers of the domain, pursued the recognition of their freehold.[70]

Beginning in 1670, a vigorous offensive was undertaken with the drawing up of the land register. Colbert excited the zeal of the intendants, d'Aguesseau and de Sève; they and their subdelegates had to require declarations in the presence of notaries commissioned by them, even for property claimed to be allodial; to order seizures against those who were recalcitrant; and to tax expenditures and costs, notwithstanding the opposition.[71] However, against the investigations and the excesses of the revenue farmers, the resistance of the affected parties developed. De Sève finished by putting off the proceedings, but not without demanding a tax of two thousand livres for the confirmation of the privileges of Agen.[72]

Under the direction of the intendant, Faucon de Ris, the proceedings resumed actively after the war with Holland. Declarations and documents of proof were harshly demanded; it was the "great storm" of which the consuls spoke in 1679.[73] The consuls were forbidden to oppose the execution of the land register under any pretext whatever, to summon assemblies on the subject, or to take the side of any individual as syndics of the region of the Agenais.[74] The community endeavored to work on Colbert through the intermediary of its lawyer to the royal council who seemed influential.[75] Conforming to the instructions of the *contrôleur générale*, de Ris authorized the consuls to present "a list of the reasons they had for opposing the land register." If they were well-founded, he would send them to the council along with his opinion, but, while waiting, it was necessary to obey. "You must follow the cautious course," he said to a deputy, "which is to make the declarations, and strive to keep the property under freehold." [76] Following a decree of the council of March 30, 1680, that obliged those possessing estates and property owing dues and obligation to His Majesty, "to make declarations of acknowledgment, even the holders of estates claimed to be freeholds, noble or common," an assembly of the three orders decided to submit, meanwhile seeking to obtain from the intendant "some moderation" of the costs of the declaration and permission to send a delegation to the council "to defend the property." [77]

Beginning in 1692, and with the increase in financial difficulties, there were new alarms.[78] A whole series of measures were directed against the allodium. There were the edicts of September and November 1692 for the recovery of the right of *franc-fief* and taxes that had to be paid by individuals possessing lands in freehold; [79] a memorandum of the intendant, Bazin de Bezons, applying the edicts; [80] other edicts of March and September 1693, which freed estates and fiefs in the king's domain from the charges of lord's due, the *cens,* and rents, on condition of paying the sums decreed by the council.[81] To prevent too heavy taxes and legal proceedings by the revenue farmers—who were "very harassed"—the intendant suggested making a gift to the king. When those involved showed little enthusiasm, he set, by virtue of a roll decreed in the council, seven thousand livres as the sum to pay, and he ordered it to be assessed.[82]

The consuls persisted in invoking their "natural freehold" and consulted with neighboring municipalities.[83] They "were not brought to their senses" and, "using vain pretexts," they delayed drawing up the prescribed rolls—"a delay prejudicial to the interests of the king." [84] In July 1696, the intendant ascertained the nonpayment of the tax and forced the consuls and six of the principal inhabitants to billet troops. At the request of the revenue farmers, seizures of property began, and the community had to bow—all the while reserving the rights, franchises, and privileges of the city.[85]

However, the payment of the tax for the exemptions did not shelter the Agenais from new inquiries. In 1696, some individuals had writs issued against them for the payment of the lord's due.[86] The subdelegate, d'Auzac, again ordered, "all individuals holding fiefs—allodial, noble, or common—depending on and owing obligations to the king's domain, to bring before the notary the declarations and acknowledgments necessary for the execution of the land register." [87] Fines and seizures were announced as a consequence. At the end of 1704, a new confirmation of the privileges and exemption from the *franc-fief* entailed the payment of a tax of thirty-three thousand livres.[88] By the beginning of the eighteenth century, the number of freeholders must have been greatly reduced. "There are not 250 houses declared in freehold," noted a deputy in 1693.[89] And Fretteau would speak of the "very small number" of estates shielded from the *directe universelle,* and that were "surrounded by property subjected to this right . . . what remains to submit does not constitute a thousandth part of the Agenais."

It was under these conditions, that the question of rights, until then "eternally undecided," was to be settled once and for all.[90] The decree of the council of September 12, 1746, "proscribed the idea of the natural freehold of the Agenais and Condomois." It declared "that the *directe universelle,* superseding all lord's dues and other seigneurial rights, belonged [to His Majesty] throughout the area of the cities, jurisdictions, and territories of Agen, Condom, Marmande, Mezin .' . . without prejudice to the particular rights and privileges, the holders of which will have to justify them by good and valid titles. . . . His Majesty consequently orders that in the places where the collection of feudal dues has been interrupted under the presupposition of the 'frivolous freehold,' it will be imposed again, in relation to what is paid in the adjacent seigneuries." [91]

Thus disappeared, and not without obstinate resistance,

the allodium in the Agenais. The interest of this episode, which it would be desirable to put into a larger framework, lies less in the example of one of the innumerable local oppositions to the fiscal demands of the royal government, than in the manifestation of an old spirit of liberty that was maintained over the centuries, and in the defense of the right of property, inherited from Roman traditions, and that the bourgeois Constituent Assembly (of 1789–91) would vigorously affirm.

NOTES

1. The essential work remains Emile Chénon, *Etude sur l'histoire des alleux en France* (Paris, 1888). There is a summary in François Olivier-Martin, *Histoire du droit français* (Paris, 1951), 256–257, 300–301, and 642–643. The term *franc-alleu* is most often used in the texts: it seems to describe the right, rather than the domain. However, according to Casenneuve, *Le franc-alleu de la province de Languedoc* (Toulouse, 1645), "one distinguishes the true and legitimate *alleus* [of fiefs] by this word, *franc*. For the Agenais, it is only a question of common *franc-alleu* [or common freehold].

2. *Archives Communales d'Agen*, CC 253, July 8, 1680. [Henceforth cited as A.C.]

3. *Ibid.*, CC 254, July 28, 1683.

4. We know that this formula was opposed in regions of the written law by the rule, "no lord without a title."

5. Best known in the seventeenth century was Galland (a *maître des requêtes*) who wrote *Du franc-alleu et origine des droits seigneuriaux* (Paris, 1637). In 1746, in his memoir cited later on the king's right of eminent domain in the Agenais, Fretteau, an inspector general of the domain, would define this pretension in the following terms: "One cannot call into doubt that the king possesses the *directe universelle*—that is original ownership, superior to all the inheritances in the kingdom."

6. Robert Boutruche, *Une société provinciale en lutte contre le régime féodal: l'alleu en Bordelais et en Bazadais du XIe au XVIIIe siècle* (Rodez, 1947).

7. In particular, series BB, nos. 55 to 67; CC, nos. 243 to 267 and 381 to 395.

8. *Archives départementales de Gironde*, C 2286. [Henceforth cited as A.D.]

9. The opponents of the *franc-alleu* thus invoked the transfer to England of the royal titles. On March 13, 1679, the intendant, de Ris, reported to Colbert that the work on the land register was difficult, because it had never been done and because all the titles of the king had been carried away to England when the English were the masters of the province (A.N. G7 131).

10. A.C., CC 248.

11. *Ibid.*, BB 58, fol. 376v.

12. *Ibid.*, BB 64.

13. For example, the homage rendered to Edward III in 1363, invoked in a memoir for the farmer general of the domain of France in 1687 (A.C., CC 256).

14. A.C., CC 256, Beaulac to the consuls of Agen, June 28, 1686.

15. The *franc-alleu* was confirmed by a decree of the council on May 22, 1667, that recognized that there was no seigneur, not even the king, without a title (Chenon, *Etude*, 212).

16. Eugène Jarry, *Provinces et pays de France: Essai de géographie historique* (Paris, 1948), II, 8–10.

17. A.C., CC 255.

18. *Ibid.,* CC 255.

19. The statement of the *procureur du roi* in the *présidial* of Agen that the affair of the *franc-alleu* was of interest "to all sorts of people of many different circumstances and qualities" appears to have applied only to the city (A.C., BB 67).

20. Aside from Agen, there were Marmande, Tournon, Villeneuve, Penne, Monflanquin, Mézin, and Condom.

21. A.C., CC 255.

22. As the memoir on crafts of 1691 shows (A.C., HH 32).

23. *De l'estendue, ressort et nombre des officiers du Présidial,* Tamizey de Laroque ed. (Paris and Bordeaux, 1874), 237–239.

24. In 1645, there were in the *présidial* 29 presidents, lieutenants, and councillors; 8 lesser officers; 39 *procureurs;* 24 notaries; and numerous lawyers. Among the consuls in 1665, one finds only 1 lawyer among 2 gentlemen, 2 bourgeois, and a doctor; but from 1674, the men of the law formed at least half of the *consulat.* On the role of the *présidial* officers, see Pierre Goubert, "Les officiers royaux des présidiaux, bailliages et élections dans la société française du XVIIe siècle," *Dix-septième siècle,* Nos. 42–43 (1959), 54–57.

25. A.C., CC 254 and CC 261. From 1693 the declarations of property in *franc-alleu* fell to less than 250 after investigations that resulted in the transformation of many freeholds into lands held under obligation (A.C., CC 259).

26. A.C., CC 256.

27. *Ibid.,* CC 255.

28. And which was to increase more and more with the growth of the population.

29. A.C., CC 243 (Gilbert, deputy of the region at Paris to the consuls of Agen, 8, 22 July, 1663 and 4 November).

30. Pierre Clément, *Lettres, instructions, et mémoires de Colbert* (Paris, 1881–1882), 10 vols., II, 303.

31. *Ibid.,* II, 334.

32. *Ibid.,* II, 303.

33. A.C., CC 259.

34. On the characteristic attitudes of the *trésoriers de France* during the Fronde crisis, see Roland Mousnier, "Recherches sur les syndicats d'officiers pendant la Fronde," *Dix-septième siècle,* Nos. 42–43 (1959), 76–117.

35. A.C., BB 58, fols. 213 and 221v.

36. A.D., C 4765 (general regulation of December 19, 1670, and the ordinances of the intendant, d'Aguesseau, of July 23 and September 8, 1671).

37. A.N. G7 131 (a letter of de Ris to Colbert of August 8, 1679, on the subject of the land register in the city of Bordeaux and its suburbs. In the same letter, he foresaw incidents over the *franc-alleu,* because of the "pretended privileges" of many cities).

38. A.N., G7 131.

39. *Ibid.,* G7 1.

40. A.C., CC 395.

41. *Ibid.,* CC 253.

42. A.C., CC 255.

43. In particular, by the regulations of December 1670 and July 1673 noted above.

44. A.C., BB 62, fols. 216 and 233; CC 264.

45. *Ibid.,* BB 65; CC 254 and 264.

46. *Ibid.,* CC 256.

47. In a letter to de Sève on September 22, 1673, Colbert wrote, "It is necessary that those like you, who by their character or their occupation must have more zeal and warmth for the service of the king, not be content to act and work only when required or pressed to it by the *traitants* (revenue farmers)." (Clément, *Lettres de Colbert,* II, 291).

48. A.C., CC 248 and CC 256.

49. A.C., CC 248 (ordinance of de Sève of January 30, 1674).

50. A.N., G7 132.

51. A.C., FF 182.

52. Abbé R. L. Alis, *Histoire de la ville d'Aiguillon* (Agen, 1895), 271–299.

53. A.C., CC 243; BB 64 and FF 203; CC 253; FF 189.

54. *Ibid.,* BB 58, fol, 221; CC 243.

55. *Ibid.,* CC 254.

56. In 1746, Fretteau declared, in his memoir already cited, that the affair "has remained undecided up to today."

57. There are many examples and quaint details, particularly concerning the trips by water from Agen to Bordeaux, in the documents.

58. A.C., CC 254, 259, 396 (for examples of legal fees and charges). The legal fees simply for obtaining a decree rose to 216 livres in 1663 (CC 243).

59. A.C., FF 189.

60. A.N., G7 131 (De Ris to Colbert, February 20, 1680).

61. A.C., CC 253.

62. Boutruche, *Une société provinciale,* 140.

63. A.C., CC 253. The assemblies were banned by de Ris in 1680.

64. For example, the tax on arts and crafts in 1674, and then in 1691, and the frequent repurchase of offices. As for the major taxes, the *taille* in the *élection* of Agen went from 443,000 livres in 1661 to 562,000 livres in 1693, to which the *capitation* would be added (A.D., C 2681, 4734, 4796).

65. A.C., HH 29.

66. *Ibid.,* BB 64.

67. *Ibid.,* CC 248.

68. Boutruche, *Une société provinciale,* 140.

69. In the *élection* of Agen, the *taille* passed from 123,000 livres in 1635 to 474,000 livres in 1659; it then stabilized at a little more than 440,000 livres until the Dutch War (A.D., C 3990, 3993, 4796).

70. A.C., AA 20; BB 55 and 58.

71. A.D., C 4765 (printed regulation of the royal council of December 18,

1670, implemented by d'Aguesseau). On August 13, 1671, de Séve and other commissioners investigating the domain lands issued a judgment ordering the owners of lands that were said to be allodial, who could not justify the *franc-alleu* with good and valid titles, to place the lands under the jurisdiction of His Majesty, because these regions no longer were part of Languedoc (A.C., CC 248).

72. A.C., CC 248. "But finally we had to give in, like the whole province," wrote one of the consuls (A.C., BB 58).

73. *Ibid.*, BB 64.

74. *Ibid.*, CC 253 (ordinance of de Ris, September 18, 1679).

75. *Ibid.*, BB 64. The deputy was Frizon, at whose death in 1685, the consuls declared, "The community has had a severe loss."

76. *Ibid.*, BB 62, fol. 240.

77. *Ibid.*, BB 63. The intendant had just written to Colbert on May 13 that the work on the land register was going well in the *généralité*, and that "soon only the *sénéchaussées* of Agen and Condom will remain" (A.N., G7 131). His true opinion appears to have been expressed in a letter to Pontchartrain on April 6, 1686: "I have always been astonished that the council did not finish the affair of the *franc-alleu* in the province of Guyenne . . . in order to complete a perfect land register" (A.N., G7, 133).

78. And also, the offensive against communal liberties that was marked by the celebrated edict of August 1692. On this question, see Charles Petit-Dutaillis, *Les communes françaises: caractères et évolution des origines au XVIIIe siècle* (Paris, 1947), 315. In 1696, the number of consuls of Agen was reduced from six to four (A.C., BB 67).

79. A.N., G7 6.

80. A.C., CC 258.

81. *Ibid.*, CC 259.

82. *Ibid.*, BB 67. This decree of 1694 set 400,000 livres as the free gift for the affranchisement of the houses in the *généralité*.

83. A.C., CC 259.

84. *Ibid.*,CC 259 (ordinance of Bazin de Bezons of July 26, 1694).

85. *Ibid.*, BB 67.

86. *Ibid.*, CC 263.

87. *Ibid.*,CC 254 (ordinance of June 23, 1704). The wording that was used tended to place all estates under the royal jurisdiction.

88. *Ibid.*, DD 32.

89. *Ibid.*, CC 259.

90. *Ibid.*, CC 267.

91. A.D., C 2289. Also see the royal letters patent of January 8, 1753, "for the continuation of the land register in the counties of Agenais and Condomois" (A.D., C 2287).

3

ABSOLUTISM AND ELITES

Because themes of conflict have so dominated the historical conception of state and society in seventeenth-century France, the harmonies that prevailed are often overlooked. Particularly the social attitudes that were shared by crown and elites alike served as a stabilizing and cohesive force. Throughout many of the articles in this anthology has run the theme of a social fear that reduced the ardor of provincial notables for revolt and promoted a certain detente between the monarchy and the privileged. The perception of the poor as a threatening class may have, as Lemarchand suggests, stimulated the social conservatism that bound all of the ruling orders together under the king. But there were also more subtle social attitudes at work, and they are illustrated in Grassby's article on the failure of France to produce a commercial nobility. Whatever the political advantages that Louis XIV drew from maintaining the old social order, there can be no doubt that the very mentality of the king was imbued with the hierarchical model of society and with the keen sense, which Richelieu shared, that honor resided in the nobility alone. Conversely, the nobles and the notables looked to the king as the ultimate sanction of the society that, by and large, served them so well. Between state and elites, then, there existed continuing sources of friction, but, as Montesquieu would later see, in the end the crown and the various nobilities stood together.

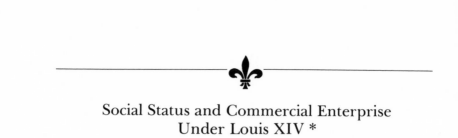

Social Status and Commercial Enterprise
Under Louis XIV *

BY R. B. GRASSBY

In Restoration England, the distinction between wealth and honour was a subject for comedy and malicious conversation, but ridicule could not permanently impair the prestige of the successful merchant, nor gossip degrade the legal status of a peer in trade. Across the channel, however, the distinction was taken more seriously. The rank and file of the French *noblesse,* those families which neither attended the Court nor sat in the *Parlements,* chose to perpetuate a scale of values and a system of rewards reminiscent of the Heroic Age. To them the *raison d'être* of the merchant was the acquisition of material wealth, his dominant motive personal gain. For his base and calculating virtues a fortune was ample recompense. Social prestige, on the other hand, should be reserved for those who displayed valour or piety, and who devoted themselves without remuneration or distraction to serve the community on the battlefield and in the chancel.

This artificial distinction sprang from the prejudices and fears of noble families, who saw their social position threatened by the wealth of the *Tiers État.* It had no basis in fact. Demographic and economic forces had transformed beyond recognition that legendary feudal *noblesse* which survived in the law books, and the status and prestige of the *noblesse* had survived, not

* Quotations from original sources have been modernized and translated, but technical terms in common use have not been anglicized. All printed works, unless otherwise indicated, are published at Paris. Of the many persons from whose criticism this paper has benefited. I am particularly indebted to Mr. K. V. Thomas and Prof. J. S. Bromley.

through military prowess or public service, but because of the wealth and privileges inherited from the past. So long as this wealth remained intact, the purchase of nobility by wealthy *roturiers* was gloomily accepted as unpleasant, but inevitable. But by the accession of Louis XIV, a redistribution of the increasing wealth of France had accelerated this natural process, and the consequent confusion in the social hierarchy had converted acceptance into hostility. As economic conditions enriched the merchant interest, and impoverished those *gentilhommes champêtres* deprived of the pensions of the Court and the sinecures of the Church, so the survival of the rural *noblesse* seemed to depend on a rigid distinction between wealth and honour. As the methods of translating money into social status were facilitated and augmented by an impoverished and calculating Crown, so determined efforts were made to draw a more distinct line between the *noblesse* and the *Tiers État*. Birth was no longer a practical criterion of nobility, because few *gentilhommes* had ancient or impeccable pedigrees, and the traditional hallmarks of nobility—the possession of fiefs, exemption from the *taille,* and an extravagant *mode de vie*—were easily accessible to wealthy *roturiers.* So the provincial *noblesse* revived in the early seventeenth century the ancient, but dormant custom of derogation, and declared the status of nobility incompatible with trade. An act of self-sacrifice, the voluntary rejection of business was expected to separate the sheep from the goats, and by renouncing the only means of restoring their economic position the rural families hoped to avert their annihilation as a class. This did not discourage the ambitious merchant. By service to the Crown, by marriage, and by the purchase of noble fiefs or legal offices, he continued to acquire both the form and substance of hereditary nobility. Indeed the attitude of the *noblesse* merely encouraged this process, for the lower the status of trade the more imperative it was for the socially conscious merchant to enter the *noblesse.* But it did separate the business from the social world.[1]

This schism constituted a severe impediment to the development of French trade. The driving force of vanity was divorced from and opposed to the creative energy of the acquisitive instinct. Where they could be combined, in the acquisition of the financial privileges of nobility, it was to the detriment of trade. Because nobility was now defined in terms of exclusion from trade, it was impossible for the merchant to revert to trade without endangering his expensively acquired dignity. The prejudice against trade immobilized therefore the capital and energies, not only of the *ancienne noblesse* but also of newly ennobled merchants who, to preserve their status, invested their commercial profits in office, land and government bonds, and lived as *rentiers*. Only those who could not afford nobility remained in trade, and they were the least well equipped to replace their more successful predecessors. The economic significance of this loss of capital and experience can be exaggerated.[2] Some of this capital did return to trade through the medium of government investment, and withdrawal from trade by the third generation of a business family was common even in commercially advanced countries like England. Nor can the slow rate of economic growth in France be explained simply by reference to the structure of French society.[3] That is to ignore the influence of geography and opportunity, the movements of population and prices, and the other objective factors that limit the role of incentive in economic development. Nevertheless, it is clear that social attitudes did create an important obstacle to French commercial expansion, and it is both appropriate and useful to ask why these attitudes persisted, what attempts were made to change them, and why they were unsuccessful.

1

The contempt of Frenchmen for trade had not escaped the attention of contemporary observers. Dazzled by the brilliant expansion of English and Dutch trade, French commentators throughout the seventeenth century had sought the elusive key which would explain why France, with her favourable geographical position, her great natural resources, and her reserve of skilled and industrious manpower, had failed to emulate her political and religious rivals. Foremost among the explanations ranked the divorce of wealth from honour. Not all writers went as far as the author who believed that 'wealth is no more sought for its own sake: it is principally desired because it can lead to honour'.[4] But throughout the profuse economic literature of the period can be detected a conviction that the desire for riches was not the only incentive to trade, and that the desire for social status should be turned to productive use. Many a pamphleteer writing about bullion or a reckoner compiling tables of compound interest felt it necessary to point out the attitude of indifference towards business, and the prejudices which alienated both the *noblesse* and the merchant interest from commerce.[5] The discussion normally centred on the sale of office, a practice attacked from its inception, but seen increasingly as a sponge absorbing the energies of the business world. This stream of comment was swollen by much repetition and imitation. Many authors were propagandists or patriots, hired to defend a private interest or eager to whip up nationalist feeling, and others through missionary zeal could not resist extravagant overstatements of their case. But a few examples from the more intelligent and original thinkers will show not only that the problem had received thorough analysis, but also that practical solutions had been devised.

At the core of the problem was seen the prejudice against trade. If commerce was considered an honourable profession the problem would disappear, because the *noblesse* would no longer fear absorption by an inferior class, and merchants would not have to abandon trade to win social respect. The obvious solution seemed therefore to elevate the status of business as a profession, and many pamphleteers charged themselves with this very task. To balance the traditional scale of values, they advanced two lines of argument, that commerce could not be ignored because it played an indispensable rôle in national life, and that it could not be scorned because it embraced both the objectives and qualities characteristic of the *noblesse*. The utility of trade in its material aspects did not require elaboration, but the extent of its influence and benefits needed further clarification. This work was best and most fully done by three well-known writers of the early seventeenth century—the irrepressible Huguenot adviser of Henry IV, Bartholomew de Laffemas, the Huguenot rebel and dramatist Antoine de

Montchrétien, and the historian, polemicist and monk Jean Eon. Laffemas abandoned the blank verse and musical scores characteristic of his early pamphlets, and vividly contrasted the limited function of the static privileged orders with the productive function and international renown of merchants, who bridged great oceans and on their letters of credit raised great fortunes.[6] Eon, in his classic work *Le Commerce Honorable,* rounded off the pioneer work of Montchrétien. He invoked the imagery and philosophy of pagan Antiquity, the wishes of the Almighty and the historical examples of primitive Israel and contemporary Europe, to show that trade was not the preserve of grasping and petty usurers, but the source of social stability, national prosperity, political power, and civilized life. He argued that overseas trade brought prosperity not only to individual merchants, but to all members of society. It provided money for the needs of government and war, markets for the agricultural produce of the landowners, employment for the younger sons of the *noblesse,* new endowments for the Church and learning, litigation for the lawyers, work for the artisans and relief for the poor.[7]

Utility however was not enough. To place commerce on an equal footing with the more traditional occupations required a purification of the acquisitive instinct, an appeal to those qualities most admired by the *noblesse.* Consequently emphasis was placed on the glory, rather than the material benefits, which resulted from trade, its aggressive instead of its sober qualities. Many pamphleteers were unashamed patriots who believed, not without justification, that the world's resources were finite, and who therefore envisaged trade as a continuous war on the prosperity of other states. There were a few men who thought that God had distributed natural resources unequally over the world to encourage peace and brotherhood. But most contemporaries were convinced that trade was not to be shared but conquered and defended, and in this belief they approached the military and spiritual objectives of feudal society. The predatory instincts of the *noblesse* could easily be identified with the conquest of markets, with territorial colonization, with the gamble of speculative investment, and with privateering, in an age when piracy was often indistinguishable from honest trade. To these elements of risk and adventure could be added the prospect of missionary work in overseas lands, the conversion of the heathen, and a crusade against the prosperous heretics of the world. These arguments had been developed by Eon, a disciple of *la gloire* and quick to notice that the military and naval power, developed under pressure of war, could further and protect French shipping and interests in time of peace. But the best example of this type of propaganda is the treatise, commissioned by Colbert and written by the *académicien* Charpentier, to attract investors to the revived *Compagnie des Indes Orientales*. The flamboyant preamble to this treatise exploited the glamour of the Orient, the brilliant success of the Dutch and Portuguese, and the infinite glory of a commercial Empire conquered from the enemies of France by the bravery of the *noblesse* and the energy and intelligence of the *Tiers État*.[8] Hard work and thrift might be the founding virtues of successful business, but honour could only derive from a display of courage and devotion.

By these arguments contemporary writers hoped to discredit the false antithesis between trade and the functions characteristic of a feudal hierarchy. They realized however that more direct action was necessary to remove the fears as well as the prejudices of the *noblesse* and merchants. The *noblesse* should be protected against loss of status should they enter trade, and some means should be found to honour merchants without forcing them to buy office and to leave business. The pamphleteers had provided a reasoned basis for the fusion of the two classes; it was the task of the Crown, as head of the social order, to translate their policies into reality. The various measures proposed do not need individual citation. Many were quickly stereotyped and others, like proposals to convert the conspicuous consumption of the Court into commercial capital, have only a bizarre significance. It will suffice to record the views of three important writers—the astonishingly precocious Louis Turquet de Mayerne, the humane Cassandra from Blésois, Du Noyer, and the spokesman of the urban nobility of Marseille, the priest Marchetti. In his *Monarchie Aris-*

todemocratique, written at the end of the sixteenth century, Mayerne argued not only that the *noblesse* was entitled to trade, but that this was the only occupation which could justify their privileges, and that merchants should by virtue of their productive function rise automatically to the *noblesse.*[9] Mayerne, who had made a fortune in business and had married his granddaughter into the *noblesse,* possessed a clearer conception of a business aristocracy than any other French writer of the period. His main ideas were echoed however by Du Noyer, who criticized the parasitic court *noblesse* and the imitative merchant, and who wanted to force the *noblesse* to invest in trade, and to ennoble merchants who invested in shipping on condition that they remained in business.[10] A different approach was made by Marchetti, writing to protect the *noblesse commerçante* of Marseille from a governmental inquiry into usurpations of nobility. Diverted occasionally by the necessity of pleasing the royal commissioners, he yet produced a coherent scheme for maintaining the social status of both the nobles and merchants actively engaged in trade.[11] Most of these scattered proposals were eventually codified by Jacques Savary, himself a descendant of a noble line which had reverted to commerce in the fifteenth century, a man who knew the risks of investment in office, and a member of the commercial aristocracy of Paris, the *corps de merciers.*[12] The best known and most widely read pamphleteer of the century, Savary did not make any original contribution to the literature of the period, but as the person employed by Colbert to help draft a new commercial Code, his words had great authority and a receptive audience. In his *Parfait Négociant* he transmitted both his own experience and the best ideas of previous writers to those with the power and inclination to reform.

Not all pamphlets enjoyed serious consideration, and many may have shared the fate of one anonymous treatise upon whose pages its purchaser composed amorous verse.[13] But the Crown, to which advice was generally directed, was both sensitive to such literature and a great publisher of this sort of material. It needed little persuasion to accept the importance of trade, and the utility and honour of commerce had been a commonplace of royal preambles since the fifteenth century. Eager to extend its authority over the total resources and population of France, the monarchy had from its earliest struggle for centralization encouraged the growth of trade, both to increase the resources available for government and war, and to maintain a level of prosperity without which the stability and security of the state could not be preserved. The social impediments to trade, outlined by professional observers and confirmed by the reports of its own officials, were therefore a source of much concern. This is indicated by the interest taken in the problem by the two greatest royal ministers of the century—Richelieu and Colbert. The Cardinal, who had personally experienced the poverty of the *hobereaux* and whose grasp of the importance of economic power pervades his *Testament Politique,* expressed a desire to attract the *noblesse* into trade, and to 'suppress offices firmly, and give value to traffic and rank to merchants.' [14] He created on paper a hereditary Catholic order of knighthood, drawn from the wealthier merchants as well as from the two privileged orders, with the express duty of extending French trade and Catholicism overseas.[15] The more pragmatic *fonctionnaire* Colbert, descended from businessmen who had won social status, also wanted to utilize all social classes to further French trade, and tried to persuade his royal master to elevate the status of commerce by showing his personal approval of businessmen.[16]

The result was that many of the measures proposed by the pamphleteers for the *noblesse* and the merchants were put into effect. The safeguards against derogation, enjoyed by nobles residing in commercial and banking centres like Marseille and Lyon, were confirmed, and investors were attracted to the companies launched by the Crown for overseas commerce and colonization by provisos protecting them from derogation in the charters of foundation.[17] No effort was spared to force the *noblesse* to invest in the *Compagnie des Indes* in 1664, including personal pressure at Court and a careful tuning of the pulpits,[18] and further protection from derogation was afforded by the sale of 'lettres de réhabilitation.' An even more direct challenge to the binding force of local custom came from royal edicts. The precocious Louis XI had projected an ordinance opening trade "by sea, land and inland waterways" to the *noblesse*,[19] but his contemporaries and immediate successors disapproved, and when the *Ordonnance* of Orléans in 1560 codified former legislation and custom concerning derogation, it withdrew the financial privileges of the *noblesse commerçante*.[20] It was not until 1628 that article 452 of the *Code Michau,* under the inspiration of Richelieu, publicly declared overseas trade compatible with nobility.[21] This article represented the limit of royal intervention up to 1701. Colbert's edict of August 1669 did maintain in an enthusiastic preamble that "there is no means more innocent and legitimate to acquire wealth than trade," but it did little more than confirm the existing law.[22] In 1701 the protection against derogation, accorded by the Crown, was still limited to overseas and wholesale trade.

Similar encouragement had been offered to merchants. The Crown recognized the nobility conferred by high municipal office, as at Nantes and Toulouse, and offered nobility to *roturiers* who invested in the commercial companies or in colonial enterprises. Twelve of the associates of the *Compagnie de la Nouvelle France* were, for example, not only granted titles of nobility, but also exempted from the terms of an edict directing the payment of *taille* by nobles of less than twenty years standing.[23] The *Code Michau* conferred the privileges of nobility upon those who maintained a merchant ship of two or three hundred tons for five years, and upon '*marchands-grossiers*' who had become *échevins, consuls,* or *gardes* of their corporations.[24] A more effective measure was the granting of individual letters patent. Louis XI had conferred nobility—though not exemption from the *taille* —upon successful merchants, and his impecunious successors periodically put up letters patent for sale.[25] The financial origin of many of these grants rendered them insecure, because the Crown was always tempted to revoke and resell them, but they were eagerly sought as the most impressive *entrée* to nobility. Only wholesale, colonial, and overseas merchants were, however, eligible for this distinction, and except in financial emergencies the Crown limited these grants to those who armed ships against its enemies, and did not grant them wholesale to the merchant interest.[26]

The limited efforts of the Crown did not make much impression. The *noblesse* was not indifferent to the advantages of trade. Indeed the supreme rôle of commerce had been a familiar feature of the *Cahiers* of the *États-Generaux* since the fifteenth century. The joint *Cahier* of the Three Estates in 1484 described trade as a necessary and useful means of creating abundance, and in 1560 and 1614 the need for government intervention and protection was strongly urged.[27] The *Assemblée des Notables* in 1627 endorsed the opinion of the *Garde des Sceaux,* that trade was a source of both prosperity and honour, and that the *noblesse* should be permitted to participate.[28] The *grande noblesse* had always possessed widespread economic interests, and the rural *gentilhommes* had engaged even in the retail trade by letting their nobility lie 'dormant' while they mended their fortunes. But the fear of social absorption, expressed in the attempts of the *noblesse* in the sixteenth century to enforce sumptuary legislation, had by the middle of the seventeenth century driven the *noblesse* away from trade back to the land.[29] Brittany, formerly the scene of the most active participation by the *noblesse* in trade, rigidly enforced the exclusion of nobles from commerce, and even the 'mystery' of glassmaking, the one trade permitted for artistic reasons by immemorial custom to the *gentilhommes,* was not widely practised.[30] As the custom of derogation grew more binding, and when after 1665 the Crown appointed commissions to enquire into usurpations of nobility, the *noblesse* were reluctant to risk participation in business, because loss of rank also entailed loss of the financial privileges without which they felt their economic position would be intolerable. The *grande noblesse* continued to dabble in speculation and to glean the financial pickings of the Court, but the rank and file of the *noblesse,* so far as can be ascertained, vegetated on the land and remained on the perimeter of trade and industry. As the *noblesse* refused to become a *noblesse commerçante,* so the merchant interest continued to play the *bourgeois gentilhomme.* Refused the opportunity of buying patents of nobility, compatible with trade, the wealthy merchant continued to seek his social salvation by the purchase of offices which could not be combined with business. Government action had therefore been both half-hearted in application and limited in effect, and contemporary writers had reason to complain that the glowing promises of royal preambles had not been fulfilled.

2

This situation might have continued unchanged but for the pressure of economic difficulties at the end of the seventeenth century. The successors of Colbert, although they followed his precepts devoutly, could not cope with the extraordinary cost and injuries of the Nine Years War, and by 1700, although the peace brought some relief, the economic position of France was far from satisfactory. At a time when the treaties of Ryswick constituted a check to the political ambitions and international prestige of France, the *mémoires* of the *Intendants* indicated economic stagnation.[31] In contrast, the heretical limited monarchies of England and Holland were humiliating examples of prosperity and *grandeur*. As an instrument to reverse this situation and restore French trade, the Crown decided in 1700 to revive the *Conseil de Commerce* used in the past by Laffemas, Fouquet, and Colbert. This was the advisory board of Colbert's *Conseil* pruned of its administrative functions and the royal presence. It gave full regional representation to the merchant interest of France for the first time, by summoning deputies from the chief commercial towns, and as their first task it instructed the deputies to present individual *mémoires* on the state of trade in general.[32] Intended as a symbol of royal determination to help French trade in every possible way, the *Conseil* marked a co-operative effort by both the leading merchants and government officials to cure the evils of the French economy. From this burst of energy was to come the final attempt to solve the dichotomy between commerce and social status.

Submitted during the winter of 1700 the reports of the deputies of the *Conseil,* although they embraced every aspect of economic life, brought the social question to the fore.[33] Many deputies doubtless spoke to justify and defend, as well as to explain, and often expressed their personal opinions rather than the views of the towns they represented.[34] Although they all had experience of business, they had normally retired before their election and now possessed private political interests in addition to the commercial interests of their home towns. But their conclusions, arrived at by independent observation and thought, proved to be remarkably similar, and taken together give an authoritative picture of France. Much time was devoted to an attack on *'Colbertisme'* as applied by Colbert's successors—the monopoly of the royal companies, the impediments of tariffs and taxation, the restriction of trade by unnecessary regulation. But they also restated in classic form the social reasons envisaged by earlier writers for French backwardness. All but two of the deputies emphasized that the profit motive must be reinforced by social recognition for merchants.

At the core of the problem they placed the fact that prestige remained identified with political and military splendour. The deputy of Bayonne contrasted republics like Holland, where prestige was unceremoniously sacrificed to profit, with monarchies like France whose 'genius prefers glory and the profession of arms . . . which had prevented serious attention being paid to commerce, which had never been regarded as a serious business.'[35] It was considered essential to reverse this order of priorities, to treat the pursuit of wealth as an end in itself, and not merely as a means to the traditional end of military glory. Du Hallay, the brilliant deputy of Nantes, hoped that the bellicose instincts of France were satisfied by the late wars, that now she would acquire the 'commercial spirit' necessary to snatch commercial supremacy from the English and the Dutch.

French merchants, they complained, were always in the pillory. According to the deputy of La Rochelle, the most eminent merchants—even those who had become *juge-consuls*—were 'no more respected than the common people'[36]; the ignorant prejudice against trade remained so strong, added the deputy of Dunkirk, that the *noblesse* remained reluctant to enter

211

commerce.[37] Indeed, such was the scorn of the *officiers* and *fermiers*, remarked Du Hallay, that a dowry of 10,000 *livres* could not guarantee the daughters of merchants a socially advantageous marriage, and civic distinctions were conditional upon leaving trade.[38] A major difficulty was the ambiguity of the term *'marchand'*.[39] The greatest merchant bore the same title as his tailor, and was associated in popular imagination with the fraudulent pedlar and the hated shopkeeper. To make it worse, pointed out the deputy of Bayonne, the only Frenchmen who did make commerce 'so to speak the sole subject of their attention' were those excluded by their religious faith from all other professions, and they were now excluded from France.[40] Reluctant martyrs for commercial progress, successful merchants abandoned trade as soon as they could afford to purchase the respect which accompanied the ownership of land or office. To the deputies this was both justified and inevitable. Had not Mésnager, the deputy of Rouen, left trade ten years earlier to become *'sécretaire du roi'*, and did not Héron, the deputy of La Rochelle, devote his time and salary, in later years, not to service in the *Conseil*, but to litigation over a similar office? [41] The blame, if any, the deputies of Lyon and Lille emphasized, was due to the endless creation and sale of posts, to which undue social superiority was attached.

Whatever the explanation, the effect was rightly considered harmful. Not only, said the deputy of Lille, did these posts 'divert the minds of the people from the attention that they should pay to trade', but merchants borrowed so heavily to purchase them that 'reasons of interest, more pressing than those of honour scarcely allow them to fill their posts with dignity'.[42] Even worse was the effect on capital accumulation and commercial efficiency of this flight from commerce. The techniques of business could not be acquired in a moment, and only rigorous training of the new generation of merchants by the old could produce skilled personnel. But, said Du Hallay, 'our young men prefer to study French airs, and to acquire polish, rather than to apply themselves to serious matters',[43] and daily bankruptcies were evidence of amateurs without capital or experience. This was not the whole story. The deputy and former mayor of St-Malo pointed out that in his port everybody lived by trade, and merchants sent their children overseas to gain experience; yet trade was depressed.[44] Nevertheless the basic problem remained. The humiliation to which merchants were reduced by French society was starving French commerce of incentives, capital and skill, and thereby contributing towards economic decay.

The solutions that the deputies advised were as familiar as their analysis. The prejudice against trade must be forcibly attacked, and various devices employed to break down the barriers between the *noblesse* and the commercial world. The right to trade without derogation should be confirmed by the Crown and extended, many deputies thought, to the *noblesse de la robe* and to include both apprenticeship and wholesale business within France. Municipal posts and consular judicatures could be confined to merchants, and their holders put on equal footing with the *avocats* and *officiers*. But the central solution offered was to grant 'some marks of honour' to those who would excel at commercial enterprise. When debating a project to create provincial counterparts of the *Conseil de Commerce* in the provinces, the deputies had firmly rejected a proposal to convert them into commercial equivalents of the *Parlements,* by making the posts in these *Chambres de Commerce* noble and hereditary.[45] But most of them did want to create an active commercial nobility, and recommended the granting of nobility to families which had remained from three to four generations in trade, and to those who would serve as deputies in the *Chambres de Commerce* once they were established. Distinction *vis-à-vis* the other orders of society necessitated distinctions within the commercial world. The majority agreed with the deputy of La Rochelle, that all those engaged in wholesale and overseas commerce should be distinguished from other '*marchands*' by the title '*négociant*', and that only those enrolled as *négociants* should enjoy the privileges and honours previously suggested.[46] The solution seemed at hand; only a warning from Du Hallay about the complexity of the problem and the technical difficulties of the solution gave any indication of the trials to come.

On the strength of these *mémoires* the commissioners of the

Conseil ordered the deputies to co-ordinate their proposals,[47] and after two weeks of discussion and revision the deputies produced a joint report.[48] This incorporated their original suggestions safeguarding the privileges, exemptions, and precedence of the *noblesse commerçante,* but was chiefly concerned with elaborating their proposals to honour merchants. To clarify the distinction between *'négociants'* and *'marchands',* they differentiated wholesale commerce from retailing by the size, weight, and value of merchandise involved.[49] When a *'marchand'* wished to become a *'négociant',* he would apply to his local *Chambre de Commerce* or consular jurisdiction with proof of his change to wholesaling; if he reverted to retailing, he would be permanently excluded from his title, usurpation of which would entail heavy fines. Similar but lower fines faced *artisans* or *ouvriers* who called themselves *'marchands'.* Certain privileges, exemptions, and rights of precedence were proposed for *'négociants',* immediately forfeited however if they went bankrupt. They would enjoy the right to hold posts as high as *Trésorier de France* and to trade freely without the obligation to enter a *corps de marchands* or to justify apprenticeship. They would be exempt from *ban* and *arrière ban* if they owned noble land, and from billeting, watch, and guard, if and when they held office as *juge-consuls;* and they would take precedence immediately after the *officiers* of the *Présidiaux.* But the crowning proposal was the prospect of nobility. Letters of nobility would be offered to the fourth generation of families which had an honourable and continuous tradition of wholesale commerce; to ensure proof of this ancestry, merchants would in future enrol their names at the consular jurisdictions. For their own efforts the deputies requested the title of *conseiller du roi.*

3

Copies of this *mémoire* were now sent to those towns which sent deputies to the *Conseil.* Several towns were slow to return their comments, and others had nothing to say. But the remaining replies, in their detail and comprehensiveness, constitute a poll of commercial opinion unparalleled since Colbert's quest for capital for the *Compagnie des Indes.* Coming as they did from every important commercial centre in the provinces, they give substance to the elaborate guesswork by which the attitudes of the merchant interest are normally deduced, and reflect the regional variations and vested interests which dominated French trade.[50] The deputies had sought a legislative formula applicable to, and in the best interests of, the whole body of French merchants. But relations between the *noblesse* and the towns varied from region to region, and even the outward forms of social status were not uniform throughout France. Consequently their formula could not meet every need and created severe problems of administration. These technical difficulties were fostered and enlarged by the predominance of powerful local interests. The commercial towns were divided not only by distance and geography, but also by historical development and private interests. Certain towns enjoyed special privileges and consideration, such as the monopoly of certain types and areas of trade, and they competed with each other for prosperity and influence. It was natural, therefore, that they should regard the proposals of the deputies not from the standpoint of the merchant interest as a whole, but from the benefits and disadvantages which would accrue to their own town and region. The Basque town of Bayonne, declining without sympathy or attention, sought direct assistance, and wished 'that a more effective method could be found to induce merchants to remain in their profession'. The Channel port of St-Malo was only concerned to confirm her right to confine municipal posts to merchants. The comments of the towns do more than illustrate the technical difficulties of enforcing the plans of the deputies; they indicate the provincialism and lack of unity among French merchants, which augured ill for the success of reform.

Much time was spent on the proposal to attract the *noblesse* into trade. The difficulties of adaptation were quickly spotted. Marseille pointed out that humility was a necessary quality in an apprentice, and Bordeaux that the landed property of the *noblesse* could not easily be converted into movable capital. These doubts do however suggest a reluctance to face competition from a *noblesse commerçante,* and the proposal by Nantes, to

215

compel a long apprenticeship for new recruits to business, probably had the profits of the older hands in mind. Similar fears arose from the proposal to distinguish wholesaling from retailing. The arguments over definition indicate how important retailing was as a source of capital, and all the towns agreed with Bordeaux that a rigid distinction would be harmful, that 'to elevate wholesaling it did not seem necessary to degrade retailing'. Nantes, where several civic dignitaries were retailers, argued that it would suffice to enforce a distinction between *'marchands'* and *'artisans'*, and to oblige *'marchands'* to hyphenate to their title the name of their particular trade. Lyon proposed as an alternative the broad and innocuous definition of wholesaling established in a legal case at Lyon in 1667, in which some local merchants had successfully defended their nobility against imputations of retailing.

Opinions varied on the efficacy of the proposal to ennoble the fourth generation of merchants. Fabre, when he reported to the *Chambre de Commerce* of Marseille, said that he had advised nobility for the third generation, since by the fourth 'a child, who had inherited a considerable fortune from his father would not take advantage (of this proposal) there being other and shorter channels to nobility'. That ancient and venerable assembly thought that this argument would apply even to the third generation, and that compulsory enrolment would prejudice other methods of access to polite society. Nor would the prospect of nobility be a great incentive in Provence, Languedoc and Dauphiné, since in those provinces the *taille* was *réelle* and nobility had less financial significance. This view was not shared by towns of more recent growth. Nantes urged the sale of letters of nobility at regular intervals to merchants, on condition that they remained in trade. Rouen suggested that they should be given and not sold. Despite the narrow outlook of the towns, it is clear that they supported the project in principle, provided that in practice it did not impinge on any of their cherished immunities and prerogatives.

Objections on principle came from an anonymous *mémoire* which restated the classic defence of the *noblesse*,[51] the distinction between wealth and honour. Although, it argued, merchants played an important role in society, yet 'it must be recognised that the wealth which is created by their efforts, enriches them first'. The *noblesse,* on the other hand, had sacrificed their private interests and fortunes to devote themselves to public service, and were therefore entitled to the compensation of honour and privileges. The emigration of merchants from commerce was not serious, because it served to redistribute wealth and to give opportunities for others to rise through business. Moreover, to prevent the buying of office, it was only necessary to exclude merchants from official posts until three years after they had wound up their businesses. Ennoblement would solve little, since experience proved that merchants who acquired nobility quickly severed and denied any connexion with trade. The author was willing to permit some reforms, including a distinction between ordinary wholesale merchants and those who rose to municipal office or seats in the *Chambres de Commerce.* But he emphasized the basic distinction between trade and honour.

Opposition was not confined to the merchants and the *noblesse.* It now came from the representatives of the Crown, the commissioners in the *Conseil de Commerce.* The proposals of the deputies, modified in the light of the comments by the towns, were submitted to the commissioners for their decision. A preliminary draft of their intentions revealed a marked change of emphasis.[52] The commissioners approved the clauses protecting the *noblesse* from derogation, and even extended this protection to guarantee succession to landed property by a noble in business. But the proposals to honour merchants were drastically pruned. The distinction between *'négociants'* and *'marchands',* and all claims to privilege, exemption and precedence by the merchants and deputies were erased. The definition of wholesale trade was considered 'too abbreviated', and the proposal to ennoble the fourth generation was supplanted by the noncommittal statement that the King would grant honours to merchants at his pleasure. Finally in September, when the commissioners moved to Fontainebleau with the Court,[53]

217

they prepared, after private discussion, a rough draft of a royal declaration which they forwarded to the deputies at Paris for their comments.[54]

Less severe than the first reaction to the deputies' proposals, the rough draft still dropped ten of the original twenty-one clauses, and only added a preamble. The *noblesse de la robe* were specifically excluded from trade, but the commissioners approved the apprenticeship of younger sons of the *noblesse d'épée,* if undergone overseas, and even permission to engage in retailing. They took as their definition of wholesale trade an elaborated version of the judgement at Lyon in 1667, and opened municipal posts to merchants who came within this definition, all existing statutes notwithstanding. They retained the proposal to institute compulsory enrolment of wholesale merchants, but left the prospect of nobility for eminent merchants vague. In sharp contrast was the benign and complimentary preamble. The Crown, this declared, had always protected commerce as an essential resource of the state, had 'always regarded wholesale trade as an honourable profession . . . which had even led it on several occasions to grant letters of nobility to some of the principal merchants, to bear witness to the esteem with which those who distinguished themselves in the profession were regarded'. Since the King had discovered that merchants ennobled in this way were excluded by social pressure from trade, and since he was eager to retain merchants and their children in commerce, he had decided to scotch any current misconceptions by public confirmation of his sentiments.

This rough draft was discussed by the deputies in a private session.[55] The preamble evoked no comment, but they objected to the exclusion of 'magistrates and other *Gens du Robe*' from commerce, a proposal which would isolate those merchants who had become office holders. The prohibition of apprenticeship within France was treated as prejudicial to the poorer *noblesse,* who could not afford to send their children overseas, and the proposed permission for the *noblesse* to become retailers was considered prejudicial to merchants. They stood by their original definition of wholesaling, and wanted to abolish all the restrictive regulations of the *corps de marchands,* thus enabling both the *noblesse* and overseas merchants to trade freely within France with foreign merchandise. Nor were the retailers forgotten. Even if they were to be denied equal footing with the *avocats* and *médecins,* they should still be permitted to hold municipal office. Greatest criticism was levelled however against the emasculation of their proposal to ennoble merchants. What had been intended as a permanent incentive to future merchants, they remonstrated, had now been reduced to a hatful of rewards, for careless distribution among those who had already succeeded in commerce.

On 30 December 1701, a Declaration was despatched to the *Parlement* of Paris and other courts for registration.[56] This was the rough draft of the commissioners couched in the plural of Majesty. The only criticism accepted from the deputies was that attacking permission for the *noblesse* to become retailers. All the other articles survived their opposition. The Edict of 1669 was officially confirmed and extended to wholesale and overland trade, but apprenticeship was not mentioned and the *noblesse de la robe* was specifically excluded. Retailers were still excluded from municipal office, and only members of the *noblesse* were freed from the regulations of the *corps de marchands.*[57] A slightly elaborated version of the judgement of 1667 was formally accepted as a definition of wholesale commerce. Some clauses from the original *mémoire* were preserved intact. Certain posts were open to wholesale merchants without obligation to leave trade or to obtain *lettres de comptabilité,* and compulsory enrolment and forfeiture for bankruptcy remained. But the key proposal of ennoblement was left obscure: the King would grant honours at his pleasure.

The Declaration was more than a confirmation of the Edict of 1669, and did provide a partial remedy for the social problem. Wholesale trade within France was permitted by law to the *noblesse* for the first time, a right extended on request in March 1702 to subsidiary manufactures.[58] Many merchants were ennobled as promised, notably deputies like Fénellon and Du Hallay, who retired with honour from the debate, and many others purchased letters of nobility from a government struggling to finance the War of Spanish Succession.[59] For merchants like Pierre Colomès, who had acquired nobility through municipal office, the Declaration was a godsend. It decided the case which he had been fighting against the commissioners into usurpations of nobility for nearly a decade, and enabled him to bring up his children in trade as he desired.[60] For those who, throughout the century, had advocated a social hierarchy based on commerce, it was nevertheless a defeat; the Crown had effectively rejected the programme of parity between the *noblesse* and the merchant interest. The issue was re-opened in 1757 and 1767 by the next generation of literary reformers, but no further legislative action was taken, and the decision of 1701 survived until the Revolution. It is significant that when, in December 1701, the deputies had to defend themselves against charges of incompetence, they did not mention the project to honour commerce in their list of achievements.[61]

4

It is tempting to dismiss these abortive attempts to create a business aristocracy as utopian. Plausible arguments can be advanced to suggest that the ideas, developed by economic writers and accepted by the commercial advisers of the Crown, were incapable of realization because they contradicted the fundamental interests of the *noblesse* and the merchant interest. On this premise, the prejudice against trade persisted because it embodied rational economic and social interests, against which the Crown was powerless to legislate. In fact the reverse was true. The benefits to the *noblesse* and merchants, which the pamphleteers and deputies had seen in the destruction of the false antithesis between land and trade, were real enough. The only victim of such a change would be the Crown, whose representatives had been responsible for emasculating the project of 1701. In the last analysis, the distinction between social status and trade was maintained by the prejudices of the *noblesse* and merchants, and by the personal interests of the monarchy.

At first glance, nevertheless, the charge of impracticability seems to carry weight. If it was poverty which forced the *noblesse* into trade, how could they raise the capital necessary to start a business? Moreover what training had they received for the skilled and exacting techniques of commerce? Even if they could surmount the initial difficulties of transition, they risked losing their social status and the financial privileges so essential to their economic survival. Were they likely to endanger their certain immunity from taxation for the unknown profits that lay in trade? It appeared more prudent to develop their own land commercially, and not to rely on royal protection against derogation, which might be withdrawn in financial emergencies by the Crown. Furthermore, by entering trade they surrendered the last justification for their financial privileges. The duties of military service and local government, in return for which their rights of immunity had originally been granted, had been rendered obsolete by a professional army and royal centralization of the administration, and only their exclusion from profit-making occupations could forestall public condemnation. It was a vicious circle from which the project to honour trade was no escape.

Similar arguments could be used to show that the merchants had nothing to gain. Was the creation of a rigid commercial caste any solution to the inclination of heirs to business fortunes to enjoy a comfortable life of security and honour? How could the Crown prevent the prodigal son from squandering his father's capital, or the aged merchant from buying an office on which to retire? If office and *rentes* provided both a more secure and a more profitable source of income, nothing but iron regulations could keep capital in trade, which the failures of the great companies and the danger of war had made a very risky source of investment. Quite apart from the technical difficulties of administering the proposals, the interests of most merchants seemed well served by the *status quo*.

It is important however to distinguish between real and apparent interests. The hard fact remains, that under prevailing circumstances both the *noblesse* and the merchants were sacrificing a potential source of income to enjoy social respect. On the other hand, by combining their capital and resources to exploit business opportunities to the full, and by making their wealth and the scale of their activities the criteria for social distinction,

221

they could preserve both wealth and honour. There was no guarantee of profits from trade, and in the process of fusion many would fall by the wayside, but this was happening in any case and at least this new policy offered the prospect of recovery. The financial privileges of the *noblesse* could not preserve them from bankruptcy, and younger sons could be apprenticed and enter trade without a heavy capital outlay. The poorer members of the *noblesse* could provide the manpower, their richer counterparts the capital. Similarly, although the sons of merchants could not be forced to follow in their fathers' footsteps, and while investment in land and office would continue to offer economic and social advantages, it was possible to establish greater fluidity between land and trade. The income from office and *rentes* was by no means secure from speculation, inflation, and repudiation, and many of the offices held by merchants were little more than clerkships. If the barriers between land and trade could be broken down, at least land, office and trade would present competitive fields of investment, between which capital could be easily transferred as needed.

Honour would also be satisfied. So long as the acknowledged symbols and trappings of social status—titles and privileges—were open for sale, little would be gained by trying to distinguish wealth from honour. Furthermore a new justification for social privilege was needed. For the *noblesse* to define their status in terms of unproductivity, and to risk bankruptcy to justify their privileges, was both absurd and dangerous. It brought values into contempt and failed in its intention to discourage merchants from entering the *noblesse*. On the other hand, by granting nobility simply to the rich and successful, irrespective of function, social distinction would be both enhanced by a smaller élite, and anchored to some productive function. The successful exploitation of both land and trade could then serve as the theoretical justification for the privileges and status of their beneficiaries, and the problem of derogation would disappear. Moreover an aristocracy of this type, linked by intermarriage and founded on wealth, would enjoy the political influence without which prestige had a hollow ring.

Both the economic and social interests of the *noblesse* would consequently be preserved by the creation of a *noblesse commerçante*. Some were unable to see this, and did oppose the project on grounds of interest. But the main opposition of the *noblesse* derived from an innate prejudice against trade, which rejected any association with merchants, even in a directorial capacity, and made the co-operative plan for a business aristocracy unworkable. The *Parlement* of Brittany rejected the Declaration of 1701, as being incompatible with the *Coutumes de Bretagne* and the status and duties of the *noblesse*.[62] In Chateaubriand's famous phrase, the age of predominance and privilege had given way to an age of vanities. The reasons for the survival of this prejudice, even when it conflicted with the real interests of the *noblesse,* are by no means clear.[63] Many arguments were advanced to defend this attitude, notably the political stability, self-sufficiency and military strength of a society based on land, the suspicion that money was made at the expense of others, and the belief that business was incompatible with the demands of morality and civilized life. These arguments were as well-worn as the prejudices they defended, and were presented without reference to the actual state of affairs. There was visible and concrete evidence to show that a commercial state could fight great wars and preserve national independence, that capital created employment, and that commercial wealth could be the basis of a leisured class. The explanation behind this sentimental ruralism and fear of change might be that both agriculture and industry, in which the *noblesse* were less reluctant to engage, are productive occupations, while trade and finance are from a layman's point of view merely concerned with exchange. But whatever the reasons, the fact was that these prejudices were much stronger than the more rational arguments advanced by the pamphleteers. Even the efforts by the deputies to use retailing as a scapegoat for the prejudice against commerce could not break down the reluctance of the *noblesse* to fuse with the merchant interest.

Merchants did not share the same prejudices, but neither did they have sufficient faith in the importance of their own profession to obviate the need to seek social respect in the ranks of the *noblesse*. Commerce was still a function, not a profession. Self-respect had not yet supplanted the need for the respect of others; respectability had not replaced honour, and the self-made man could not stand on his own feet. This lack of self-confidence shows that the commercial world still lacked an ideology independent of traditional values, the coherence of a separate class. It had a well-developed hierarchy—a political élite, the *corps de merciers,* and an administrative élite, the *noblesse de la cloche.* But it was difficult to maintain even the basic distinction between wholesalers and retailers, and there was little interest in founding commercial dynasties on the Dutch model. This lack of unity is not surprising, when the disunity of economic life in France is considered. Different regions and towns had developed independently, and local rivalries and jealousies were rampant. There was no dominant commercial centre around which a merchant class could develop, and no system of political representation to bring local interests together. The major fault lay however in the restricted horizon of the merchants themselves. Colbert's impression of French merchants as selfish, narrow-minded individuals, indifferent to public needs and concerned only with preserving their own interests, was not too exaggerated.[64] They were not interested in increasing national prosperity, and bitterly opposed the Huguenots and alien merchants, whose productivity created serious competition. They were reluctant to gain social prestige at the price of economic competition from the *noblesse,* and even when the government took the initiative they were loth to follow. Their ambitions were therefore those of the conservative *rentier* rather than the speculative entrepreneur—the respectability and safe, if modest, income of a small office. So limited and dependent an attitude could not compete with the traditional values of the *noblesse.* Consequently French merchants accepted the social system as it stood, and sought recognition on its terms. So long as they could buy the profitable immunities of the old order and the prestige that accompanied land and office, there was no pressure to develop a different social hierarchy or to join forces with the *noblesse* in business.

Against such opposition the proposals of the deputies could make no headway. They had tried to give commerce the outward forms of nobility, but commercial organization was not amenable to the rules of social precedence. Reform had to come from the bottom as well as from the top, and the merchant preferred to exploit rather than to change the structure of society.

The guarantor of this social system was however the King, and the monarchy was in the strongest position to reform. Nobility on one definition was simply recognition by the Crown, and by throwing the weight of royal prestige and authority into the scales, the prejudices and preferences of the *noblesse* and merchants could have been overcome. Why therefore did the Crown withdraw from a policy created by its own initiative? Although the *noblesse* had received more thorough protection from derogation, the monarchy refused to exploit its power of ennoblement on behalf of merchants, and rejected the project of a business aristocracy. This was partly because Louis XIV did not want to change the structure of society, partly because he could not afford such a change. Although the Crown was the representative of national interests, *vis-à-vis* the interests of local pressure groups, matters of state were inextricably bound up with the person of the monarch and the interests of the dynasty. The proposal to equate commerce with social status, though in the overall interests of the kingdom, was a danger to these private interests.

Fundamentally Louis XIV yearned for the glory of territorial expansion and military power, and preferred the social class most closely associated with these ends. Sometimes these ambitions could be identified with economic interests—the defence of French trade against the English or the attack on Dutch commerce—and Louis never forgot that the financial burden of his military ambitions could only be borne by a prosperous society, and by ruthless exploitation of the social system for financial ends. Consequently the Crown provided the resources, energy and initiative lacking among French merchants to extend, plan, and regulate French trade, and fought tariff and trade wars with economic weapons. The King had assumed responsibility for national welfare, and sought if possible to achieve both plenty and power. But in a crisis, when commercial interests conflicted with the demands of war, ends were distinguished from means and profit was sacrificed to prestige and order. Despite the unparalleled economic supervision of his reign, Louis' heart still cherished the ideals of the *noblesse*.

This was not however just a vague preference. A *noblesse commerçante,* as Montesquieu later pointed out in the *Esprit des Lois,* was incompatible with the real interests of the monarchy.[65] The Crown had appealed to the *Tiers État* in its struggle to emasculate the military *noblesse,* and had supported merchants against the hostility of the *noblesse.* But it would also support the *noblesse* against the pretensions of merchants, because the claim to prestige by business was, in the long run, more dangerous to royal supremacy than the old social power of the *noblesse.* The royal prerogative of raising to the nobility was more than a backstairs source of income; it was a political weapon that had to be used with care and not too often. The monarchy had by the reign of Louis XIV broken the military power of the *noblesse,* and channelled their surplus energy into foreign wars. By the timeless principle of divide and rule, by distinguishing between *grandeur* and *pouvoir,* it had created a situation in which the *noblesse* was compensated by social supremacy and privilege for the political power which the Crown exercised through its own instruments, the *Intendants.* This internal balance of power would be upset by any fusion between rank and wealth, by a *noblesse* enjoying independent and hereditary wealth, acting in accord with a merchant aristocracy enjoying independent and hereditary prestige. On the other hand, by selling offices, the monarchy not only raised the money needed for its wars, and the pensions of the court; it put the merchants who became office holders in a position of dependence. Thus, although eager to expand trade, and to increase the wealth upon which external glory and internal solvency ultimately depended, the crown would not eliminate the buying of office by direct ennoblement on a large scale. The preambles to royal edicts show the policy which was dictated by the interests of the *noblesse* and the merchants; their clauses reveal the private political interests of the Crown. The merchant could not find his place in the sun, because he might eclipse the *Roi Soleil*.

The divorce of wealth from honour was therefore a question not only of prestige but also of power. Just as an equitable system of taxation would increase demand for political representation, so a fluid social system would release energies dangerous to royal power. It has become fashionable to soften the contrast between absolute monarchy in France and the mixed constitutions of England and the United Provinces, to emphasize the great efforts made by French Kings to develop French trade. But the failure of the attempt to equate social status with trade suggests that absolute monarchy was only superficially compatible with commercial enterprise. If the French Crown was responsive to the needs of its commercial subjects, it could afford to ignore them, whereas it could not afford to abandon the social *status quo*. The author of a *mémoire* in 1701 was not far from the truth, when he remarked that honour for trade was all very well in republican states, where merchants ruled, but France was a monarchy.[66]

NOTES

1. The evidence for this paragraph is drawn from a profuse and scattered literature. The classic *exposé* of the *noblesse* remains E. Lavisse, *Histoire de France: Louis XIV* (1908), VII, Part I, 372–86, and the best study of derogation, La Bigne de Villeneuve, *Une curieuse théorie: la dérogeance* (Thèse, Rennes, 1918), pp. 57–126. Important also are H. Lévy-Bruhl, 'La Noblesse de France et le Commerce', *Revue d'Histoire moderne,* N.S. VIII (1933), 209–235, and M. Szeftel, 'La Règle de vie exemplaire des nobles', *Revue de l'Institut de Sociologie,* XVI (1936), 608 *et seq.* Further information is given by C. A. Foster, *Honoring Commerce and Industry in Eighteenth Century France* (unpub. Ph. D. thesis, Harvard, 1950), pp. 84–111, and G. Zeller, 'Une notion de caractère historico-sociale: la dérogeance', *Cahiers internationaux de Sociologie,* N.S. XXII (1957), 40–74. See also R. Mousnier, 'L'évolution des finances publiques . . .', *Revue historique,* CCV (1951), 9, and a discussion by the same author with V-L Tapié, printed in the *Revue d'Histoire économique et sociale,* XXXIII (1955), 338–9.

2. No detailed analysis of this problem has, to my knowledge, yet been made. The authorities on the sale of office in France, M. Göhring (*Die Aemterkäuflichkeit im Ancien Régime,* Hist. Stud. 346 Berlin, 1938) and R. Mousnier (*La Vénalité des Offices,* Rouen, 1945) have not dealt with the economic effects of this major distraction to trade, and W. Sombart (*Der Bourgeois,* Leipzig, 1920, p. 180) and H. Hauser ('French economic development . . .', *Econ. Hist. Rev.* IV [1933], 262) have accepted without further investigation the analysis of Savary in the *Parfait Négociant.* Some brief remarks by G. Roupnel (*La Ville et la Campagne,* 2nd ed. 1955, pp. 229–233) suggest that at least in Burgundy capital investment was a more complex problem than Savary indicates.

3. The difficulties of relating social attitudes to economic development are well illustrated by a controversy over modern France in the *Explorations in Entrepreneurial History,* VI (1953–4), 1–15, 181–3, 245–297, and VII (1954), 111–119; the interaction of social and economic factors also tends to undermine the theoretical patterns imposed on French society by M. Kolabinska, *La Circulation des élites en France* (Lausanne, 1912), and by E. Barber, *The Bourgeoisie in Eighteenth Century France* (Princeton, 1955).

4. Bibliothèque de l'Institut de France Ancien MS. 787, fol. 325, Discours de la police en général, 1684.

5. For the mathematical handbooks see N. Z. Davis, 'Sixteenth Century French Arithmetics', *Journal of the History of Ideas,* XXI (1960), 29, 45.

6. B. Laffemas, *Traité de commerce . . .* (1601), p. 4.

7. J. Eon, *Le Commerce Honorable* (Nantes, 1646), pp. 1–9, 44–53.

8. E. Charpentier, *Discours d'un fidèle sujet . . .* (1664), pp. 3–4, 16. A more colourful version of his argument is found in the advertisements displayed for investors, e.g. Archives Communales Lyons, HH 372, 12 July 1664.

9. R. Mousnier, 'L'opposition politique bourgeoise . . . L'oeuvre de Louis Turquet de Mayerne', *Rev. Hist.* CCXIII (1955), 8–9.

10. L-A Boiteux, 'Un économist méconnu: Du Noyer de Saint Martin et ses projets', *Revue d'Histoire des colonies,* XLIV (1957), 31–2.

11. M. Marchetti, *Discours sur le négoce des gentilhommes de . . . Marseille* (1671), pp. 4–9, 65–70.

12. J. Savary, *Le Parfait Négociant* (1675), pp. 1–4, 38–41; H. Hauser, *Les Débuts du Capitalisme* (1928), pp. 266–308.

13. *Utilité de la Navigation et Commerce* (1627) (Bibliothèque Nationale copy).

14. A marginal note added by Richelieu to his *Utilité du commerce* (c. 1628), printed by G. d'Avenel, *Lettres . . . de Richelieu* (1853–77), III, 178–9; H. Hauser, *La pensée et l'action économique du Cardinal de Richelieu* (1944), pp. 186–7, 191–2.

15. Bib. Nat. Ancien Français MS, 4870, fol. 144; see also C. de la Roncière, *Histoire de la marine français* (1899–1932), IV, 488–9.

16. *Mémoire touchant le commerce avec l'Angleterre* (c. 1650), reprinted by P. Clément, *Lettres de Colbert* (1861–2), Coll. des Dccs. Inéd. II, Part 2, 405–9; see also C. W. Cole, *Colbert and a Century of French Mercantilism* (N.Y. 1939), I, 361–2.

17. Marseille first received this protection in 1566, Lyons in 1609. The originals are preserved in Archives Communales Marseille, AA 121, and Archives Communales Lyon, BB 114. Printed versions of many company charters are listed by L. André, *Les Sources de l'histoire de France; XVIIe siècle* (1934), VII, 133–246, and summarized by Savary des Bruslons, *Dictionnaire universel de commerce* (1723–30), II, 866–8, s.v. Noblesse.

18. P. Boissonade, *Colbert et le souscription aux actions de la Compagnie des Indes* (Poitiers, 1909), pp. 4–9.

19. This is printed as an ordonnance by J. Toubeaux, *Les Institutes du droit consulaire* (2nd ed. 1700), p. 31, but for reasons given by G. Zeller ('Louis XI, la noblesse, et les marchands', *Annales: Economies, Sociétés, Civilisations,* II (1946), 337 n. 4) this could only have been a project.

20. F-A Isambert, *Recueil général des anciennes lois françaises* (1821–33), XIV, 94.

21. *Ibid.,* XVI, 339.

22. The preamble is printed by Isambert, *Lois,* XVIII, 217–18, with a curious footnote; the text by D. Jousse, *Recueil chronologique des ordonnances . . .* (1757), I, 255–7.

23. Bib. Nat. Anc. Franc. MS. 16, 738, fol. 133. Decree of 10 March 1635. See also H. P. Biggar, *The Early Trading Companies of New France* (Toronto, 1901), p. 137.

24. Isambert, *Lois,* XVI, 339. The article was ambiguously phrased.

25. Zeller, 'Louis XI', *Annales E.S.C.* II (1946), 333–7.

26. Statistics for the sale of letters patent to merchants in this period are still incomplete, although much information is collected by L. N. R. Chérin, *Abrégé chronologique d'édits . . . concernant le fait de noblesse* (1788). Some details are provided for Brittany by Bourde de la Rogerie, 'Étude sur la Réformation de la Noblesse en Bretagne', *Mémoires de la Société d'Histoire et d'Archéologie de Bretagne,* II (1922), 250–76; for Nantes by the pioneer work of H. du Halgouet, 'Gentilhommes commerçants et commerçants nobles', *Mém. Soc. d'Hist. et d'Arch. de Bretagne,* XVI (1935); for la Rochelle by M. E. Garnault, *Histoire du commerce rochelais* (La Rochelle, 1887–1900), pp. 35–7; and for Rouen by R. Rouault de la Vigne, 'L'ascension social et l'anoblissement des négociants et commerçants rouennais', *Précis analytique des Travaux de l'Académie de Rouen* (1955), 185–195.

27. *Journaux des États-Généraux de France . . . en 1484,* ed. and trans. by A. Bernier (Coll. des Docs. Inéd. 1833), p. 698; Isambert, *Lois,* XII, 810. Lalource & Duval, *Recueil des pièces originales et authentiques concernant la tenue des États-Généraux* (1789), IX, 84.

28. *L'Assemblée des notables tenue à Paris ès années 1626 à 1627* (1652), pp. 32, 182.

29. Regional studies of noble participation in trade are still too few to permit accurate generalizations about France. But they do support the contention of Bourde de la Rogerie (*Inventaire des Archives du Finistère,* Ser. B. III, Introduction (Quimper, 1902), pp. clxi–clxv) that the later seventeenth century witnessed a movement back to the land.

30. W. C. Scoville, *Capitalism and French Glassmaking* (Berk. & Los Angeles, 1950), p. 166.

31. For the general state of the French economy after Colbert, see C. W. Cole, *French Mercantilism, 1683–1700* (N.Y. 1943).

32. Archives Nationales (subsequently abbreviated as A.N.) F^{12} 51, fols. 1–4. Register of the *Conseil de Commerce,* 24 November 1700.

33. These *mémoires* exist both in manuscript and print. The Bibliothèque Nationale has three manuscript collections, of which, for reasons given by J. Cain ('Les Mémoires de Députés . . . en 1700', *Rev. d'Hist. mod.* XVII, 1913, 5–19) the copy Anc. Franc. 8038 is the best. Another virtually complete manuscript copy is in the Archives Departementales Loire-Inférieure, C 894, and this has been collated here with the other texts. Of the various printed versions, the most accessible is the edition of A. M. de Boislisle (*Correspondance des Controleurs-généraux.* Coll. des Docs. Inéd. 1874–83 II, App. IV), which prints the four *mémoires* delivered by Mésnager, Du Hallay, Anisson, and Pelletier from Anc. Franc. 8038.

34. Short biographical notices of the deputies will be found in P. Bonnassieux & E. Lelong, *Inventaire analytique des Procès-Verbaux du Conseil de Commerce* (1900), pp. lxv–lxxii.

35. Anc. Franc. 8038, fols. 425–6.

36. *Ibid.* fol. 321.

37. *Ibid.* fol. 151v°.

38. Boislisle, *op. cit.* pp. 484–5.

39. The term *'marchand'* was, as A. Kuhn (*Die Französische Handelsprache im XVII Jahrhundert,* Inaug. Diss. Leipzig, 1931, pp. 35–43) suggests, already being superseded in commercial usage at the end of the seventeenth century by the word *'négociant'*, and even the term *'commerçant'* was coming into use. For examples of the great diversity within the commercial world see P. Goubert, 'Types de Marchands Amiénois au début du XVIIe siècle', *XVIIe Siècle,* No. 33 (1956), 655–6.

40. The full statement is printed by W. C. Scoville, 'The Huguenots in the French economy', *Quart. J. of Econ.* LXVII (1953), 442.

41. Vicomte d'Estaintot, 'Nicholas Mésnager député de Rouen', *Précis anal. des trav. de l'Acad. de Rouen* (1871–2), 10–14; Héron's nefarious activities are recorded in Bibliothèque Municipale La Rochelle MS, E supp. 1195.

42. Anc. Franc. 8038, fols. 114v°–115.

43. Boislisle, *op. cit.* p. 484.

44. Anc. Franc. 8038, fols. 291–2. He was not quite correct since P. Langlet ('Les principaux courants commerciaux du port de St-Malo en 1681 et 1682', *Annales de Bretagne,* LXIV (1957), 326) shows that merchants of St-Malo did withdraw their capital to buy land and respect.

45. A.N. F^{12} 908–909. 'Proposition de créer des Chambres de Commerce'. The proposals are undated, and the replies of the deputies are dated 1707. This is almost certainly an error, since on internal evidence the proposals must have preceded the deputies' own resolutions on the *Chambres de Commerce* in April 1701.

46. Anc. Franc. 8038, fols. 321–2.

47. A.N. F^{12} 51, fols. 27–8, 8 April 1701. For biographical details of the commissioners see Bonassieux, *Conseil de Commerce,* pp. xxxvii–xxxviii; for the constitution of the *Conseil* A.M. de Boislisle, *Mémoires de Saint-Simon* (1884), App VII, 426. No debates in the *Conseil* are in fact recorded—only brief summaries of decisions—but the drafts of *mémoires* with corrections inserted are preserved in A.N. F^{12} 847–854A. By close comparison of these the trends in debate can be calculated with considerable precision.

48. A.N. F^{12} 52, fols. 30–33. 'Mémoire sur les veues que le Roi a d'exciter ses sujets au commerce', 22 April 1701.

49. The full definition is printed by Lévy-Bruhl, *La Noblesse de France et le Commerce,* 218 n. 2.

50. The replies of Bordeaux, La Rochelle, Lille, Dunkirk, Rouen, Lyon, Nantes, St-Malo, and Bayonne are preserved in A.N. F^{12} 847–854a. Neither Paris, Toulouse nor Marseille sent official replies, but the opinion of the *Chambre de Commerce* of Marseille is expressed in their correspondence with Fabre, in Archives de la Chambre de Commerce de Marseille, B 152, fols. 269–275, and Archives Communales Marseille, B 153. Further indications of Bordeaux's reaction are supplied by correspondence between the town and Fénellon in Archives Departementales Gironde, 7. B. 4. fols. 8–14, parts of which have been printed without indication of origin by V. Labraque-Bordenave, *Histoire des Députés de Bordeaux* (Actes de l'Acad. de Bordeaux, 1889), pp. 282–298.

51. A.N. F^{12} 641. 'Mémoire sur la décoration des Commerçants', which can be dated approximately between April and November 1701. It has been printed by C. van Renynghe de Voxrie in the *Tablettes de Flandres,* VII (1957), 258–267.

52. A.N. F^{12} 847–854A. A corrected draft of the proposals of 20 April 1701.

53. A.N. F^{12} 114, and F^{12} 662–670.

54. A.N. F^{12} 51, fol. 73, 26 October 1701. No fair copy of this project survives—only copies upon which the secretary of the *Conseil* had scribbled the comments of the deputies, preserved in A.N. F^{12} 847–854a. But by subtracting the criticisms which the deputies finally submitted to the commissioners from these drafts, it is possible to reconstruct what the original project contained.

55. A.N. F^{12} 847–854a. 'Observations de MM. les Députés sur le projet de la déclaration du roi pour la décoration du commerce', 17 November 1701.

56. The full text is printed by Boislisle, *Correspondance des Contrôleurs-généraux,* II App VII, 509. It is sometimes incorrectly described as an Edict.

57. For the significance of this article see A. Des Cilleuls, *Histoire et régime de la grande industrie* (1898), p. 319 n. 484. It was virulently opposed by the *Corps,* and blackened the Declaration in the eyes of the merchant interest.

58. A.N. F^{12} 847–854A, 29 March 1701. For what details are known of the participation of the *noblesse* in industry see G-L Martin, *La Grande Industrie en France sous le règne de Louis XV* (1900), pp. 210–217, and Foster, *Honoring Commerce and Industry,* pp. 297–303, and Apps. xiii–xv.

59. The number of letters patent, sold under financial pressure at this time, misled C. Z. Louandre (*La Noblesse française sous l'ancienne monarchie* (1880), p. 41) to remark that Louis made nobles by *dragonnades.*

60. A.N. F^{12} l. Arrêt du Conseil d'État, 1702.

61. Archives des Affaires Etrangères, Mémoires et Documents France, No. 306, fols. 73–4. 'Replique au mémoire intitulé commerce'.

62. Archives Departementales Loire-Inférieure, C 695, 'Mémoire sur l'exercise du commerce par rapport aux Nobles . . . de la . . . Bretagne'. For the literary debate which continued on this question see E. Depitre, 'Le Systeme et la querelle de la noblesse commerçante', *Rev. d'Hist. écon. et soc.* VI (1913), 143, 158; H. Carré, *La Noblesse de France et l'opinion publique au XVIIIe siècle* (1920), pp. 137–148; and M. Reinhard, 'Elite et Noblesse dans la seconde moitié du XVIIIe siècle', *Rev. d'Hist. mod. et contemp.* III (1956), 13–19.

63. For some broad suggestions see H. Lévy-Bruhl, 'Commerce', *Revue de Synthèse historique,* VIII (1938), 44–50.

64. Cole, *Colbert,* I, 334–5. Colbert's attitude can partly be explained by his authoritarianism and dislike of opposition. His major criticisms were made against the merchants of Marseilles who opposed his bullion policy and his Edict of March 1669.

65. *Oeuvres Complètes* (ed. A. Masson), I (1950), 462–3.

66. A.N. F^{12} 641.

Economic Crises and Social Atmosphere in Urban Society Under Louis XIV

BY GUY LEMARCHAND

Under Louis XIV, grave economic crises shook the whole country, and popular troubles revealed a profound distress. However, internal revolts appear to have been less numerous than during the preceding period under Richelieu and Mazarin. Does this mean that a certain relaxation occurred? Was there, under the government of the Sun King, a transformation of attitudes? The study, within a limited geographical framework, of certain aspects of the famines of the period can provide a few answers. Those crises are, in effect, the only time in which the documents tell us about those who were most numerous, but who, nevertheless, elude us—the poor. They equally reveal latent tensions in society that hunger alone could actualize and magnify; social protests, that formed a permanent theme, were finally given clear expression. This is, then, a means of approaching the collective psychology of the past. It permits us to see if the mental attitudes characteristic of the reign of Louis XIII and of the Fronde did not, more or less, linger on. From this perspective, we have tried to exploit the vast documentation concerning the famines of 1661–62, 1693–94, and 1709–10, in two cities of Upper Normandy—one of medium size, Dieppe, that numbered nearly thirty thousand inhabitants; the other, Rouen, that was very large, perhaps the second largest in the kingdom during the seventeenth century. Three categories of sources are essential: the correspondence of the intendants of the *généralité* of Rouen, the local and regional judicial archives, and the deliberations of the municipalities.

Let us specify here the general sequence of events, in order that we may take up, henceforth, only those aspects that were properly psychological in nature. During the first serious famine of the personal reign of Louis XIV, the price of wheat in Upper Normandy began to rise as early as the winter of 1660–61.[1] A popular antifiscal revolt broke out in Dieppe on June 20–21, 1661, in the wake of a rumor spread throughout the city that a new duty was to be levied on grain. Three houses belonging to the farmers of different taxes and some finance offices were looted.[2] In the spring of 1662, at Rouen, some incidents occurred in the marketplace, and the authorities feared an insurrection.[3] In 1693–94, a certain tension was revealed at Dieppe, and the poor were numerous; at Rouen, mobs formed and bakeries were attacked.[4] In 1709, finally, threatening bands of beggars formed in Dieppe; and, at Rouen, there occurred a violent uprising, as the crowd demonstrated in the street for two days, laid siege to the intendant's town house, and devastated the house of a subdelegate [of the intendant] and of a police commissioner.[5] A certain agitation persisted until the harvest of 1710. The outline of events at the time of these famines was the same as in other cities of the Old Regime: "high prices, unemployment, the beginnings of workers' revolts, charity measures, contagion." [6]

What was the general attitude of the different groups toward royal policy? Did not, as a consequence of the crisis, hostility mount against the monarchy? What was the climate of relations among the social groups within the city? What were the solutions adopted to meet the crisis, and did all social classes follow the people in revolt? Let us take up these questions successively.

Famine made the tutelage of the absolute monarchy heavier for each social class and generalized discontent. It took place in an atmosphere that was already unfavorable to the king, and that could only confirm the public in the idea that government was responsible for the crisis.

At Dieppe and Rouen, as in the rest of France in 1661–62, 1693–94, and 1709–10, it was the popular classes that were most heavily hit by high prices. In the capital of Normandy, brown bread rose, at the legal rate, to at least two sols, four deniers the pound in 1662, and to two sols in 1694 and 1709.[7] The real price was still more elevated, because the bakers, profiting from scarcity, did not neglect to cheat on weight. Brown bread cost more than two sols during at least six months in 1693, three months in 1694, and five months in 1709. Moreover, wages were from ten to fifteen sols daily in normal times, which, counting 270 workdays a year, left to the workers in fact about seven sols, four deniers to eleven sols, one denier each day.[8] But we know that a subsistence crisis always brought with it a decrease in nominal wages that, in Rouen, appears to have been very great.[9] In the public workhouses, the salary in Rouen was some six sols and at Dieppe in 1709, seven sols, five deniers. Consequently, with high prices, the normal individual minimum of some three pounds of bread took, at times of great crisis, at least two thirds of daily earnings or even more. If we also imagine the indispensable expenses for rent (two to three hundred sols yearly), and for candles and wood, we see that in 1661, as in 1693 or 1709, single individuals were able to nourish themselves only with difficulty, and that, in the homes of married men with two children, they ate less than a pound of bread each. Naturally, unemployment accompanied high prices: it was reported in Rouen from the end of 1660 until July 1662, and from March 1693 until June 1695.[10] Thus we observe at each crisis the same phenomena—sickness due to improper nutrition (some bran boiled in water in 1693); streets "filled with poor families who sleep there without any shelter"; [11] and the stacked bodies of the destitute—dead of hunger. But, as was noted by the *lieutenant-général* of Rouen, Boisguilbert, the people still attributed the crisis to a "failure of police"—that is to bad administration.

Moreover, in this conjuncture, the weight of the principal taxes, which essentially hit the popular masses, became unsupportable. If Dieppe and Rouen were both exempt from the *taille* and *gabelle*,[12] their inhabitants, nevertheless, were faced with heavy royal demands. Between 1640 and 1665, the monarchy claimed by right of the *ustensile* up to 120,000 livres yearly at Rouen, and 50,000 livres yearly at Dieppe.[13] Each war, then, was the occasion for gifts and forced loans. Rouen granted 240,000 livres in 1674, 300,000 livres in 1689, again 300,000 in 1692, and 226,000 in 1706.[14] To pay these sums, it was each time necessary to create new "provisional" municipal taxes—in fact they were almost permanent under Louis XIV—on drink, livestock, and firewood, because the king had taken over since 1662–65 the ordinary municipal taxes, which he also increased.[15] Other taxes were equally created by the city councillors in order to raise the money necessary for the repurchase of certain municipal offices intentionally created by Louis XIV for this purpose.[16] In addition, the *aides* in Normandy were very heavy, particularly hitting beverages, meat, eggs, and wood.[17] In this manner, the king drew already in 1672 more than a million livres annually from the municipal taxes and *aides* levied at Rouen—which did not prevent him from further increasing the *aides* in 1680. The Norman capital was more burdened with taxes, than was Paris.[18] Evidently, the result of this policy was a rise in the price of common commodities. Toward 1680, a pig that was worth 5 or 6 livres at the farm paid 4 livres, 11 sols in duty to the king at Rouen—and in 1699, 7 livres. The situation was nearly the same at Dieppe, where municipal taxes were increased in 1703, despite the partial destruction of the city in 1694 from the bombardment by the English fleet.[19] To these royal or municipal duties were added diverse seigneurial and individual charges. In 1646 at Dieppe, the count of the place received 15,380 livres from various taxes levied on the city's commerce. His most important revenue derived from the "boette"—a customs duty on three hundred products entering and leaving by land or by sea.[20] In 1695, the archbishop of Rouen, titular of the county, succeeded in augmenting substantially his tariffs, which would have allowed him to double his profits.[21]

The merchant bourgeoisie of the two cities also had good grounds for being discontented with royal policy. The companies of commerce created by Colbert had always been rather poorly received by the merchants. Those of Dieppe refused in 1665 to join the West Indies Company, despite an invitation from the provincial governor.[22] Seignelay, who sought in 1684 to found a new society for the fisheries, wrote that the inhabitants of Dieppe, who refused, showed "stubbornness and disobedience." [23] In addition, beginning in 1680, the sale of offices multiplied, striking the merchants and the guilds. The edict of 1703 imposed a levy of 180,000 livres on the guild masters of Rouen who were to enjoy the privilege of heredity.[24] In 1704 the important corporation of retail clothiers was obliged to buy back offices of inspector of manufactures (150,000 livres); in 1706 there were offices [created] for cloth measurers; and then in 1708, for supervisors of the account books (100,000 livres).[25] The many currency changes after 1686 were a serious impediment to business—there were four of them, for example, between March 1708 and March 1709—and disrupted activity in the cities that were particularly devoted to commerce.[26] Paper currency, the acceptance of which for a quarter of all payments was made obligatory in 1707, had the same consequences.[27] But the most serious subject of discontent among the bourgeoisie was the stagnation of business during the reign of Louis XIV, which became more pronounced with each subsistence crisis. Tariff or fiscal policies were always held responsible for the difficulties that were encountered, and protest was continual. In 1661–62, in order to explain the stoppage of manufacturing, people blamed the insufficiency of customs duties in the kingdom that allowed too great an importation of foreign cloth and linen.[28] By contrast, the duties on exports were judged excessive. At Dieppe in 1665, the merchants declared that the burden of taxation since 1659 prevented them from increasing the export of textiles to Spain.[29] In 1700, again, the deputy of commerce from Rouen, Ménager, called in vain for their reduction.[30] Complaints against the duties levied on local products were general. People blamed equally the manufacturing taxes and state regulation of work for paralyzing certain branches of the artisan industry.[31] The royal administrators, themselves, were obliged to agree that these accusations did not lack foundation. An investigator sent by Colbert to Dieppe in 1665 noted that, because of the excess taxes on boats at the entry and exit of the port, "of the twelve to fifteen ships that previously went each year to

America, there are no longer more than one or two, and, indeed, often none at all." Thus the treasury, by its excessive pressure, managed to reduce the amount of taxable goods and harmed its own profits—as Boisguilbert did not fail to stress. Even the Controller General [Colbert] recognized that the commerce of Dieppe would not be able to reestablish itself as long as foodstuffs were so burdened with taxes.[32] From the psychological point of view, as well, the bourgeoisie, or the merchants at least, was not satisfied. According to the merchants of Rouen, "commerce in France was choked by the sword and the robe (and even, they added, by the haughty empire of customs clerks), and the merchants who had earned something in trade immediately withdraw their investment from the particular companies in which they participated and give it all up in order to buy judicial offices for their children or noble lands for themselves." [33] In 1700, again, Ménager urged that the condition of merchant be "an honored one."

The officers of the sovereign courts, who were numerous at Rouen—the seat of Parlement, of the Chambre des Comptes, and of the Cour des Aides—also had grievances against the monarchy. Fiscal questions too played an important role. As under Louis XIII, the Parlement showed a certain hostility in regard to the tax contractors. In 1660 it allied with the other two courts to defend the privileges of the councillors against the greed of the farmers-general who sought to tax the products from the farms of the "messieurs" that entered Rouen duty-free. In the legal proceedings, it supported only an indirect tax on the resisters.[34] Beginning in 1695, a new motive for discontent appeared, the creation of the *capitation* [head tax]. In 1709, for example, the *parlementaires* showed a great deal of ill will in fulfilling their contribution.[35] In another area, on the political side, Parlement did not easily resign itself to the near total loss of its right to remonstrate. Only the threats of Colbert and the exile of a *président à mortier* reduced it to silence in 1673. Nevertheless, in July 1709, it sent a firm protest to the king regarding the prohibition against the forced sale of livestock belonging to debt-ridden farmers who worked their [i.e., the judges'] lands.[36] The *parlementaires* thus secretly kept to their old pretensions against the royal power. And their relations with the intendant of the area were often rather bad— each claiming the right to regulate and judge in all domains. At the time of the revolt of Dieppe in 1661, two councillors were sent by the court to investigate on the spot. But the intendant, Champigny, judged the rebels, and this led the court to complain to the king. The organization of food supplies was also a subject of conflict with the representative of the monarchy. In 1662, Parlement oversaw the provisioning of Rouen.[37] But in 1693 and 1709, the powers of the intendant having been expanded, the court had to be content with fixing the price of bread and with the supervision of the city's granaries. However, the intendant, La Berchère, was resentful to see the court interfere in this domain in 1693. In 1709, the conflict was violent. The councillors reproached the intendant, Courson, for sending, in place of the ordinary judges, commissioners to investigate sales contracts in the countryside. This reduced to nothing the appellate jurisdiction of the Parlement.[38] The court tried to retake the initiative by issuing an edict to suppress hoarding. But on May 7, the king gave the supervision of the grain trade to the intendants,[39] which raised the irritation with Courson to its highest pitch. Thus there took place a veiled battle around this regulatory power that made Parlement only an administrative cog.

Moreover, certain aspects of royal policy aggravated the subsistence crisis and risked increasing hostility against [the crown]. Above all, it was the controller-general's constant concern to provide for Paris, which deprived neighboring provinces, such as Upper Normandy, of wheat. The grain that went up the Seine was reserved for the capital. In 1662, Colbert scolded Parlement, which had retained a portion of the convoy for the provisioning of Rouen.[40] Norman merchants were forbidden to purchase provisions in the neighboring provinces of Picardy and Beauce—regions responsible for nourishing Paris. And even the Parisian provisioners came to carry away foodstuffs from the markets that provided for the needs of Rouen, without any attempt by the *contrôle-générale* to stop them. Thus the provincials had the impression that the government initiated hoarding at their expense.

Then war, so frequent under Louis XIV, made the solution to the subsistence crisis more difficult and paralyzed the economy of Dieppe and Rouen. The famine of 1661 came right after the long French-Spanish conflict that ended in 1659; those of 1693 and 1709 took place during the most severe wars of the reign. Thus the actions of the Dutch and English made the importing of wheat difficult. In April 1694, Breton grain boats, chartered by some Rouen traders, were not able to leave Saint-Malo for lack of escort vessels. At Dieppe in 1708, they complained about the activity of enemy privateers. This partial blockade led to a recession in the commerce of the two ports. During the War of the League of Augsburg, when the enemy blocked the Seine estuary, the customs at Rouen reported [receiving] 167,271 livres, compared to 1,247,687 livres in 1688. At Dieppe, fishing, which was the essential resource of the city, nearly stopped. It was followed by a decline in those crafts working at the export trade—the production of serge, tanning, the manufacture of objects from bone and horn at Dieppe, and the decline of cloth manufacture at Rouen after 1706.[41] The war also touched more directly certain elements of the cities' population. At Dieppe, it entailed the drafting of sailors from among the fishermen, who sought, moreover, to avoid this obligatory military service.[42] In Rouen, the king requisitioned the boatmen who did not show much more eagerness.[43] Finally, the provisioning of troops on the coasts or along the nearby frontiers of Flanders led the intendant to undertake to purchase foodstuffs in Caux and Vexin, regions that ordinarily fed Dieppe and Rouen. At a time of scarcity, this provoked a rise in prices.[44] At the beginning of 1709, great quantities of oats were sent from Upper Normandy to the troops in the north—then, in the spring of 1710, twenty-two thousand sacks of wheat.

Thus, due to the subsistence crisis, each social group supported the weight of royal policy only with great difficulty, and each was led to challenge, if not the principle of absolute monarchy, at least its concrete application—the authority of the intendant and the demands of the tax farmer. Each had reasons to complain about the royal government. Certainly the principal cause of the economic difficulties, perhaps more than the general policies of Louis XIV, was the reversal of [economic] conditions that had struck the country in the 1650s. But contemporaries evidently had no awareness of this. And it is true that nonproductive investment, the increase in government finances, and the unfortunate maritime war could only accentuate the depression. But the question is to know just how far this discontent would go—a platonic or legal protest, or violent revolt against the established order?

In this context, where the totality of royal policy was submitted to lively criticism by the majority of the population, famine exposed a characteristic feature of the relations among the social groups within Dieppe and Rouen—the fear of the bourgeoisie and of the authorities before the popular masses.

The sensitivity of the people to the problem of provisioning and to the price of grains was dreaded by contemporaries. The documents constantly repeat such phrases as, "the necessity to avoid greater disorders," or people "who might rise up in revolt." Agitation by the lower classes was considered a permanent possibility. The intendant, Courson, thus wrote: "The spirit of the people is so difficult to govern, above all in an affair as delicate as this one (the provisioning of grain), that I always fear lest it break loose." [45] The subdelegate at Dieppe declared more brutally in regard to the poor, "We must admit that it is a terrible beast to govern." [46] Even Colbert, when sending his orders to an intendant on the subject of a small demonstration by some women dissatisfied with the changing of a parish priest, recalled, "You must notice that the greatest number of rebellions of this sort begin over petty things; and if one does not suppress them, they grow and subsequently take other forms." [47] Crowd disturbances were dreaded, because they were the acts of unprincipled people who had no respect for property, persons, or the authorities. Thus wrote a bourgeois of Rouen:

241

Popular disturbances ordinarily happen only in very great cities; and to confront them will mean to oppose the impulsiveness of a raging torrent that no dike can hold. Because those who cause these disorders are nearly always persons from the dregs of society, it is not surprising that, being sensitive only to the ills that press upon them, they give little attention to the designs and the will of God, who wishes us to obey without dissent Princes and those who are appointed on their behalf, whatever excess they commit in the taxes that they require.[48]

A profound mistrust was thus expressed toward the lower classes. Any assembly of poor people was considered dangerous *a priori,* because "all these assemblies can have very great consequences."[49] The *bailliage* of Rouen often ended the pronouncement of its judgments in craft matters by recalling the prohibition upon journeymen "to gather together under any pretext whatever." As for the beggars, always numerous in the cities, people accused them of stealing and of causing "an infection that there is reason to fear, because, the air becoming corrupt, epidemics might return."[50] Such a fear was justified by the picture that the propertied classes and the authorities had of the popular mentality. Concerning the journeymen, the intendant, Courson, explained that the inhabitants of Bolbec, "are very bad, because it is a manufacturing region where there are many workers who have nothing to lose."[51] The vagabonds constituted "a riffraff composed ordinarily of people who are godless, who are without religion, and without instruction; who live in license and dissoluteness and in a shameful and even horrible way, without distinction of sex, kinship, or relationships, like animals; who were conceived and nourished in vice, passing their life there, and proceeding easily to all kinds of crime."[52]

Thus workers and beggars formed dangerous classes. Evidently, this idea was not without foundation: physical violence, both individual and collective, was common in the popular *milieux.* It has already been noted, regarding seventeenth-century trials in a *bailliage* near Rouen, that criminality mainly consisted of fights and murders.[53] In truth, abuse and blows with fists or

242

sticks were very frequent. Of fifty-three cases judged in the criminal *bailliage* of Rouen in 1710, we find twenty-six cases of assault and battery, three of abuse and intimidation, two murders, and one rape.[54] One can classify the occasions for these outbursts of individual violence under three categories. Quarrels over money were the most frequent. Participants hardly bothered with subtle arguments, hitting out immediately with fist or foot.[55] One senses that in this society, money was rare and difficult to earn. Defense of honor was another occasion for violence. The least disapproving remark about the behavior of a subject was frequently followed by acts of brutality in reply. There was, perhaps, a factor of social mimesis in this: in a hierarchical society, each person wants to maintain his rank, just as the great persons of the city. Finally, there was some gratuitous violence that seemed to relate to a certain nervous disequilibrium. Such were the cabaret riots, the disturbances of the peace at night with threats and the breaking of windows and doors, and the rapes.[56]

But more formidable to the bourgeoisie and the authorities were the collective acts of violence emanating from the people. Under Louis XIV, they still carried on openly against fiscal agents and particular taxes. It was always easy to assemble a menacing crowd, when one did not want to pay what the collector of any tax demanded.[57] The famous cry of "monopolist" was uttered again in 1663 and provoked the arrival of a "great number of people" in a hostile mood. There were also work conditions that drove the journeymen to collective and violent demonstrations. Even some associations were formed for the economic struggle. The prohibitions in the sentences handed down by the *bailliage* of Rouen allow us to observe, among the journeymen cloth workers, linen workers, weavers, and hatters, the existence of a syndicate or confraternity, the president or *syndic* of which was elected, and which possessed a communal treasury filled by the "levying of dues on the members." [58] The goal of these organizations was to direct the boycott of certain masters and [to organize] strikes. Salary levels were, directly or indirectly, the essential object of work conflicts. Sometimes, it was a question of preventing masters from using outsiders—

workers from the countryside who accepted lower wages and thus depressed the salaries of urban journeymen. Finally, the scarcity of certain products—meat and wood—stimulated small disturbances.

In times of serious subsistence crises, popular violence was even more likely to erupt. In Dieppe, on July 21, 1661, "the populace" that pillaged the house of one of the tax contractors took care to leave nothing: they threw out the furnishings on to the quai and from there into the water, "so as not to leave a trace." [59] In Rouen, from July 3 to July 4, 1709, the mutineers—journeymen in the wool, lace, and hat industries—sought to seize the intendant and to knock him about. It was not a question, as in the eighteenth century, of accusations or of taking some wheat, but rather of angry vengeance. We are dealing here not only with hunger, but also with the social indignation that, in France, involves a kind of "tradition of popular revolt," according to the expression of M. Mandrou,[60] and which appears due to diverse factors. The spectacle of inequality was for the poor a primary cause of anger; to their awful misery during the famine was opposed the situation of the bourgeoisie and the officers who remained comfortable. At Rouen in April 1694, they had "threatened to harm some important bourgeois for reasons that were unknown, and which they wanted to use in order to assuage their passion either out of animosity or something else, up to the point of having abused them and thrown rocks against their doors." [61] Thus was born the idea of burning the houses of the rich at Dieppe and Rouen in 1709.[62] Secondly, the demonstrators could hardly endure the sight of wealth that they had reason to believe to have been acquired at their expense through unjust manipulations and speculations. In 1661 at Dieppe, they reproached the municipal officers, who had ordered them to disperse, for not opposing the tax contractors.[63] Now, some of the rich bourgeois who composed the city council were already tax farmers for the count of the city.[64] It was thus possible that they were also involved with the tax contractors. In 1693–94, two great traders in wheat from Rouen and Dieppe were threatened. In 1709, the intendant, Courson, and his collaborators were suspected of having hoards of wheat, because they had undertaken to purchase grain in the region for the provisioning of Paris. The last cause for the people's irritation was, without doubt, the contempt that the rich showed for the poor, and which derived from the very sharp sentiment of social superiority under the Old Regime. To designate the inhabitants of the poor sections, we encounter in the texts at Rouen—particularly from the pens of several presidents of *Parlement*—the pejorative term *purains* or *pauvres purains*. The rich retail merchant, Jacques Papavoine, spoke of the "scum" and the "wicked." In 1709, it was rumored among the demonstrators in the Norman capital that the wife of the intendant, to whose house the unemployed had gone to demand work, had responded that they had "only to throw some of their children in the river," adding, "you are tramps and scoundrels; we should hang some of you as an example to the others." [65] This was doubtlessly a made-up story, but one which conveyed, nevertheless, what the poor imagined the state of mind of the prosperous classes to be. We perceive here their bitter humiliation.

The habitual practice of violence was related to the totality of conditions for the lower classes in the urban environment. The precapitalist economy, characterized by a mediocre production and unstable economic conditions, could only provide the propertyless with a standard of living that constantly bordered on the physiological minimum, or even less. There is no need to insist on the precariousness of the means of subsistence linked to the crisis of high prices and unemployment. Even outside of these tragic times, nutrition was insufficient. We have on this point only some rather incomplete information provided by the hospital archives during the famines. We can estimate that the diet of these establishments corresponded, more or less, to the maximum diet of the popular classes in time of crisis, and to a level only a little below the general average for normal periods. At Dieppe in 1694, the hospital did not distribute bread, but rather a soup composed of forty-six grams of meat per person, fifty-six grams of bread, and an unspecified quantity of vegetables.[66] In 1709 at Rouen, the poor in the general hospital received a pound of bread each day, ninety grams of meat for three days, and, during the four fast days, thirty-four grams of butter, some boiled vegetables, and some fish, the weight of which was not given. Nonetheless, we see a lack of fresh fruits and vegetables, of meat and milk products. Lodging was equally defective. During the seventeenth century, the popular sections of Rouen offered the classic aspect of narrow streets where the sun did not penetrate because of the overhung roofs. Numerous artisans lived in only one room with their families.[67] Working conditions were not better: the workshops were unhealthy, and the working day was long (for cloth makers in Rouen, from 6 A.M. to 7 P.M. in winter, and, in summer, from 5 A.M. to 8 P.M.).[68] Finally, a truly repressive administration weighed on the workers and the vagabonds. Very often salaries were fixed in a unilateral fashion by the *bailliage* or by the city councillors. The prohibition against the formation of confraternities and against the gathering of crowds was sanctioned by fines of fifty livres or by corporal punishment. Punishments, varying according to circumstances, were meted out for begging—from the pillory and banishment to the galleys for life. However, masters frequently used outsiders, despite the regulations. It was also necessary to submit to the arbitrariness of the police agents.[69] The hopes for social mobility—that is to say, the possibility of leaving that sort of ghetto—were probably diminished during the course of Louis XIV's reign. As at Amiens, the masterships became more closed with the coming of economic depression.[70]

This popular violence was not subject to the restraints that might have existed among the superior social groups. Education was still very weak. The clergy had little influence on the workers and beggars. The latter did not hesitate to persuade the parish priests, frequently by force, to give them alms. At Dieppe, the Capuchins complained that the sailors and fishermen plundered their gardens, thus indicating little respect for their status.[71] At Rouen, the inhabitants of the ramparts declared "that every feast day and Sunday, there assembled at the said place several workers from the cloth factory and others who occupied themselves by playing dice during the divine service, and that oaths and execrable blasphemies were uttered by the said players." [72] At the time of the crises of 1661 and 1694, some "disorders" and "scandals" caused in the cathedral by the wool workers were reported.[73] Evidently, these workers are not to be considered apostles of free thought; they were certainly religious (their banned confraternities sometimes celebrated masses). But we can ask if they were ever perfectly christianized, and if their religion was not a simple aggregate of superstitions and rites over which the clergy, assimilated more or less to the rich, had little influence. The question has recently been posed, whether the popular classes in the diocese of Orleans had really been catholic before the nineteenth century.[74]

The fear of the bourgeoisie and the authorities is equally explained by another consideration—the recognition of the numerical balance of forces as between potential rebels and the defenders of the established order. It is naturally difficult to know the number of inhabitants of our cities under Louis XIV and their social composition. One is forced to make very rough estimates.

For Dieppe, a census made in 1664 gave a figure of 23,303 inhabitants, which, if we add the large suburb of Pollet and take into account information supplied by Claude Pellot, suggests a total population of some 25,000 to 30,000 inhabitants.[75] The city lost population in the second half of the seventeenth century, because of the plague of 1668, the departure of the Huguenots, and the great mortality in 1693. Therefore, we can support a figure of 15,000 to 20,000 inhabitants for the period 1700–10, which would correspond to the supposed evolution of the eighteenth century.[76] This population was composed of 9000 to 10,000 lace makers, wool-combers, and weavers, and as many fishermen and sailors—these figures probably include both workers and their families. In addition, we find some merchants (160 in 1664), some shopkeepers, and some judicial officers. That is to say that the lower classes—journeymen, self-employed workers, lesser artisans, and beggars—together with their families—must have constituted more than half the population.[77] It seems unlikely that this proportion had been significantly modified during the reign of

Louis XIV, because, if the poor were more affected by demo-graphic crises, many prosperous people, following an economic depression, retired to the countryside or went to other cities.[78] In January 1694, 1500 persons registered for alms—that is to say that they were totally deprived of resources. Naturally, this figure is far from covering the total number of indigents. Thus we see that the situation was delicate for the authorities in times of crisis.

At Rouen, the danger presented by an eventual popular uprising was still more serious. In the years 1660–70, the popu-lation appears to have been about 80,000 inhabitants and, around 1700, only 60,000.[79] The notes of Pellot indicate that there were, about 1670, 12,000 cloth workers, 10,000 linen makers, 800 wool combers, and 400 tanners. Thus the popular classes, including boatmen—who were numerous and less well off than fishermen—represented three quarters of the popula-tion. Moreover, the situation was made more difficult by the fact that near Rouen, there existed two large centers of the tex-tile industry, Darnetal and Elbeuf, the population of which was almost exclusively workers—numbering perhaps, in each place, 8000 inhabitants at the beginning of the reign of Louis XIV and 5000 around 1700–10. Now, in moments of crisis, there was an incontestable solidarity among the journeymen of neighboring places. In July 1709, rumor had it "that the people of Darnetal and Elbeuf were to come to join with the rebels," and the councillors immediately had the city gates closed.[80]

Moreover, at Dieppe as at Rouen, the peril was aggravated by the influx of beggars from the countryside at times of bad harvest—a phenomenon reported everywhere in the seven-teenth century. And there was also an active solidarity linking the laboring classes of the cities and the vagabonds. Frequently, Parlement and the governor of Dieppe prohibited the lodging of vagrants.[81] Those among the people who gave it [shelter] to them, and who even used violence to prevent their arrest, were accused of multiplying their numbers in the city. In a period of famine, the city found itself infested by bands of vagrants who roamed around its walls, and who could indeed enter and join the rebels within. In July 1709, the mayor of Dieppe explained that it was necessary to fill gaps in the city's defenses in order "to save it not only from the enemies of the state, but also from the peasants and inhabitants of Picardy who, because of famine and the lack of grain in their region, came a little time ago in great numbers to the region of Caux, so that, assembling as they do daily, it would be easy for them, when they want, to scale the walls of the ramparts." [82] At Rouen, during the same period, they reported that 2000 to 3000 Picards were at the edge of the city, after having pillaged Neufchâtel on their way.[83] Reciprocally, the rebels found refuge in the neighboring villages after the troubles.[84]

Thus we see the enormous pressure that was exerted on the bourgeoisie and the authorities during a crisis. In May 1693, there were at Rouen 21,000 to 22,000 paupers registered for alms, 3000 who begged in the streets, and many artisans out of work.[85] In July 1709, there were 25,000 "paupers and laborers" unemployed, more than one third of the population. As early as the month of May, with the cessation of manufacturing in the region, the intendant feared having "more than 40,000 persons on charity." [86] A witness to the uprising of July 3 estimated the rebels at 10,000 persons in Rouen and 4000 in Darnetal. To contain this crowd, the forces of order appeared very weak. At Dieppe, the councillors had at their disposal only 32 soldiers, in garrison at the *chateau,* and the bourgeois militia, which numbered from 500 to 1000.[87] At Rouen, there were 50 horse soldiers, 104 musketeers, and 3000 to 4000 members of the bourgeois militia. Furthermore, the military value of the latter diminished during the second half of the seventeenth century, because the bourgeoisie had fallen into the habit of paying poor people to serve in their stead. However, in serious situations this practice was not tolerated, as in 1709. The militiamen lacked training, the majority had no weapons, and it had been necessary to borrow and buy some hurriedly.[88] Finally, the authorities could not trust the lackeys, who were numerous in Rouen because of the presence of the nobles of the sovereign courts. They formed a turbulent and unsettled society, and Parlement often forbade them to fight armed and denounced the help that they gave the vagabonds.[89]

In the face of the danger of popular rebellion, the intendant, the Parlement, and the councillors took precautionary measures. They encountered great difficulties in this task—opposition was widespread among the property owners who supported the burden of these arrangements. Each one, arguing his special privileges, sought to shift the burden to others. Yet, in spite of everything, a minimum of unity before the peril that came from the popular classes was managed.

A policy of charity was first attempted to lessen the economic crisis, and the same justification was always openly stated—it was a question of "preventing disorders among the poor." At Rouen, a poor office oversaw the administration of the hospitals, of which it named the administrators. It was headed by the first president of the Parlement and consisted of two parlementaires, two canons, and two councillors. In case of necessity, an enlarged assembly met, including members of the two other sovereign courts, of the *bailliage* and of the *vicomté*, the archibshop, priests from the poorer parishes, and some city notables. All of the groups of property owners participated in the formulation of measures to help the poor.

The hospitals that received the indigent sick and gave sustenance to the unemployed proved to be very inadequate during the famines. The *Hôtel-Dieu* of Rouen could ordinarily hold 500 persons and the general hospital, 700 to 800. But in January 1710, there were 2000 poor in this latter establishment. The conditions there became very bad. In 1693, there were four patients for each bed, instead of the usual two.[90] Food rations diminished. Thus the epidemic could bring havoc inside the hospitals, just as outside.[91] The financial means that these charitable institutions had at their disposal were, in truth, very limited—real estate; different rents and revenues, such as municipal duties; collections; and the sale of objects made by the pensioners. At each crisis, the receipts diminished because of the economic paralysis, while expenses increased rapidly. In addition, the decline of rents and the monetary instability at the end of Louis XIV's reign led to a diminishing patrimony. In order to meet current deficits, the administrators sold some of the institution's lands—a solution that brought in fresh money, but that compromised the future.

It was necessary, then, to seek remedies for the misery. Thus it was that the general assembly of the poor office suggested, each time, the organization of a "subscription," the acceptance of which was entrusted to the Parlement. From winter to the month of July, in each parish of the city, commissioners, [who were] councillors of the sovereign courts, prepared, with the help of priests and of "bourgeois or merchants," the register of the poor on charity; calculated the sums necessary to feed them—on the basis of a pound of bread daily for each person; and taxed the inhabitants in proportion to the value of their house or their rent. In its functioning, the system ran up against many a difficulty. First, the principal taxpayers, that is to say the courts and institutions represented in the assembly for the poor, showed hardly any eagerness to comply. Everyone tried to fix themselves the amount of their gift. In 1662, the cathedral chapter obliged the secretary of the archbishop to erase the register on which he had inscribed, without consulting them, the sum that the canons had furnished.[92] Each institution took a long time to pay what it had promised, and the administrators of the hospital had frequently to repeat that it was important to deposit funds rapidly. The royal officers, like the ecclesiastics, were careful, above all, to have their prerogatives upheld.[93] The less powerful members of the assembly of the poor received insulting reproaches from the others. On January 10, 1661, the deputies of the sovereign courts "charged the city for the greatest part of these expenses [for the poor] . . . they criticized the amount of expenditures that were made at city hall." [94] Often quarrels over precedence broke out.[95] But the most serious difficulty stemmed from the fact that these subscriptions took place at a time when money was scarce. Consequently, the results obtained remained modest, and it was even necessary to threaten the subscribers with the seizure [of their goods] in order to collect the needed sums—in vain. In March 1694, when 20,000 livres were needed each month to tend to the needs of the poor, the administrators of the general hospital, charged with the distribution of the aid, had received only 11,201 livres. They were waiting for 1200 livres that the archbishop was to contribute and for 450 livres from the cathedral chapter. There remained, in spite of everything, a deficit of 7149 livres.[96]

Two other solutions might have been at once more efficacious in the battle against poverty and more useful for all of the city's inhabitants. First off, there were public works designed to put the unemployed to work. This remedy, used in time, perhaps prevented serious trouble at Rouen in 1661–62. In 1709, by contrast, these workshops were opened only after the uprising of July 3. Next, there was the stockpiling and sale of wheat by the municipality that could influence the price of this commodity. Such an operation was organized at Rouen in the spring of 1693 and in March 1709. However, these solutions at Rouen, in 1693 and in 1709, had only minimal success because of the insufficiency of the municipal finances that carried the burden. The king monopolized a good part of the urban resources. In July 1709, 2000 to 3000 men were employed on public works, and even some money was loaned to manufacturers, so that they could resume their activity.[97] But it was necessary to create a new municipal tax in order to cover the expenses, which, in a time of inflation, added more to the price of goods. Moreover, the authorities showed a certain distrust of these public workshops that brought together crowds of the disinherited. "I am always afraid," wrote the intendant in 1709, "that there will be some trouble from this mob, given the temper of the people." [98]

These charity measures did not prevent the authorities from resorting to force at the same time. At each crisis of high prices, they proceeded to expel the beggars who had come from elsewhere. They were given twenty-four hours to leave the city under penalty of whipping or the galleys; almsgiving in the streets was forbidden, guards were placed at the city gates to prevent them from reentering. Justification for this was that the "tramps" were only "good-for-nothings" who deprived the "true poor of the city"—the invalids—of the help they could expect and that everyone had to return to live in his parish of origin. The urban authorities thus purged their city at the expense of the countrymen, for whom they showed hardly any concern. As for the beggars living inside the walls, they began by confining them, as soon as possible, in the general hospital, where they were subject to forced labor, under penalty of life in the galleys for men and imprisonment for life for the women, if they refused.[99] The goal of these purifying operations was undoubtedly to prevent the formation of an aggressive coalition of beggars and workers.

When rebellion broke out, in spite of the precautions that were taken, it was necessary to mobilize the bourgeois militia. How events developed depended on its attitude. At Dieppe in 1661 and at Rouen in 1709, it was the militia that broke the popular movement; in the two cases, it appears that it fired into the crowd. At Dieppe, it pursued the mutineers and arrested a few of them.[100] At Rouen, it prevented them from attacking the mills and other buildings, and all witnesses agreed that it "performed marvels." [101] The city councillors showed the same kind of loyalty in regard to the king. At Dieppe, as early as the day after the riot, they reestablished the financial office that had been pillaged,[102] and they convened an assembly of bourgeois who swore that they were "all ready to take an oath in blood and do their duty by risking their lives to execute the orders of His Majesty." In 1709, they put themselves at the head of the militia and prevented the crowd from assembling.[103] From the beginning of the troubles of July 3 and 4 at Rouen, they remained in permanent session and distributed small sums to the rioters to try to calm them down. However, it is necessary to note that the bourgeois militia took a certain time to mobilize. At Dieppe and Rouen, rioters were able to attack several houses before running up against the forces of order. It is possible that at the beginning of the riot, the militiamen watched with some satisfaction, as the crowd went after certain people whom they too disliked. Croisé, bourgeois of Dieppe, reported complacently that Dubuc, one of the monopolists assaulted in 1661, had invented a tax on linen put out to dry on rocks at the beach, that he had died the following year, perhaps in punishment for the dishonest profits that he had made. Papavoine, a cloth merchant of Rouen, criticized the financial aid that Louis XIV sent to the Spaniards and Hungarians during the War of Spanish Succession, and he held that the intendant, Courson, a victim of the riot, speculated on grain. But this irresolution when the guard was called may also be explained by the disaffection, already noted, of numerous bourgeois from that institution. In any case, once assembled, the bourgeois companies executed orders punctually. Without doubt, the bourgeoisie had grievances against the monarchy, but it did not go so far as to side with the rioters, not even passively. What dominated their behavior was still social fear. The intendant, Courson, noted that the members of the militia, "since they have seen that their houses were also threatened with pillage, and that the people had visited several . . . have indeed understood that it was in their interest to prevent disorder." [104] Moreover, they feared that the government would send troops that they would have to lodge. Some days after the troubles in Dieppe in 1661, as at Rouen in 1709, the city councillors begged the lieutenant of the king not to force the city to receive soldiers, pointing out to him, "the good will and affection of all the bourgeois who have been put under arms." [105]

The Parlement of Normandy, responsible for the policing of Rouen, equally kept close watch. It ordered patrols in the streets of Rouen in 1661 and 1662, and it summoned the militia in 1709. It threatened with death any individual arrested in a mob. Nevertheless, its repressive actions appeared rather moderate. In 1693, it was content to admonish the women who assembled near the Palais du Justice, and it released, after five days of detention, two individuals arrested when they incited a crowd at the market place to riot. Can we speak here of the complicity of the court and the rebels, as has been done regarding the popular uprisings under Louis XIII? [106] In reality, it was only a question of prudence on the part of the Parlement: recognizing the weakness of the troops, police, and militia that it controlled, it sought not to excite further popular anger, in order to avoid a test of strength that it was not sure of winning. After the outbreak of the riot of 1709, the president of the Chambre des Comptes explained that, since there were no royal soldiers at Rouen, "we shall disperse the storm by gentleness, after which we shall put the bourgeois militia on alert to prevent and oppose similar disorders." [107] The first president of Parlement wrote that he thought of arresting several rioters after they had returned home, but, he added, "as we were not the strongest," he did nothing.[108]

On the other hand, that did not prevent the intendant, Courson, from insinuating in his letters to the controller-general that the riot was due to a conspiracy of the Parlement, accusing it of having, out of jealousy, spread the rumors among the people that he had hoarded wheat, and that he was responsible for the repurchase of the head tax. According to him, the plotters had profited from a time when he was absent from Rouen to warn the people that he had prevented the distribution of grain. That was why the poor revolted. Next, they had dissuaded the first president from mobilizing the militia, and they had "preferred to see the people pillage with impunity, than to oppose them." [109] Courson equally exaggerated a few words of little importance uttered by two councillors after the riot.[110] He sought to overwhelm them at any price. If it was true that the Parlement had been extremely annoyed with the intendant (to the point of believing that he had hoarded wheat),[111] it was no less true that all evidence suggested that the councillors had actively participated in the repression of the popular movement—a *président à mortier* and a councillor even prevented the crowd from pillaging Courson's town house. Thus it seems, that in attacking the Parlement, the intendant sought to divert the controller-general's attention from his own responsibilities in the riot, which, at the least, had taken him unawares. When the harvest of 1708 had been bad in the *généralité*, when, as early as February, that of 1709 promised to be among the most mediocre, and when the price of foodstuffs began to rise at the end of the autumn in 1708, Courson still wrote, in the month of May 1709, that provisioning was easy and the region very tranquil.[112] He clearly sought to draw an optimistic picture of the situation in order to demonstrate the efficiency of his administration, not failing to emphasize that through measures he had adopted, he had prevented illegal transactions, and that he had "the confidence of the people." [113] Very naturally, as a consequence, he put the responsibility for an event that he had not forseen on his enemies in the sovereign courts. We must take into account the spirit of flattery toward ministers and the king that characterized the high administration. Each sought to push aside possible rivals and to make the most of his services.[114] The governor of the province in 1709, the Duke of Luxemburg, had a few difficulties with the president of Parlement and harshly criticized the president of the Chambre des Comptes.[115] He prided himself on rapidly restoring order, writing that he had been received at Rouen on July 7 with acclamations, but begging the minister, modestly, not to speak of his merits to the king. Evidently, some days after, he received "signs of satisfaction" from the sovereign. On the other hand, we must note that the thesis of a conspiracy was equally supported by another observer, who had a different explanation: the archbishop of Rouen had heard that the Protestants contributed to the rebellion by having women and young people drink brandy in order to make them more violent.[116]

Thus it seems that, regarding the social situation in these two cities of Upper Normandy at the end of the seventeenth century, we can speak of the existence, as under Louis XIII, of two fronts of opposed classes—a union of the popular classes against a union of the property owners.[117] Those who were well-off confounded the laboring classes with the dangerous classes, as later at Paris under the constitutional monarchy.[118] The two groups were difficult to distinguish. The urban masses were not passive, and their violence maintained among the bourgeois and the authorities a latent fear that was underlined, for example, in the monotonous repetition of the edicts of Parlement against beggars—at least seventeen between 1658 and 1679. At the time of famine, the behavior of the antagonistic social forces was very reminiscent of the period of Richelieu's ministry. However, we must ask why the popular disturbances in our cities, as in the rest of France, were less numerous under Louis XIV than under Louis XIII.[119] Rouen, particularly, had experienced riots nearly every year between 1623 and 1639. The low price of grain from 1661, except for the years of bad harvests, and when it was not accompanied by underemployment, might have produced a slight increase in the well-being of journeymen who had work.[120] And the demographic crises, which particularly struck the lower classes, probably decreased the labor supply and allowed workers to better protect their income.[121] Above all, the attitude of the bourgeois militia had changed: while at the beginning of the great revolt of August 1639, it had strongly supported the rioters, under Louis XIV it vigorously maintained order.[122] Touched by economic depression, the bourgeoisie withdrew into itself out of fear of impoverishment, and it separated itself more clearly from the people. The city council of Dieppe from the middle of the seventeenth century, and that of Rouen after 1665, were controlled by a narrow circle of notables.[123] Thus the bourgeoisie, along with the new nobles of the sovereign courts, indeed had grievances against the absolute monarchy, but what linked them to the sovereign was stronger than what separated them: social fear led them to adjust to royal demands, because the soldiers of the monarchy were the best guarantors of property (provided they did not have to lodge them, which happened at Dieppe in 1661 and at Rouen in 1709). Their arrival in these two cities prevented the repetition of the riot. Their presence in the neighboring region of Caux in 1693 diminished, without doubt, the magnitude of the popular disturbances.

Besides, it seems that under Louis XIV, the theme of "the disturbance" changed: from an antifiscal [manifestation], it became, above all, a question of subsistence, as during the following period. Economic development, which would reduce the burden of taxes, constitutes, perhaps, a useful explanation for this change in the eighteenth century. One can understand why under Louis XV and Louis XVI, in Upper Normandy at least, antifiscal disturbances were rare. But expansion did not appear before 1730–50: the hypothesis, then, cannot be supported for the reign of Louis XIV. Nor can one argue a reduction of fiscal pressures between 1660 and 1715. But it is possible that there had been a change in the social effects of taxes that were created then, by comparison to those that were established under Richelieu and Mazarin. During the latter period, new taxes, in the cities above all, struck the professions and the circulation of goods. Now it was largely a question of taxes directly levied on revenues: an increase in the *taille,* from which Dieppe and Rouen were free; the *capitation;* and the *dixième* [or tithe]. Without doubt, the popular masses paid the king important and even increasing sums in the form of *aides* and municipal duties. But the primary increase in the tax burden imposed by Louis XIV fell mainly on the bourgeoisie and the peasantry. Moreover, the two forms of disturbance could be linked: the uprising at Dieppe in 1661 had been caused by peasants and common city people come to get wheat from a boat at the docks.[124]

One can also note that the attitude of the central power toward the rioters changed. Whereas in 1661, the intendant had one of the rebels at Dieppe executed and several others condemned to the galleys, at Rouen in 1709 there had not been one arrest, even after the arrival of the troops of the Duke of Luxemburg. This was probably a sign of the serious difficulties that overwhelmed Louis XIV at the end of his reign and that forced him to act prudently. Finally, we must note that in our two cities, despite the difference in their size, the social atmosphere was nearly the same. Nevertheless, at Dieppe, trouble was less frequent and less violent than at Rouen. This divergence stemmed from the fact that Dieppe, being a seaport and less populated, was more easily provisioned. In 1662, a famine ended there in June, thanks to an abundant catch of mackerel.[125] But, above all, the economy was more traditional, capitalism less developed there, and, consequently, the journeymen, who provided most participants in the riots, were less numerous. Because of a social structure that was less evolved, there was a more relaxed social climate within the city.[126]

NOTES

1. Unfortunately, we have no official price statistics, except for Rouen in 1709, but the evidence on prices is still rather abundant.

2. *Bibliothèque Municipale de Rouen,* Y 28-12, Croisé, "Histoire de la ville de Dieppe" (1710); *Bibliothèque Nationale,* Ms. fr. 17, 400. [Henceforth we shall use the following abbreviations to designate archival sources: *Archives Nationales,* A.N.; *Archives Départementales de la Seine-Maritime,* A.D.S-M.; *Archives Communales de Rouen,* A.C.R.; *Archives Communales de Dieppe,* A.C.D.; *Bibliothèque Nationale,* B.N.; *Bibliothèque Municipale de Rouen,* B.M.R.].

3. B.N., *Mélanges de Colbert,* 108, fol. 150, April 16, 1662.

4. Célestin Hippeau, *Le gouvernement de Normandie au XVIIe et au XVIIIe siècles* (Caen, 1863), 9 vols., IX, 204; A.C.D., *Déliberations,* Iaa, January 8, 1694; A.D.S-M., B, *Registre secret,* April 17 and 24, 1694.

5. A.C.D., *Registre d'audience de police,* VII, July 13, 1709; A.C.R., A 30, July 3 and 4, 1709.

6. Pierre Goubert, *Beauvais et le Beauvaisis de 1600 à 1730* (Paris, 1960), I, 302.

7. The pound of Rouen weighed 489 grams.

8. A.D.S-M., G 7371.

9. At the time of the crisis of 1685, the intendant ordered the wool workers to take only eight sols each day in place of the usual fifteen (Arthur Boislisle, *Correspondance des contrôleurs généraux des finances avec les intendants des provinces* (Paris, 1874–1897), 3 vols., I, 44.

10. There is no point in insisting on the dramatic character of the crisis in prices. In his work, already cited, Pierre Goubert has decisively done that, and for us, it is only a question of verifying the spread of the phenomenon to Rouen and Dieppe.

11. Boislisle, *Correspondance,* I, 319.

12. Voysin de la Noiraye, *Mémoire de la généralité de Rouen* (1665), Edmond Esmonin ed. (Paris, 1913), 137, 142.

13. Edmond Esmonin, *La taille en Normandie au temps de Colbert* (Paris, 1913), 267.

14. Georg B. Depping, *Correspondance administrative sous le règne de Louis XIV* (Paris, 1850–1855), 4 vols., III, 219; A.C.R., A 28, March, 1689 and August, 1692; A 29, December 4, 1706.

15. Esmonin, *La taille,* 267–268.

16. A.C.R., A 29, June 30, 1704: Provisional creation of municipal duties to cover the expenses of 95,000 livres necessary to repurchase offices of lieutenant to the mayor, assessors, alternate receivers—all newly created.

17. B.M.R., Ms. Y 169, "Mémoire sur la généralité de Rouen, 1699."

18. *Notes du Premier Président Pellot sur la Normandie, 1670–1683,* G. Prévost ed. (Rouen, 1915), 135.

259

19. A.D.S-M., B *Chambre des Comptes,* 103, fol. 55.

20. A.D.S-M., G 901 (*Inventaire* Gilbert Le Breton); G 903, "Motifs pour parvenir au bail nouveau, 1648."

21. A.D.S-M., G 905.

22. Depping, *Correspondance administrative,* III, 389.

23. *Ibid.,* 887.

24. A.D.S-M., C 124, edict of March 1703.

25. A.D.S.-M., *Arts et métiers,* E 528, December 3, 1704; September 4, 1706; July 17, 1708.

26. A.N., G7 499, May 13, 1709. [According to a letter of the intendant, Courson] commerce was disrupted at Rouen by the rumor of a coming currency depreciation, and it was impossible to borrow money.

27. Boislisle, *Correspondance,* II, 358, 442.

28. B.M.R., Ms. Y 91, "Abrégé historique du Parlement de Normandie par Pavyot de Bouillon, 1722."

29. "Rapport du Chevalier de Clerville touchant le rétablissement du commerce dans les ports de Normandie (1701)," *Mélanges de la Société de Normandie* (Rouen, 1891), I, 263.

30. Boislisle, *Correspondance,* II, 477.

31. *Mémoire de l'intendant de la généralité de Paris, 1699,* Arthur de Boislisle ed. (Paris, 1881), 615.

32. Pierre Clément, *Lettres, instructions, et mémoires de Colbert* (Paris, 1861–1882), 10 vols., IV, 144.

33. *Rapport de Clerville,* 282.

34. In 1693, for example, it prevented the tax farmer in the *vicomté* of L'Eau from taking action against several merchants of Rouen who owed taxes (A.D.S-M., B, *Cour des Aides, Requêtes,* August 14, 1693).

35. A.D.S-M., F, *Correspondance de Bernières de Bautot,* I, January 11, 1709.

36. A.D.S-M., B, *Registre secret,* July 10, 1709.

37. *Ibid.,* April–June 1662.

38. Boislisle, *Correspondance,* III, 140.

39. Arthur de Boislisle, "Le grand hiver et la disette de 1709," *Revue des questions historiques,* XXIX (1903), 442–509.

40. Paul Bondois, "La disette de 1662," *Revue d'histoire économique et sociale,* XII (1924), 51–117.

41. *Mémoires pour servir à l'histoire de la ville de Dieppe par M.C. Guibert, prêtre,* Samuel Hardy ed. (Dieppe, 1878), I, 219; A.D.S-M., *Arts et métiers,* E 528, 1706–1708.

42. Clément, *Correspondance de Colbert,* III, 489.

43. A.D.S-M., B, *Vicomté de L'Eau de Rouen, Procédures criminelles,* August 19, 1689.

44. Germain Martin, "Les famines de 1693 et 1709 et la spéculation sur les blés," *Bulletin du Comité des Travaux Historiques et Scientifiques* (Paris, 1908), 150–172.

45. A.N., G7 1650, April 4, 1709.

46. A.D.S-M., C 192, July 18, 1709.

47. Clément, *Correspondance de Colbert*, IV, 119.

48. *Histoire de la ville de Rouen en six parties par un solitaire* (Rouen, 1731), I, 535.

49. Boislisle, *Correspondance*, I, 361.

50. A.D.S-M., B, *Registre d'arrêts*, November 17, 1693.

51. A.N., G7 1650, April 24, 1709.

52. G. Panel, *Documents concernant les pauvres de Rouen* (Rouen, 1917–1919), 3 vols., II, 72.

53. B. Boutelet, "Etude par sondage de la criminalité dans le bailliage de Pont-le-Arche," *Annales de Normandie*, No. 4 (1962), 235–262.

54. A.D.S-M., B, *Bailliage de Rouen, Liasse criminel*, 1710.

55. For example, Pierre Regnault, who rented two rooms from Jean Coustel, began to remove the furniture when the landlord unexpectedly arrived. He beat the latter and then quietly went back to work (A.D.S-M., B, *Baillage de Rouen, Criminel*, 1710). Returning to Rouen with his family, Pierre Poison met . . . three men who were beating a child. His wife remarked to them that it was wicked to harm one so young. The men fell upon her, hitting and kicking her, shouting, "death, idiot, whore, we must kill her" (B, *Bailliage de Rouen, Criminel*, May 11, 1687).

56. On July 5, 1708, an investigation was opened: several girls from the popular quarter of Saint-Hillaire had been kidnapped and raped on the walls by some men (A.D.S-M., B, *Bailliage de Rouen, Plumitifs*, 1680–1709).

57. Lubin Jouenne, collecting certain municipal fees, complained that, in broad daylight, merchants "shouted and gathered a large crowd around him to prevent him from collecting the fees . . ." (A.D.S-M., B, *Bailliage de Rouen, Police*, 1704).

58. A.D.S-M., B, *Bailliage de Rouen, Registres de police*, 1701–1723.

59. B.M.R., Ms. Y 2811.

60. Robert Mandrou, "Les soulèvements populaires et la société française au XVIIe siècle," *Annales: Economies, Sociétés, Civilisations*, No. 4 (1959), 756–765.

61. A.D.S-M., B, *Parlement, Registres d'arrêts*, April 24, 1694.

62. A.D.S-M., C 192, July 18, 1709; A.N., G7 1650, July 5, 1709.

63. Demarquet, *Mémoires chronologiques pour servir à l'histoire de Dieppe et à celle de la navigation française* (Paris, 1785), 2 vols., I, 410–415.

64. A.D.S-M., G 901.

65. "Extrait du journal de Jacques Papavoine, bourgeois de Rouen, 1673–1732," *Bulletin de la Société d'Histoire de Normandie* (1896).

66. A.D.S-M., *Hôpital général de Rouen*, E 13, January 30, 1694.

67. Jacques Levainville, *Rouen: Etude d'une agglomeration urbaine* (Paris, 1913), 303–316.

68. P. Jubert, "La juridiction et l'inspection des manufactures à Rouen de 1670 à 1699," *Bulletin de la Société Libre d'Emulation du Commerce et de l'Industrie de Siene-Inférieure* (1930–1931).

69. A.D.S-M., B, *Bailliage de Rouen, Plumatif,* January 17, 1704.

70. Pierre Deyon, "Mentalités populaires: un sondage à Amiens au XVIIe siècle," *Annales: Economies, Sociétés, Civilisations,* No. 3 (1962), 448–458.

71. A.D.S-M., B, *Amirauté de Dieppe,* 214 B27, November 11, 1711.

72. A.D.S-M., B, *Bailliage de Rouen, Police,* October 31, 1704.

73. A.D.S-M., G 2195, March 30, 1661; G 2209, February 15, 1694.

74. Christiane Marcilhacy, "Un tentative de rechristianisation au XIXe siècle: le diocèse d'Orléans de 1849–1878," *Information historique,* No. 4 (1964).

75. Voysin de La Noiraye, *Mémoire,* 143.

76. Charles de Robillard de Beaurepaire, "Recherches sur la population de la généralité et du diocèse de Rouen avant 1789," *Mémoires de la Société des Antiquaires de Normandie,* VIII (Caen, 1872), 371–433.

77. The preceding figures include even those master artisans who were well-off. Moreover, a number of fishermen owned a boat and were not exactly members of the popular classes.

78. Boislisle, *Correspondance,* II, 433.

79. The figures are drawn from B.M.R., Ms. Y 169, and Voysin de La Noiraye, *Mémoires,* 140.

80. A.C.R., A 30, July, 1709.

81. A.D.S-M., B, *Bailliage de Rouen, Plumatif,* 1703–1723. On August 14, 1711, G. Breton, already condemned because of the salt tax, was punished with three hours in the iron collar and nine years of exile for lodging poor people from Lower Normandy and charging a sol a night.

82. A.D.S-M., C 105, July 7, 1709.

83. "Journal de Jacques Papavoine."

84. Demarquet, *Mémoires chronologiques,* 408.

85. Boislisle, *Correspondance,* I, 319.

86. A.C.R., A 30, July 19, 1709; A.N., G7 1650, May 3, 1709.

87. The estimates on the numbers in the militia follow.

88. A.C.R., A 30, July 7, 1709.

89. A.D.S-M., B, *Registre secret,* July 27, 1693.

90. A.D.S-M., *Hôpital général,* E 17, January 17, 1710; *Hôtel-Dieu* de Rouen, E 46, August 19, 1693.

91. A.D.S-M., *Hôpital général,* E 13, February and March 1693. Dysentery was reported.

92. A.D.S-M., G 2195, April 12, 1662.

93. *Ibid.,* G 2209, January 30, 1693. The cathedral chapter sent two canons to the assembly of the poor "to preserve the place and rights of the chapter."

94. A.C.R., A 27, February 10, 1661.

95. A.D.S-M., *Hôpital général,* E 12, July 26, 1693. The deputies of the Chambre des Comptes and those of the cathedral chapter fought over who would sit at the left of the president of Parlement.

96. A.D.S-M., B, *Registre secret,* March 26, 1694.

97. A.N., G7 1650, July 10, 1709.

98. *Ibid.,* July 7, 1709.

99. The edict on the establishment of the *Hôpital général* is to be found in Panel, *Pauvres de Rouen,* II, 91.

100. Demarquet, *Mémoires chronologique,* 408.

101. A.N., G7 1650, July 8, 1709.

102. A.C.D., *Registre de l'Hôtel de Ville,* June 23, 1661.

103. A.D.S-M., C 105, July 7, 1709.

104. A.N., G7 1650, July 7, 1709.

105. A.C.R., A 30, July 9, 1709.

106. Roland Mousnier, "Recherches sur les soulèvements populaires en France avant la Fronde," *Revue d'histoire moderne et contemporaine,* V (1958).

107. A.N. G7 1650, July 4, 1709.

108. *Ibid.*

109. *Ibid.,* July 5, 1709.

110. *Ibid.,* July 3, 4, 5, 7, 1709. Two councillors had spoken in public of the intendant's wheat, which confirmed the rumor that Courson was a speculator. In fact, they meant only the reserves kept by the intendant to provision the city, but they were not understood by the crowd.

111. B.M.R., Ms. Y 91.

112. Boislisle, *Correspondance,* III, 141.

113. A.N. G7 1650, March 16, 1709, and April 6, 1709.

114. Already in 1662, the intendant Champigny complained of being persecuted by "a few individuals" for a year (B.N., *Mélanges de Colbert,* 112, fol. 270), and he asked the chancellor for a position as councillor of state (B.N., Ms. fr. 17899).

115. A.N., G7 499, July 23, 1709.

116. *Ibid.,* G7 1650, July 13, 1709.

117. Boris Porchnev, *Les soulèvements populaires en France de 1623 à 1648* (Paris, 1963), 261–299.

118. Louis Chevalier, *Classes laborieuses et classes dangereuses* (Paris, 1958), 454–465.

119. Pierre Clément, "Les émeutes sous Louis XIV," *Séances et travaux de l'Academie des Sciences Morales et Politiques,* No. 4 (1865).

120. Pierre Léon, "La crise de l'économie française à la fin du règne de Louis XIV," *Information historique,* No. 4 (1956).

121. The study of the crisis of 1693 at Lyon—a city comparable to Rouen—shows this clearly. See Richard Gascon and Claude Latta, "Une crise urbaine au XVIIe siècle: la crise de 1693–94 à Lyon," *Cahier d'histoire,* VIII (1963), 371–404.

122. A.C.R., *Tiroir* 409, Uprising of Rouen in 1639.

123. S. Deck, "Les municipalités de Haute-Normandie," *Annales de Normandie,* No. 4 (1961), 279–300; No. 2 (1962), 77–92; and No. 3 (1962), 151–168.

124. A.C.D., *Registre de l'Hôtel de Ville,* 1640–1661, June 26, 1661.

125. D. Asseline, *Les antiquitez et chroniques de la ville de Dieppe,* Samuel Hardy ed. (Dieppe, 1874), II, 318.

126. This article was in press when E. Le Roy Ladurie's thesis, *Les paysans de Languedoc* (Paris, 1966), appeared. It would be interesting to compare his facts concerning urban troubles in the Midi with what we have found. . . .

GLOSSARY OF TERMS

Aides. Although once a form of feudal dues, the *aides* were by the seventeenth century excise or consumer taxes paid to the monarchy.

Bailliage. Important middle-level courts of justice that received certain civil and criminal matters in the first instance, and others on appeal.

Ban and *arrière-ban.* The convocation of feudal levies for royal military service. Service had largely been converted to a money payment by the seventeenth century.

Cahiers. Petitions or lists of grievances presented by the three legally recognized social orders to the Estates General or to provincial estates.

Capitation. A tax established in 1695 that was suppressed and renewed several times. The tax fell upon all classes but the most poor, and it was regarded as egalitarian by the privileged.

Chambre des Comptes. A sovereign court that dealt with cases involving the royal domain and also served as an audit court in cases arising out of the accounts of royal agents.

Chambre Tournelle. A criminal chamber in the Parlement.

Consuls. A name applied to municipal officials in parts of southern France.

Contrôleur général des finances. Originally a lesser financial office, it was transformed by Colbert after 1661 into the central ministry and most powerful agency of the royal government. Outside of judicial administration, most domestic affairs fell under its jurisdiction.

Cour des Aides. Sovereign courts that dealt with cases arising from certain taxes—the *taille, gabelle,* and *aides*—and served as an appeals court in tax matters.

Cour des monnaies. A sovereign court with jurisdiction in civil and criminal cases involving the currency.

Directe universelle. The royal claim, particularly under Louis XIV, to be the ultimate seigneur of all territories in France and, especially, of the freeholds.

Droit annuel (or *annuel*). An annual tax paid by royal office-holders to the crown in order to maintain the heritability of the office.

Election. A lower court that judged tax matters, and that had a role in assessing the *taille.*

Elus. Royal officers in the *élection.*

Franc-alleu. Property held free of seigneurial obligations or feudal tenure—the allodium or freehold.

Franc-fief. A fee paid by a commoner who acquired a noble property. By the seventeenth century, the monarchy collected the fee.

Gabelle. The salt tax.

Généralité. The principal administrative district in France for purposes of royal finance. Once administered by the *trésoriers de France,* they became in the seventeenth century the jurisdiction of the intendant.

Grand jours. Special sessions of sovereign courts held to investigate and punish official and noble corruption.

Greffier. A clerk of court.

Intendant. The principal field agent of the seventeenth-century monarchy. Although commissioners of the royal council, the intendants, from the time of Colbert, were particularly agents of the *contrôleur général.*

Mazarinades. Pamphlets and polemics written against Cardinal Mazarin during the Fronde (1648–53).

Octroi. Municipal taxes absorbed by the state in the seventeenth century.

Parlement. The highest and most powerful of the royal courts of justice. The Parlement of Paris and those in the provinces were not only courts of appeal, but also important administrative bodies as well.

Paulette. Another name for the *droit annuel.*

Pays d'élection. A region where there existed an *élection,* and where *élus* assessed the *taille.* This was opposed to the *pays d'états,* where the provincial estates levied the *taille.*

Présidial. In 1551, the crown created a new set of appeals courts (*présidiaux*) to handle less important appeals in both civil and criminal cases.

Prévoté. A low-level royal court that mainly dealt with minor affairs of civil justice.

Procureur fiscal. An officer of the seigneurial courts.

Sénéchaussée. Similar to the *bailliage.*

Sol pour livre. A surcharge placed upon an existing tax to increase royal revenues.

Taille. The principal royal levy in seventeenth-century France, and one from which the privileged were exempt. Depending on the region, it was levied on persons (*taille personnelle*) or on property (*taille réelle*). Increasingly, the intendants came to supervise the assessment and the collection of the *taille.*

Taillon. A surcharge on the *taille.*

Trésorier de France. A royal officer of the *bureau des finances* who was concerned with the distribution of the *taille* among the *élections* and with other financial affairs.

Ustensile. A royal surtax to provide for the upkeep of troops.

Vicomté. The Norman version of the *prévoté.*

BIBLIOGRAPHICAL ESSAY

The following bibliographical essay is not meant to be exhaustive, but rather to suggest a short list of recent work on problems of state and society in seventeenth-century France.

Rorbert Mandrou, *La France aux XVIIe et XVIIIe siècles* ("Nouvelle Clio," Paris, 1967), provides the best introduction to the historiography of seventeenth-century France. The most stimulating general treatment of problems of state and society will be found in Pierre Goubert's two volumes, *L'ancien régime: La société* (Paris, 1967) and *L'ancien régime: Les pouvoirs* (Paris, 1973). Some of Goubert's revisionist ideas are contained in his, *Louis XIV and Twenty Million Frenchmen*, Anne Carter trans. (New York, 1970). Although not all of the book directly concerns the seventeenth century, J. H. Shennan, *Government and Society in France, 1461–1661* (London, 1969) has a useful introduction to the problem and a good selection of documents.

A convenient introduction to Roland Mousnier's interpretation of the period is his collection of essays, *La plume, la faucille, et le marteau* (Paris, 1970). For a short statement of Boris Porchnev's conception of seventeenth-century French society, see his, "The Legend of the Seventeenth Century in French History," *Past and Present*, No. 8 (1955), 15–27. Another Marxist viewpoint, quite different from Porchnev's, is to be found in A. D. Lublinskaya, *French Absolutism: The Crucial Phase, 1620–1629*, Brian Pearce trans. (Cambridge, England, 1968). David Parker, "The Social Foundations of French Absolutism, 1610–1630," *Past and Present*, No. 53 (1971), 67–89, refines the Porchnev thesis on the basis of a close study of the city of La

Rochelle. Menna Prestwich, "The Making of Absolute Monarchy, 1559–1683," in J. M. Wallace-Hadrill and John McManners eds., *France: Government and Society* (London, 1957), offers a balanced interpretation.

On the typology of absolutism in France, see Fritz Hartung and Roland Mousnier, "Quelques problèmes concernant la monarchie absolue," *Relazioni del X Congresso Internazionale di Scienze Storiche,* IV (Florence, 1955), 3–55. Orest Ranum, *Richelieu and the Councillors of Louis XIII* (Oxford, 1963), analyzes the structure of government under Richelieu and the role of the high administrative elite. In his *Etudes sur la France des XVIIe et XVIIIe siècles* (Paris, 1964), Edmond Esmonin provides some excellent case studies of field administration under the Bourbons. Georges Livet, *L'intendance d'Alsace sous Louis XIV* (Paris, 1956), is good on the relations of the central government and the social orders.

Much of the discussion of state and society in the seventeenth century has focused on elites. Davis Bitton, *The French Nobility in Crisis, 1560–1640* (Stanford, 1969), describes the declining public role of the landed nobility. On the relations of the state and the great nobility, see Jean-Pierre Labatut, *Les ducs et pairs de France au XVIIe siècle: Etude social* (Paris, 1972). Pierre Goubert's "Les officiers royaux des présidiaux, bailliages, et élections dans la société française au XVIIe siècle," *Dix-septième siècle,* No. 33 (1956), 648–670, is a model essay on the provincial notables. For a solid study of one important group of officials, see Jean-Paul Charmeil, *Les trésoriers de France à l'époque de la Fronde* (Paris, 1964). A. Lloyd Moote, "The French Crown Versus its Judicial and Financial Officials, 1615–1683," *Journal of Modern History,* XXXIV (1964), 146–160, describes the ongoing struggle of the crown to contain its officials. Gaston Roupnel, *La ville et la campagne au XVIIe siècle: Etude sur les populations du pays dijonnais* (2nd ed.; Paris, 1955), is a classic older work that analyzes the political and social dominance of a provincial elite of officeholders. Among the major recent works of social history, Pierre Deyon, *Amiens, capitale provinciale: Etude sur la société urbaine au XVIIe siècle*

(Paris and The Hague, 1967), is best on the impact of the state upon urban society. Yves-Marie Bercé, "La bourgeoisie bordelaise et le fisc sous Louis XIII," *Revue historique de Bordeaux et du Département de la Gironde,* XIII (1964), 41–66, presents a case study of the resistance of an urban elite to the financial demands of the crown.

The literature on popular revolts is increasing. It is reviewed by Robert Mandrou in, "Vingt ans après, ou une direction de recherches fécondes: Les révoltes populaires en France au XVIIe siècle," *Revue historique,* CCXLII (1969), 29–40. Another good overview is to be found in J.H.M. Salmon, "Venal Office and Popular Sedition in France," *Past and Present,* No. 37 (1967), 21–43. Madeleine Foisil, *La révolte des nu-pieds et les révoltes normandes de 1639* (Paris, 1970), is a detailed local study. On the midcentury revolt of elites against the crown, Ernst Kossmann, *La Fronde* (Leiden, 1954), still remains the best single study. A. Lloyd Moote, *The Revolt of the Judges: The Parlement of Paris and the Fronde, 1643–1652* (Princeton, 1971), gives a good account of the role of the officers in the Fronde.

Eugene Asher, *The Resistance to the Maritime Classes: The Survival of Feudalism in the France of Colbert* (Los Angeles, 1960), examines the capacity of provincial society to resist the absolute monarchy of Louis XIV. In his *Documents relatifs à la communauté villageoise en Bourgogne* (Paris, 1962), Pierre Saint-Jacob documents a case of local resistance to the reforms of Colbert. Marcel Giraud argues that there was a general breakdown of royal authority during the late seventeenth century in his, "Crise de conscience et d'autorité à la fin du règne de Louis XIV," *Annales: Economies, Sociétés, Civilisations,* VII (1952), 172–190, 293–302. Lionel Rothkrug, *Opposition to Louis XIV: The Political and Social Origins of the French Enlightenment* (Princeton, 1965), is a somewhat controversial book that seeks to establish the intellectual origins of the opposition to the Sun King.

The French experience of crisis and revolt may be compared to that of other countries in the two following volumes: Roland Mousnier, *Peasant Uprisings in Seventeenth-Century*

France, Russia, and China, Brian Pearce trans. (New York, 1970); and Robert Forster and Jack P. Greene eds., *Preconditions of Revolution in Early Modern Europe* (Baltimore, 1970).

For further bibliographical information, consult the Mandrou volume listed at the beginning of this essay and Jacques Lelièvre, "Eléments d'une bibliographie de l'histoire du droit public français au XVIIe siècle," *Dix-septième siècle,* Nos. 58–59 (1963), 83–104.

INDEX

Abbeville, interception of wheat by, 136
Abonnements, 75–76, 87, 90
Actes Royaux, 19, 20
Affaire des airiements, 139–41ff.
Agen, 6, 9ff., 14, 15, 19ff., 29, 181–92
Agenais, 5–6, 10, 11–12, 19, 23–24, 180–93
Agriculture. *See* Farms and farming
Aguesseau, de (intendant), 190, 195, 197
Aides, 29, 236. *See also* specific places
Aigrefeuille, Charles d', 177
Aiguillon, Duchess of, 186ff.
Airieurs, 139–41ff.
Aix, 70, 96–123
Albisson, J., 91
Albret, Marshal d' (governor), 166–67
Alis, Abbé R. L., 196
Allodium (*franc-alleu*), 180–97, 266
Amiens, 8, 33, 105, 130–54
André, Louis, 41, 229
Anjou, 49
Annales de Bretagne, 64, 66
Annales: Economies, Sociétés, Civilisations, xxi, 176, 229, 261, 262
"Annales" school, xxi
Annuaire-bulletin de la société de l'histoire de France, 24, 126
Annuel. See Droit annuel
Apt, 118
Arbassier, C., 88

Argouges, d' (president of Parlement), 60, 61, 66, 90
Arles, 98, 117, 118, 128
Armagnac, 5–6, 19, 23
Army. *See* Military
Arras, 146
Arrêts du conseil, 89
Arrière-ban, 29–30ff., 214
Artisans. *See* Workers; specific crafts, places
Asseline, D., 264
Assemblée des Notables, 209, 230
Aubenas, 164–65
Aubray, d' (intendant), 101ff., 118, 120, 121, 128
Audijos, Bernard, 162–63
Augustinians, 132, 140
Aumont, Duc d', 160
Auxerre, 73–74, 77–81, 85–86, 90ff.
Auzac, d' (subdelegate), 192
Avallon, 93
Avenel, Georges d', 124, 129, 229
Aveyron, 23
Avignon, 119

Bacr, P., 88
Baehrel, René, 124, 125
Bailliage, 68, 72. *See also* specific places
Bailly, de (greffier), 147
Baizieu, 146
Ban, 29–30ff., 214
Bapaume, 146

Military (army, soldiers), 30, 32–35, 37–38, 45, 98, 240, 249, 253 (*see also* War; specific wars); lodging of troops, 37–38, 72
Milk products, 246
Mimata, de (canon), 124
Monarchie Aristodemocratique, 205–6
Monchrétien, Antoine de, 203–4
Monflanquin, 195
Monier, de (president), 119
Monks, 132, 140
Mons, de (councillor), 144, 145, 147
Montbas, H. de, 131, 148, 155
Montesquieu, Charles de Secondat, Baron de, 199, 226
Montgaillard, Marquis de, 171
Montluc, A. de, 41
Montmorency, 121
Montpelier, 14
Morant (*intendant*), 70
Morbihan, 48
Moret, Countess of, 15
Mortgage loans, 32
Moulin, de (doctor), 141
Moulins, 70, 78, 80–81ff., 90ff.
Mouret (councillor), 148, 151
Mousnier, Roland, xv–xvii ff., 4–5, 8, 18, 20, 24, 40, 63, 124ff., 157–60, 176, 195, 228, 263
Moutiers, 101, 102
Musée Arbaud, 128

Nantes, 49, 92, 170, 208, 211, 215–16, 230, 231
Napoleon, codes of, 48
Navy, 45
Necker (minister), 74
Negociants, 214, 231
Netz, Nicolas de, 14
Neufchâtel, 249
Nibles, Sieur de, 129
Nîmes, 97
Nine Years War, 210
Nobility, xvi ff., 2, 11, 25–43, 52, 158ff.; social status and commercial enterprise, 200–1, 209–10ff.

Nogent-le-Roi, 37
Normand, C., 88
Normandy, 19, 27, 28, 42, 233–64
Noyers, Sublet de, 144, 145, 150
Noyon, 150

Oats, 97–98, 240
Octrois, 29, 68, 69, 72, 79, 80, 82ff., 93. *See also* specific towns
Offices, 44–45ff.; heredity of, 4–5, 8, 45ff., 99–100 (*see also* Paulette); selling of (*rachat des offices;* venality of offices), xvi–xvii, 8, 15, 35, 44–45ff., 53–54ff., 76ff., 86–87, 91, 237
Oliver-Martin, François, 194
Oppède, d' (president of Parlement), 99, 101, 102, 106
Orléans, Gaston d', 37, 121
Orléans, 247; Ordinance of, 88, 208
Ornano, Marshal, 9, 10, 13ff., 22, 23
Ouvriers, 214

Pagès, Georges, 18, 24, 90
Pagès, J., 136, 155, 156
Panel, G., 261, 263
Papavoine, Jacques, 245, 254
Paper: currency, 237; legal (*papier timbré*), 58–59, 61, 166, 169
Parfait Négociant, 206, 228, 229
Paris, 6, 7, 28, 47ff., 85, 86, 90, 91, 93, 100, 144–45, 150, 160, 162, 184, 188, 219, 256; deprives Upper Normandy of food, 239–40; market for Amiens, 132; Selves in, 10ff.
Pas de Suse, 97
Paule, de (councillor), 107, 126
Paulette, 4–5, 8, 16, 45ff., 53ff., 99–100
Paupers, 249. *See also* Beggars; Vagabonds
Pays d'élections, 81, 267
Pays d'états, 81, 267
Peasants, xviii, 158ff. *See also* Farms and farming; specific places
Pecquet (doctor), 141
Peiresc, Nicolas Fabri de, 98, 100, 119
Pelissanne, 109, 126